Applied TinyML

End-to-end machine learning for microcontrollers with examples

Ricardo Cid

bpb

www.bpbonline.com

First Edition 2025

Copyright © BPB Publications, India

ISBN: 978-93-65890-716

LIMITS OF LIABILITY AND DISCLAIMER OF WARRANTY

To View Complete
BPB Publications Catalogue
Scan the QR Code:

Dedicated to

My dear daughters:
Dianna
and
Luna

About the Author

Ricardo Cid is a mechanical engineer specialized in mechatronics who has been working with embedded systems for more than 20 years. At school, he was already helping a team at the engineering institute (UNAM) connect a washing machine to the internet even before the term IoT was coined (to this day, he has not figured out why connecting a washing machine to the internet is necessary). After finishing school, he moved to NYC to design stage robots for artists in his free time while working as the head of engineering for a very successful company in the travel industry, where he pioneered creating systems in the early days of the cloud, acquiring extensive experience in big data and massive traffic volumes.

Around 2015, he took a six-month residency at the Museum of Arts and Design at Columbus Circle with a project that earned him multiple awards, consisting of creating 3D-printed mechanisms that danced to music. Because of his unique skill set, which included mechanical engineering, electronics, enterprise software, APIs, cloud, and big data, one of the biggest and most prestigious real estate portfolios in NYC offered him the unique opportunity to build a smart building operating system from scratch, using more than 15 skyscrapers as a sandbox.

During that amazing gig, Ricardo experimented with massive amounts of data and conceived a series of applications for a then-new type of technology called machine learning. Ricardo and his team conceived dozens of prototypes, some of them never saw the light, but they laid the foundation for a series of algorithms that eventually saved hundreds of megawatts in multiple buildings across the U.S., including those of the federal government and the largest bank in the world.

At the end of his sixth anniversary at that company, Ricardo realized there was a massive opportunity to bring much of that intelligence to edge devices, avoiding critical cybersecurity and reliability single points of failure. In 2023, Ricardo created a design studio exclusively dedicated to architecting and building edge solutions that run ML models in constrained environments.

About the Reviewer

Martin Yanev is a highly accomplished software engineer with nearly a decade of experience across diverse industries, including aerospace and medical technology. Over his illustrious career, Martin has carved a niche for himself in developing and integrating cutting-edge software solutions for critical domains such as air traffic control and chromatography systems. Renowned as an esteemed instructor and computer science professor at Fitchburg State University, he possesses a deep understanding of the full spectrum of OpenAI APIs and exhibits mastery in constructing, training, and fine-tuning AI systems. As a widely recognized author, Martin has shared his expertise to help others navigate the complexities of AI development. With his exceptional track record and multifaceted skill set, Martin continues to propel innovation and drive transformative advancements in the field of software engineering.

Acknowledgement

I would like to thank, first of all, you, the reader, for picking up this book. I hope that by the end of it, you are inspired to create awesome systems and gadgets that inspire more people to join you in this adventure.

I would also like to express my gratitude to my entire family for supporting me during the creation of this book. They actively participated in the data acquisition of many of the use cases by driving me around while I was holding an accelerometer, placing sensors in the refrigerator for me, playing notes on the piano to test the classification model, taking pictures of their hand signals, holding a sensor while they jumped to simulate free fall, and many more. We did this together.

Nothing could have happened without the BPB team, to whom I am eternally grateful. From believing in the book concept, being patient during the revisions, accepting my changes, guiding me through the process, and helping me get to the finish line; all with the best attitude and kindness there could be.

And finally, I need to recognize the entire TinyML ecosystem and its awesome community. All the tools, all the SDKs, books, blog posts, etc are pure gold, thank you. Special thanks to Nordic, Bluetooth, Arduino and Edge Impulse.

Preface

The idea for this book was born from my fascination with the intersection of machine learning and embedded systems. In the last few years, I have seen how AI has transformed industries. Many of the most powerful applications remain locked within cloud servers and large computing infrastructures. My goal with this book is to help bridge that gap by showing readers that it is possible to bring intelligence to edge devices and make TinyML accessible to engineers, makers, and innovators who want to deploy machine learning in real world, low power environments.

TinyML is the latest frontier for AI and ML models, as its constraints are everywhere. Memory is scarce, and computing is smaller by orders of magnitude compared to traditional computing used to train and run the models. Therein, however, lies one of the greatest opportunity windows in many years. When you think about the future, you do not imagine just text editors that help you write a letter but an interactive physical world, appliances and stand-alone devices transacting with people in the most natural way, friendly furniture, smart clothing, and personalized gadgets. All of that is the great promise of TinyML. It is our once-in-a-lifetime opportunity to not only live in the future but to create it.

Another important aspect about this book is its breadth. The principles of each concept are explained lightly; however the variety of domains covered is wide. Instead of focusing solely on the data science aspect of the TinyML models, we include system design (requirements are mapped to an hypothetical business problem that needs to be solved), data acquisition challenges (rather than just assuming the existence of a ready made data set available on the internet), feature extraction (which is directly impacted by data quality, a real issue in production environments), model design (understanding how the model works under the hood is critical in constrained environments where resource waste is not an option), electronic component configuration (using existing electronic components instead of just running in simulators), networking (since real world solutions are often distributed across a surface rather than confined to a single location), power considerations (as connection to the electric grid cannot be assumed), and bill of materials research (because cost is a fundamental metric in real-life systems).

Chapter 1: Foundation and Methodology - This chapter walks the reader through the concepts and terminology used throughout the book. It also established the scope of each one of the use cases in this book.

Chapter 2: Sound Classification - This chapter focuses on identifying the features that define sounds according to their specific use cases. We utilize Mel Frequency Cepstral Coefficients (MFCC) for human voices, which excel in recognizing linguistic attributes such as inflection rhythm and silences. Fourier Coefficients are employed for transient sounds to delineate the sound by its power distribution across frequencies, which is essential for capturing the unique energy profile of each sound. Periodic tones are analyzed through spectrum analysis to uncover their distinctive frequency signatures. We employ Convolutional Neural Networks to leverage the spatial representation of sound (across time and magnitude) for pattern recognition, training the model to convert the output layer into a probability distribution used to classify the sound sample.

Chapter 3: Movement Classification - In exploring movement classification, we gather data from three orthogonally placed accelerometers to accurately describe object movement. By breaking down the accelerometer readings into thirteen distinct features and segmenting the wave into small time windows, we calculate metrics such as root mean square, kurtosis, spectral kurtosis, and skewness. These metrics reveal critical aspects of movement, from the average power indicating the movement's energy to kurtosis and skewness, offering insights into the frequency and suddenness of movements. The rich dataset feeds into a dense neural network, enabling precise classification of movements ranging from gentle to vigorous.

Chapter 4: Image Classification - Focusing on image classification, we acquire images through a direct connection to a digital camera interfaced with a microcontroller. Preprocessing steps include adjusting the image to a square format and, if color is not critical, converting it to 8-bit grayscale to streamline object recognition models' application. Images are resized to a standard size to accommodate the neural network's capacity. Rather than training from scratch, we apply industry standard TinyML models and a technique called transfer learning to efficiently train the model with our dataset, achieving a fast and accurate system applicable across various machine vision scenarios.

Chapter 5: Object Tracking - This chapter introduces tracking, a technique often paired with Image Classification to consistently identify an object across sequential video frames. Whether tracking moving or static objects, the method involves first classifying objects with a Convolutional Neural Network and then comparing their sequential positions to deduce if they are the same based on proximity. Successful tracking assigns consistent

IDs to objects, maintaining identity even through temporary classification lapses or visual obstructions, showcasing the robustness of a good tracking algorithm.

Chapter 6: Sensor Fusion - Sensor Fusion is examined as an advanced method of combining data from multiple sources to generate new insights. We categorize sensor fusion into complementary, competitive, and cooperative types. Complementary fusion brings together different data perspectives of the same event, while competitive fusion seeks reliability through redundancy in data acquisition. Cooperative fusion merges data from unrelated events to synthesize new information, highlighting the technique's versatility in enhancing system perception.

Chapter 7: Deep Learning Regression - This chapter explores using deep neural networks to infer numerical values from one or more data sources. We demonstrate how integrating feature engineering with deep learning can expand the realm of regression applications. We discuss developing control systems using regression models with multiple inputs and outputs that apply continuous learning and adaptation to current conditions. This chapter illustrates how regression can forecast future conditions based on historical data, opening new possibilities for predictive analytics.

Chapter 8: Anomaly Detection - This chapter examines the anomaly detection method, which aims to identify occurrences that deviate from expected patterns. Distinguishing itself from classification, anomaly detection focuses on detecting behaviors or events previously unseen by the model.

Code Bundle and Coloured Images

Please follow the link to download the
Code Bundle and the *Coloured Images* of the book:

https://rebrand.ly/m6t6yc9

The code bundle for the book is also hosted on GitHub at
https://github.com/bpbpublications/Applied-TinyML.
In case there's an update to the code, it will be updated on the existing GitHub repository.

We have code bundles from our rich catalogue of books and videos available at **https://github.com/bpbpublications**. Check them out!

Errata

We take immense pride in our work at BPB Publications and follow best practices to ensure the accuracy of our content to provide with an indulging reading experience to our subscribers. Our readers are our mirrors, and we use their inputs to reflect and improve upon human errors, if any, that may have occurred during the publishing processes involved. To let us maintain the quality and help us reach out to any readers who might be having difficulties due to any unforeseen errors, please write to us at :

errata@bpbonline.com

Your support, suggestions and feedbacks are highly appreciated by the BPB Publications' Family.

Did you know that BPB offers eBook versions of every book published, with PDF and ePub files available? You can upgrade to the eBook version at www.bpbonline. com and as a print book customer, you are entitled to a discount on the eBook copy. Get in touch with us at :

business@bpbonline.com for more details.

At **www.bpbonline.com**, you can also read a collection of free technical articles, sign up for a range of free newsletters, and receive exclusive discounts and offers on BPB books and eBooks.

Piracy

If you come across any illegal copies of our works in any form on the internet, we would be grateful if you would provide us with the location address or website name. Please contact us at **business@bpbonline.com** with a link to the material.

If you are interested in becoming an author

If there is a topic that you have expertise in, and you are interested in either writing or contributing to a book, please visit **www.bpbonline.com**. We have worked with thousands of developers and tech professionals, just like you, to help them share their insights with the global tech community. You can make a general application, apply for a specific hot topic that we are recruiting an author for, or submit your own idea.

Reviews

Please leave a review. Once you have read and used this book, why not leave a review on the site that you purchased it from? Potential readers can then see and use your unbiased opinion to make purchase decisions. We at BPB can understand what you think about our products, and our authors can see your feedback on their book. Thank you!

For more information about BPB, please visit **www.bpbonline.com**.

Join our book's Discord space

Join the book's Discord Workspace for Latest updates, Offers, Tech happenings around the world, New Release and Sessions with the Authors:

https://discord.bpbonline.com

Table of Contents

CHAPTER 1

Foundation and Methodology

Introduction

If asked what can analyze its surroundings, understand ongoing events, and respond without external help, your likely response would be a living organism, particularly an animal. This is correct, but you could also accurately say an **Applied TinyML** system. A TinyML application gathers data, analyzes it, extracts insights, and reacts to the environment at or near the data source. This method offers significant advantages: it ensures privacy by keeping data local, enables real-time decision-making without cloud delays, eliminates single points of failure by distributing decision-making, reduces communication costs, and creates a scalable system with thousands of devices working towards a goal. Additionally, distributing computation lowers power consumption, making battery or solar power feasible for off-the-grid use.

In this chapter, we begin with an overview of data acquisition, discussing ideal data types and frequencies, peripherals, labeling techniques, and noise reduction. Next, we guide you through processing, feature selection, and extraction. We then examine **machine learning** (**ML**) model types, suitable architectures, and hyperparameter tuning for enhanced accuracy. After obtaining the model's refined result, we show how to write a program to use or communicate this result, including issuing commands to actuators and displays.

In distributed applications, data acquisition, processing, and actuation rarely occur on the same device, requiring a network for device communication. You will learn to use a pub/sub paradigm for scalable, decentralized communication. Finally, understanding power consumption and selecting appropriate power sources is essential, as is preparing a bill of materials to ensure your project's financial and maintenance viability.

Structure

The chapter covers the following topics:

- TinyML in AI
- Designing and building a TinyML application

Objectives

The goal of this chapter is to introduce the terminology and concepts covered throughout the book. We begin with an overview of TinyML and its role within **artificial intelligence (AI)**, then explore what constitutes a TinyML application. We outline the steps to create one, from defining the problem and developing the concept, to deciding on data acquisition, selecting features, creating the model, and crucially, deploying it while considering hardware, network, and power usage.

TinyML in AI

TinyML applications operate on devices with limited computational capacity and low power requirements. However, these constraints are technological, not goal oriented. If we could integrate the power of a **graphic processing unit (GPU)** into a microcontroller lasting a decade on one battery, the objective would remain a self-sufficient entity operating at the Edge. Thus, the industry often refers to these applications as EdgeML.

In a standalone application, each design decision affects every subsystem. The data's size and frequency determine the sensor type, exchange protocol, transmission network, processing microcontroller, storage memory, display interface, and power source.

TinyML is a subset of AI specifically tailored to apply AI's capabilities to the smallest and most energy-efficient hardware. While AI encompasses many technologies and applications, TinyML focuses on making a subset of these technologies work in the most resource-constrained scenarios.

The core concept behind minimizing AI model sizes lies in the realization that you can train models in powerful machines but deploy them in significantly lower-power microcontrollers. Typically, the training of TinyML models occurs on powerful cloud-based GPUs, utilizing vast datasets amounting to hundreds of gigabytes. Through employing various optimization strategies that reduce the model's dimensionality and accept minor, often imperceptible, losses in accuracy, the model's size can be reduced to just a few megabytes. This size reduction makes it feasible to deploy the models onto microcontrollers. However, this approach applies only to specific models with certain types of inputs and outputs. Despite these limitations, the research community remains exceptionally vibrant, frequently publishing new white papers introducing advanced AI models into the TinyML sphere. The progression began with sound classification for microphone activation, extended to image classification, followed by anomaly detection, and eventually to compact language models.

Level of experience and knowledge required to use TinyML

The landscape of TinyML application development is transforming, making it more accessible and intuitive than ever before. Historically, modeling and implementing physical behaviors into applications required a deep understanding of mathematics and seasoned software engineering skills. However, ML has created a new, more natural methodology for development that is easier to understand and mirrors the human learning process. Just as individuals acquire language skills through trial and error rather than memorization of grammatical rules, ML models learn from examples. By presenting a dataset and indicating the desired outcome, the Model iteratively adjusts through multiple attempts, improving its accuracy over time.

This evolution in the development paradigm is significantly lowering the barriers to entry in the field of TinyML. By equipping non-technical individuals with user-friendly tools for data collection, modular processing components, model training interfaces, and practical usage examples, ML technology is becoming accessible to a broader audience. This democratization of technology empowers anyone interested in learning and applying ML, paving the way for widespread adoption and innovation across diverse domains. The implications of this shift are profound, offering the promise of unleashing creative solutions and applications by people who were previously excluded from the technological development process due to the complexity of traditional methods.

Designing and building a TinyML application

A TinyML application is a solution that tackles a practical problem that exists in a business, organization, or location. This book teaches readers how to define, design, plan, budget, and build TinyML applications.

A TinyML application has elements of data science, software, ML, electronics, networking, power management, and **user interfaces** (**UI**), among many others. It is, nevertheless, possible to simplify its components as abstract building blocks.

The best way to stay on track is to follow a methodology that allows us to see the big picture, eliminate unnecessary complexity, and tackle one aspect of the system at a time while staying focused on creating something valuable that delivers value.

Throughout this book, we use a 10-step method to define the problem, develop concepts that could become a solution, select the suitable model, select the right features, use the right tools to train the model, test it, and integrate all this into an embedded solution that can be deployed to a real environment.

The method's steps are as follows:

1. Define the problem
2. Concept development
3. Data acquisition
4. Feature engineering
5. Model creation
6. Integrating the ML model
7. Hardware, electronics and connectivity
8. Networking
9. Power management
10. Materials and costs

These steps have been explained in detail in the further sections.

Step 1: Defining the problem

This step involves delineating the current situation, essential requirements, and metrics for success while remaining open to various potential solutions. You should be able to answer the following ten questions before starting any project. The document with the answers will guide the design decision-making in the following steps and validate the final implementation:

First, we define the problem:

- What is the current state?
- What is the desired state?
- What obstacles are preventing the transition from the current to the desired state?
- In what manner will this solution be utilized?

Next, we identify the data available for addressing the problem and establish a metric for tracking your progress:

- What data is accessible to tackle this issue?
- What output would you like the system to produce to demonstrate its effectiveness?
- Does the solution require any changes to the environment?

Finally, we specify the constraints of the solution:

- Where must the solution be implemented?
- Is it necessary for the solution to operate on an independent power source?
- Must the solution offer real-time updates?
- What is the allocated time and money budget for this solution?

Recognizing that this document is dynamic and will evolve over time is crucial. As the project advances through its various phases, you may realize that your initial goals could be more ambitious and require refinement or that the data you intended to use is challenging to obtain, needing an alternative approach. Additionally, changes in the project's location or shifts in environmental conditions may occur. View these developments as part of an iterative process where adjustments are acceptable and expected. The key is to remain focused on addressing the problem at hand.

Step 2: Concept development

In this step, we sketch a preliminary diagram showcasing a potential solution leveraging TinyML technology. This phase is inherently iterative, often requiring multiple iterations to align with expected metrics, functionality, and operational costs.

The core idea behind concept development is to generate multiple options to reduce the risk of choosing a suboptimal solution, which is achieved by exploring the solution space. To do this, we draft at least three different ways to solve the same problem. You need at least three, not only one, because usually, the first concept is the recipient of all our biases and assumptions of a solution, which is not necessarily the optimal one but, in most cases, based on personal preferences. The second concept will allow you to explore new approaches to solve the same problem. The third concept will be a good mix between the first and second concepts.

Creating the concept

The best way to create a concept is to represent its functionality in blocks. Each block should do one and one thing only. Each block can be represented as a black box with an input and an output.

Methodology

You can translate an idea like this one, there should be a people counting sensor on each one of the three doors communicating wirelessly to an LED panel showing the total people count, into a diagram.

Draw a diagram with as many boxes (or blocks) as components, name each, and list its main characteristics (color, type, voltage, etc.). Indicate what data is moving between blocks by writing it using the arrows that link the blocks (temperature signal, inference results, image, etc.). Try to estimate the cost of each component. Write the number by the blocks.

Once you have a couple of different concept diagrams, qualify them against each other by comparing their commonalities:

- Create a spreadsheet that lists the total cost of components. Is the project cost within a reasonable budget?

- Are components easy to find?

- Do you know how to implement every component?

- Is this the solution that uses the least number of components?

- Is this the solution that solves the problem the best way?

Step 3: Data acquisition

Edge computing is the act of bringing computation to the data instead of data to the computation. Edge devices are naturally well-positioned to acquire data via cameras, microphones, accelerometers, or any other available sensor.

The components that make data acquisition possible are sensors, UI and drivers.

Sensors

A sensor is a device that converts physical signals into electrical signals. A physical signal could be anything from changes in acceleration, temperature, sound, or the light that produces an image. Among the most relevant sensors for TinyML applications are microphones, cameras, displacement, position, and proximity sensors, temperature sensors, light sensors, velocity and motion sensors, IR sensors, touch sensors, UV sensors, and air quality sensors. The characteristics you need to consider when selecting a sensor for your application are:

- **Range**: Minimum and maximum limits of the input.

  What are the minimum and maximum values your application needs to acquire from this sensor? Sensors are usually designed to capture a range that is used by typical use cases (e.g.: Most temperature sensors cover the range of temperatures that a thermostat can operate on). However, if your application needs to capture corner cases like sub-zero temperatures or temperatures in an oven, your choices might be limited to a couple of sensors. Additionally, you want most of the readings in your application to fall in the middle of the range of the sensor, this is to have some room for your system to capture all readings without saturating. Saturation happens when your sensor tries to read out of its range, the output will not show the real temperature but the limit temperature your sensor can read which might cause your application to draw incorrect conclusions.

- **Accuracy**: Degree to which the reading conforms to the correct value.

  What is the risk of getting a wrong value every so often in your application? A sensor's accuracy is usually directly proportional to its price. In most cases, average accuracy is more than enough for your application. Accuracy is essential when false positives are much more expensive than false negatives. In other words, if missing an event is more costly than having a false alarm, you want to invest in an accurate sensor.

- **Sensitivity:** The ability of a system or instrument to detect small changes in the reading.

  Does your application care about slight variations in the readings? Sensitivity measures a sensor's ability to discern and extract meaningful information from faint stimuli, defined as the minimum signal level at which it can operate effectively. Two main constraints limit a sensor's sensitivity; the first is its resolution, defined as the most minor change a sensor has been designed to perceive. The second constraint is the noise the sensor components allow to be introduced to the signal. Sensors with higher resolution and good shielding against noise are generally more expensive. Ask yourself if your application needs high sensitivity before investing in one.

- **Stability**: Ability of a sensor to maintain consistent output over time despite external changes or disturbances.

  Will your application operate in an unpredictable environment? A sensor should be able to measure one and one thing only, disregarding what is happening around it. The degree to which a sensor is not affected by other factors is its stability. Consider this characteristic if you want to design your system once and install it in multiple environments. An example is a car counting system that should work everywhere. You want to ensure the count is the same on a rainy or sunny day, whether inside a garage or outdoors. You can only measure this parameter by trial and error, as every environment differs. You can always use a complementary sensor to reduce the error using sensor fusion (refer to *Chapter 7, Deep Learning Regression*).

- **Repeatability:** Ability of a sensor to consistently produce the same results under unchanged conditions over repeated trials.

  Is your application trying to detect change over long periods? Or will the readings be used as a point of reference? Every sensor should always return the same result if it measures the same event. Repeatability characterizes the error that a sensor introduces to the reading over time. Knowing this error is essential to countering it by using filters, periodically resetting the sensor, or accounting for it in the result.

- **Response time:** Duration a system or component takes to react to a given input and produce an output.

  How fast does your application need to respond to changes? This parameter is essential when the readings are part of a control system that must react to an event quickly. A delay in the response time can be caused by a phenomenon called hysteresis that impedes the sensor to change state caused by a temporary resistance to change in its components. A different cause for delay is the use of filters. Many sensors clean their data before returning it. Passing the signal through a filter comes with the cost of a delay. The better the filter, the shorter the delay, and the better the results.

- **Ruggedness:** Sensor's durability and ability to operate reliably under extreme environmental and mechanical stresses.

  Will the application be outdoors or in a rough environment? This characteristic concerns every sensor installed in a real implementation. Ruggedness has many dimensions. The obvious one is the mechanical stress a device needs to endure, but there is also electrical and thermal stress. Will the sensor survive a power surge? Will it melt on a scorching day?

User interface

Not all inputs are acquired using a sensor; in many instances, a user pressing a button, activating a switch, moving a slider, or rotating a dial is what the system uses to trigger a process, infer data, or issue control commands to actuators. The difference between a user input and a sensor is not clearly defined. For example, an optical switch is a proximity sensor that flushes a toilet. TinyML has created even more examples where the UI is expanded thanks to classification and regression models. For example, a classification and tracking sensor that detects and recognizes faces could replace a keypad that authenticates users.

There are many types of basic **user input devices**, such as buttons, switches, sliders, dials, and keypads. Like sensors, they share the same characteristics: range, accuracy, sensitivity, stability, repeatability, response time, and ruggedness.

The outputs of the UI components are similar to those of sensors and can be either analog or digital. Similarly, once their signal reaches the microcontrollers, it is converted to an 8-bit or 16-bit digital signal.

Drivers

Drivers are software components in charge of receiving the signal from the sensor and making it readily available to the software running the TinyML model.

Drivers play a crucial role in facilitating communication between computing systems and sensors. Each driver has unique capabilities tailored to specific needs. Some drivers are designed to interface with sensors using well-established protocols (I2C, UART, ISP), ensuring seamless data transmission. However, custom-built drivers are required to enable communication when sensors operate on proprietary or non-standard protocols.

Driver data handling varies significantly. While some drivers are designed to receive a continuous stream of data passively, others actively request data from the sensor. Additionally, certain drivers can convert analog signals into digital format, making the data more accessible for digital processing.

Some drivers offer advanced data management features beyond basic data transmission. They may aggregate data to provide a comprehensive overview, buffer data to prevent loss during connection interruptions or use moving windows to calculate and output an average of recent readings. Other drivers can handle data in packages, ensuring structured and efficient data processing.

Security and data integrity are also vital considerations. Some drivers can receive encrypted data, maintaining the confidentiality and security of the transmitted information. Acknowledgment of received data is another feature that ensures the data transmission process is reliable and errors are promptly identified.

Some drivers offer additional processing capabilities to enhance data quality and usability. They can correct errors, interpolate missing data to maintain continuity, filter out noise to improve signal clarity and translate or convert data into more useful formats. Furthermore, some drivers have resampling features that allow the adjustment of data sampling rates to match the application's requirements.

There are many parts and variations in a driver architecture. However, there are three main steps:

1. The driver communicates with the sensor and brings the bytes to memory.

2. The driver interprets the bytes and translates them into a format the system can use.

3. It takes care of the additional functionality (if any) such as buffering, encrypting, correcting, filtering, resampling, etc.

Drivers are located inside the microcontroller and are usually written in the same language as the system's primary language. They are also often referred to as libraries of the sensor.

Step 4: Feature engineering

Feature engineering is the process of selecting, modifying, or creating new features from raw data to improve the performance of ML models. It involves using domain knowledge to extract and transform the most relevant information from the data, making it more suitable for modeling. Effective feature engineering can significantly enhance model accuracy by providing the most pertinent, insightful data representations, which might not be immediately apparent in the raw data. This step is crucial because the quality and relevance of the features used directly influence the model's ability to learn and make accurate predictions or decisions.

Feature engineering for images

Feature engineering for images involves the process of transforming raw image data into a structured format that an ML model can understand and use to make predictions or classifications. This process is crucial because it helps highlight the important elements of an image that distinguish one category from another, enhancing the model's learning efficiency and predictive accuracy. Here is how feature engineering for images typically unfolds:

- **Preprocessing**: This initial step involves cleaning and normalizing the images. Cleaning could mean removing corrupted images or those that do not meet certain criteria. Normalization usually involves scaling pixel values to a standard range, often between 0 and 1, to reduce variability between images and help the model learn more effectively.

- **Size reduction**: Images are often resized to a uniform dimension before being fed into an ML model. This not only ensures consistency across the dataset but also reduces the computational load. The choice of size depends on the model's requirements and the balance between retaining enough detail for accurate classification and minimizing computational demands.

- **Color space conversion**: Depending on the application, converting images from one color space to another (e.g., from RGB to grayscale or HSV) can be beneficial. For some tasks, color may not be relevant, and converting images to grayscale can simplify the model without significantly impacting performance. For other applications, different color spaces might highlight relevant features more effectively than the standard RGB.

- **Augmentation**: Image augmentation artificially increases the size and diversity of the training dataset by applying a series of random transformations to the images, such as rotation, scaling, flipping, and cropping. This helps the model generalize better and reduces the risk of overfitting, especially when the available dataset is limited.

Feature engineering for accelerometer readings

Feature engineering for accelerometer readings involves processing raw time-series data from accelerometers to extract meaningful attributes (features) that effectively capture the underlying patterns of motion. Accelerometers, which measure acceleration forces in one or more directions, generate data that can be rich in information but challenging to interpret directly. The goal of feature engineering in this context is to transform this data into a form that makes it easier for ML models to recognize patterns, such as walking, running, or other physical activities.

The process starts with preprocessing the raw accelerometer data, which may include filtering to remove noise and normalizing the data to a consistent scale. Given the time-series nature of accelerometer data, it is common to segment the continuous stream into smaller, fixed-size windows. This segmentation is crucial because it allows the model to analyze discrete chunks of data, making it easier to identify and classify short-term patterns of movement.

For each window of data, a variety of statistical and time-domain features are typically extracted. These can include basic statistics like the mean, median, standard deviation, and range of the acceleration signals, which provide a summary of the data's central tendency and variability. More complex features, such as the **root mean square (RMS)**, **signal magnitude area (SMA)**, and zero-crossing rate, help capture the energy, intensity, and frequency of movements. Additionally, frequency-domain features, obtained through techniques like Fourier Transform, offer insights into the dominant frequencies of motion, which can be indicative of specific types of activities.

Feature engineering for soundwaves

Feature engineering for sound inputs in ML is a critical process that involves transforming raw audio signals into a set of descriptive features that capture the essential characteristics of the sound. Given that audio signals are complex and can contain a wide range of frequencies, durations, and intensities, extracting meaningful features is essential for training ML models to perform tasks such as speech recognition, music genre classification, or environmental sound detection.

The process begins with preprocessing the audio data, which may include normalization to ensure consistency in volume levels across different recordings and possibly converting the audio into a uniform format and sampling rate. Noise reduction techniques might also be applied to clean up the recordings and improve the quality of the features extracted.

A fundamental step in feature engineering for sound is the extraction of relevant features from the audio waveforms. Time-domain features, such as zero-crossing rate (the rate at which the signal changes from positive to negative and vice versa) and energy (the sum of squares of the signal values, normalized by the length of the signal), capture basic properties of the sound. However, much of the useful information in an audio signal is better represented in the frequency domain or as a combination of time and frequency domains.

Spectral features, extracted through techniques like the Fourier Transform, provide insights into the distribution of power across different frequencies within a sound. Common spectral features include spectral centroid (indicating the *center of mass* of the spectrum), spectral bandwidth (the width of the spectrum), and spectral roll-off (the frequency below which a certain percentage of the total spectral energy is contained). Another powerful set of features are the **Mel-Frequency Cepstral Coefficients (MFCCs)**, which mimic the human ear's response to different frequencies and are particularly effective for speech and music processing.

In addition to these, more advanced feature extraction methods can explore the modulation of sound signals, harmonic patterns, and even the use of deep learning models like **Convolutional Neural Networks (CNNs)** to automatically learn optimal features from spectrograms (visual representations of the spectrum of frequencies of a signal as it varies with time).

Feature engineering for timeseries from sensors

Feature engineering for time series data captured from sensors involves transforming the sequential data collected over time into a structured format that ML models can effectively use for prediction, classification, or anomaly detection tasks. Given the ubiquity of sensors in domains such as industrial monitoring, healthcare, environmental tracking, and wearable technology, the ability to accurately interpret sensor data through feature engineering is critical for extracting meaningful insights and making informed decisions.

The process typically begins with preprocessing steps to ensure data quality and consistency. This may include cleaning the data to remove noise or irrelevant signals, normalizing to standardize the range of data values, handling missing values through imputation, and potentially segmenting the continuous data stream into manageable, discrete windows of time. These windows can then be analyzed individually, enabling the model to recognize patterns over specific intervals.

For each window or segment of the time series, a variety of features can be extracted:

- **Statistical features**: Basic statistical measures such as the mean, median, standard deviation, variance, minimum, and maximum values provide a summary of the data's central tendency and dispersion. These features are easy to compute and can give a quick overview of the data's characteristics within each window.

- **Temporal features**: Including lag features (values at previous time steps) and moving averages can help capture the temporal dependencies and trends in the data, essential for forecasting and trend analysis.

- **Frequency domain features**: Applying Fourier Transform or Wavelet Transform converts the time series into the frequency domain, allowing the extraction of features related to the dominant frequencies and cyclical patterns in the sensor data. This is particularly useful for identifying periodic behaviors or distinguishing between different types of signal modulation.

- **Autocorrelation features**: The autocorrelation function, which measures how the data points in the series correlate with each other at different lags, can reveal the presence of repeating patterns or seasonality in the data.

- **Domain-specific features**: Leveraging domain knowledge to create features specific to the application or sensor type can significantly enhance model performance. For instance, in wearable technology, features capturing the intensity and frequency of human activity, such as steps per minute or heart rate variability, can be particularly informative.

- **Derivative and integral features**: Calculating the derivative (rate of change) or integral (cumulative sum) of the time series can highlight changes in the sensor readings over time or the accumulation of a quantity, respectively.

Feature selection follows feature extraction, where the most informative and relevant features are identified and retained for model training, while redundant or irrelevant features are removed. This selection process is crucial for improving model accuracy, reducing overfitting, and enhancing computational efficiency.

Step 5: Model creation

With the data acquired and the features defined, the next step is to decide which model is better suited to perform the task and help us fulfill our goal.

A machine learning system is a mathematical construct that learns patterns from data. It adjusts its structure and parameters through training to minimize errors between its predictions and actual outcomes. Once trained, an ML model can make predictions or decisions based on new, unseen data. These models are central to ML and can range from simple linear regression to complex deep neural networks, depending on the task and the amount of data available. They are used across various applications, including image recognition, natural language processing, and predictive analytics, adapting and improving their performance as they are exposed to more data. The tasks to prepare a model involve choosing an algorithm, splitting the data, training the model, evaluating the model, monitoring and updating the model.

Choosing an algorithm

Select an appropriate ML algorithm based on the problem type, the nature of the data, and the desired outcome. Classification helps you identify classes, regression allows you to infer quantities, and anomaly detection finds uncommon patterns in your data. Let us look at these in detail:

- **Sound classification:** It is a process where ML models are trained to identify and categorize sounds into predefined classes or labels. By analyzing audio data, these models learn to recognize patterns and features that distinguish different sounds, such as human speech, music, environmental noises, or animal sounds. This involves extracting relevant features from the audio signals, such as frequency components, amplitude, and temporal characteristics, and feeding them into neural networks.

  - **Applications**: Voice recognition, surveillance for unusual sounds, noise monitoring, etc.

- **Movement classification:** It involves training ML models to recognize and categorize types of physical movements or activities based on sensor data. This process typically uses data from accelerometers, gyroscopes, or other motion sensors embedded in devices. The models learn from patterns in the sensor data, such as movement, speed, direction, and acceleration.

  - **Applications**: Health and fitness tracking, driving styles, Free falling object detection, etc.

- **Image classification:** This is a technique where ML models are trained to identify and categorize images into predefined classes or categories. This process involves analyzing visual data, extracting relevant features from the images, such as textures, colors, shapes, and spatial relationships, and using these features to teach the model how to differentiate between various types of images. Deep learning models, particularly CNNs, are commonly used for this task due to their effectiveness in handling complex image data.

- o **Applications**: Facial recognition systems, medical imaging diagnosis, object detection, content categorization, etc.

- **Regression:** ML based regression is a predictive modeling technique for estimating the relationships between a dependent variable and one or more independent variables. The goal is to understand how the dependent variable changes as the independent variables are varied. Unlike classification, which predicts discrete labels, regression predicts continuous outcomes. Various types of neural networks are employed to model and predict these continuous outcomes, making regression a versatile tool for analyzing and forecasting numerical data.

- o **Applications**: Prediction of sensor values, real-time control, weight estimation, etc.

- **Anomaly detection**: This is a technique for identifying unusual patterns or outliers in data that do not conform to expected behavior. This is achieved by training ML models on data representing normal operations or states, allowing them to learn the underlying patterns and distributions. Once trained, the model can detect deviations from these patterns in new data, signaling potential anomalies.

- o **Applications**: Outlier detection, water leak detection, intrusion.

Splitting the data

The rationale behind splitting datasets is a foundational practice in ML designed to evaluate the performance of models accurately and prevent overfitting. The dataset is split into training, validation and testing subsets and is used as follows:

- **Training set:** This data set is used to train the model, allowing it to learn the underlying patterns and relationships in the data. Based on the feedback from this data set, the model's parameters are adjusted to minimize errors.

- **Validation set**: The model is tested against the validation set after training. This data set is not used for training but serves to evaluate how well the model generalizes to new data. It is crucial to tune the model's hyperparameters and make decisions about the model architecture without touching the test set. Using a validation set helps detect overfitting early on, as performance on this set can indicate when the model starts to learn the noise in the training data rather than the actual signal.

- **Testing set**: This is the final, untouched set of data used to evaluate the model's performance after it has been trained and validated. Testing the model on this separate set provides an unbiased assessment of its generalization ability to new, unseen data. To ensure the accuracy of this evaluation, this data must be only used once, at the end of the process.

Training the model

The training process of a ML model is a crucial phase where the model learns to make predictions or decisions based on data. Initially, the model is fed a large set of training data, including the input features (data points) and the corresponding target values (labels or outcomes). This data set is representative of the real-world scenarios the model is expected to handle. The training process aims to adjust the model's parameters (e.g., weights in neural networks) so that its predictions closely match the target values in the training set.

Training involves an iterative process where the model makes predictions based on the training data, and adjustments are made to its parameters based on the accuracy of these predictions. The difference between the model's predictions and the actual target values is calculated using a loss function, which measures the model's error. An optimization algorithm, such as gradient descent, is then used to minimize this error by iteratively adjusting the model's parameters. This process is repeated over many cycles (or epochs) until the model's performance on the training data reaches an acceptable level of accuracy or until further improvements become negligible.

Monitoring the model's performance on the training data and a separate validation set is vital during training. This helps to ensure that the model is learning to generalize from the training data to new, unseen data rather than merely memorizing the training set (a problem known as overfitting). Various techniques, such as regularization and dropout (for neural networks), can be employed during training to prevent overfitting and improve the model's ability to generalize. Once the training process is complete, the model's final performance is evaluated using a separate test set, which provides an unbiased assessment of how well the model will perform in real-world applications.

Evaluating the model

The evaluation process of a ML model is a crucial step that follows the training phase, aiming to measure how well the model performs on unseen data. This step is essential for assessing the model's generalization capability, which is its ability to apply what it has learned to new, similar problems. Evaluation involves using specific metrics appropriate for the type of ML task (classification, regression, clustering). For example, classification tasks might use accuracy, precision, recall, F1 score, and the area under the ROC curve (AUC-ROC). In contrast, regression tasks could use **mean squared error (MSE)**, **root mean squared error (RMSE)** or **mean absolute error (MAE)**.

The process typically involves a separate data set known as the testing set, which the model has not seen during its training phase. This ensures that the evaluation reflects the model's performance under real-world conditions. In many cases, cross-validation techniques are also employed to ensure that the evaluation is not biased by how the data was split into training and testing sets. Cross-validation involves dividing the dataset into several subsets, then training and evaluating the model multiple times, using a different subset as the test set and the remaining data for training. The final performance is averaged across all these iterations, providing a more robust estimate of the model's performance.

Tuning and optimizing the model

A ML model's tuning and optimization process is critical in enhancing its performance by systematically adjusting its parameters and configuration. After an initial model is trained and evaluated, tuning involves experimenting with various hyperparameters that control the learning process and model architecture. Hyperparameters include learning rate, the complexity of the model (such as the number of layers in a neural network), regularization strength, and many others, depending on the type of algorithm being used.

Optimization uses techniques like grid search, random search, or more sophisticated methods such as Bayesian optimization. Grid search evaluates the model performance for a comprehensive combination of hyperparameters within a specified range, while random search randomly selects combinations, providing a quicker but less exhaustive exploration. On the other hand, Bayesian optimization uses the results of previous evaluations to intelligently choose the next set of hyperparameters to evaluate, often leading to more efficient finding of the optimal configuration.

The process is inherently iterative, requiring multiple rounds of training and evaluation to identify the set of hyperparameters that yield the best performance according to the chosen metrics (e.g., accuracy, precision, recall for classification tasks, or MSE, RMSE for regression tasks).

Additionally, model optimization may involve feature engineering and selection to improve model input quality or explore different model architectures. The goal of the tuning and optimization process is to arrive at a well-performing model that fits the training data well and effectively generalizes to new, unseen data.

Deploying the model

Deploying a ML model to an Edge device with limited connectivity presents unique challenges that require careful planning and optimization to ensure the model operates effectively within the constraints of the device. The process begins with optimizing the ML model to suit the Edge device's limited processing power, memory, and storage capabilities. Techniques such as model pruning, quantization, and knowledge distillation reduce the model's size and computational demands while maintaining its predictive performance. This optimization phase may involve using specialized tools and frameworks designed for Edge deployment, like TensorFlow Lite or PyTorch Mobile, which can convert the model into a more efficient format for execution on low-power devices.

Once the model is optimized, it is packaged for deployment, often alongside a minimal runtime environment that facilitates model inference on the Edge device. The deployment process must consider the device's operating system, hardware specifications, and the software stack required to run the model. Given the limited connectivity, the model is designed to perform inference locally, process data directly on the device, and make decisions without constantly communicating with a server. This not only conserves bandwidth but also ensures the device can operate independently, even in the absence of a network connection. When connectivity is available, a strategy for data synchronization is implemented, allowing the device to update model parameters, send aggregated insights, or download new models and updates as needed.

Monitor and update

Monitoring and maintenance mechanisms are also crucial components of the deployment process. These systems can be designed to operate with minimal data transmission, focusing on essential metrics that indicate the model's performance and the device's health. Updates to the model, driven by changes in data or improvements in the algorithm, are carefully managed to minimize bandwidth usage and disruption. Often, differential updates are employed to transmit only the changes since the last version.

Step 6: Integrating the ML model with the application code

Application code refers to the set of computer programs or software instructions written to perform specific tasks, functions, or operations within a software application. This code forms the backbone of any application and dictates its behavior, functionalities, and interactions with users, other applications, and hardware resources.

Integrating an ML model into application code effectively turns a static application into a dynamic, AI-enhanced system capable of learning from data, making decisions, and adapting to new information over time. The integration involves writing code within the application that interacts with the ML model. This includes loading the model into the application environment, preparing or preprocessing input data in the format the model expects (for e.g., scaling images, encoding categorical data), and invoking the model to make predictions. After receiving predictions, the application may need to post-process the results (e.g., decoding output, applying thresholds) before presenting them or acting based on them.

Step 7: Hardware, electronics and connectivity

A TinyML application is a ML system that runs on low-power, resource-constrained devices such as microcontrollers.

A TinyML application can do the following:

- Connect to sensors and other input peripherals.

- Run stand-alone ML models.
- Execute application code.
- Control switches, motors, and other actuators
- Communicate with other devices
- Run on batteries, solar power, or low-voltage power sources

In its simplest form, a TinyML application consists of a single device that acquires its data, runs a model, and performs an action with the resulting information.

In cases where the data sources are spread across a wide area, like a warehouse or a hotel, keeping the TinyML application in one single device (e.g., one sensor in every area analyzing readings independently) is challenging. Furthermore, it is not only difficult to achieve but not even recommended. The resource-constrained nature of the devices will not be able to sustain the analysis of multiple sources, let alone run a couple of ML Models and control several actuators on a single device. The solution to this scalability issue is to spread computation across multiple devices.

Using multiple devices requires us to think about data differently. The legacy paradigm, which would require capturing and forwarding raw sensor data to the cloud for further examination, cannot and should not be replicated in an Edge-based system. The fundamental shift is based on the principle that data and information are not the same. Data captured by sensors should be processed locally, and only information should be shared between different devices.

Data versus information

Data and information are related concepts, but they differ significantly in meaning and Function within the context of processing and analysis.

Data refers to raw, unprocessed facts and figures without any context. It can come in various forms, such as numbers, text, images, or sounds, and is typically collected from measurements, observations, or responses. Data on its own may not convey direct meaning; for example, a list of numbers representing temperatures over a period is just data without context.

Information, on the other hand, is data that has been processed, organized, or structured to add context and make it meaningful and useful. After analyzing data, interpreting it, and putting it into context, information is what you get. Using the previous example, if the collected temperature data is organized to show trends over time, such as an anomaly, it becomes information that can inform decisions.

Sending data between devices

Information requires only a few bytes and can be transmitted at intervals less frequently than raw data. For that reason, for devices limited by resources, transmitting information is substantially more manageable in terms of memory and battery usage than sending raw data.

Sending and receiving a few bytes at low frequencies is the key to running a network of devices for a TinyML application with constrained resources (low memory, small computation capacity, and, in many cases, battery-powered).

Low-energy network technology exists for many use cases. LoRa enables low-energy communication for very long ranges, LTE-M enables low-energy communication using cellular infrastructure, and Bluetooth Mesh enables low-energy communication in local area networks, to mention a few. By design, each of these technologies has incredibly low bandwidth. The fewer bytes that need to be sent out, the less energy, memory, and computation you need. This makes low energy networks a perfect match for TinyML applications.

Using a network requires extra hardware. A microcontroller can run a TinyML model and manage its wireless network communication simultaneously; however, it is not recommended. A secondary microcontroller is the way to go for network communication. Most examples in this book use an Arduino as the primary microcontroller to run the TInyML model and an NRF52840 Dongle as a secondary microcontroller to receive and send wireless messages using a Bluetooth Low Energy Mesh Network.

Connection schematic

The following figure illustrates how devices and components in a TinyML application can be interconnected with a low energy network:

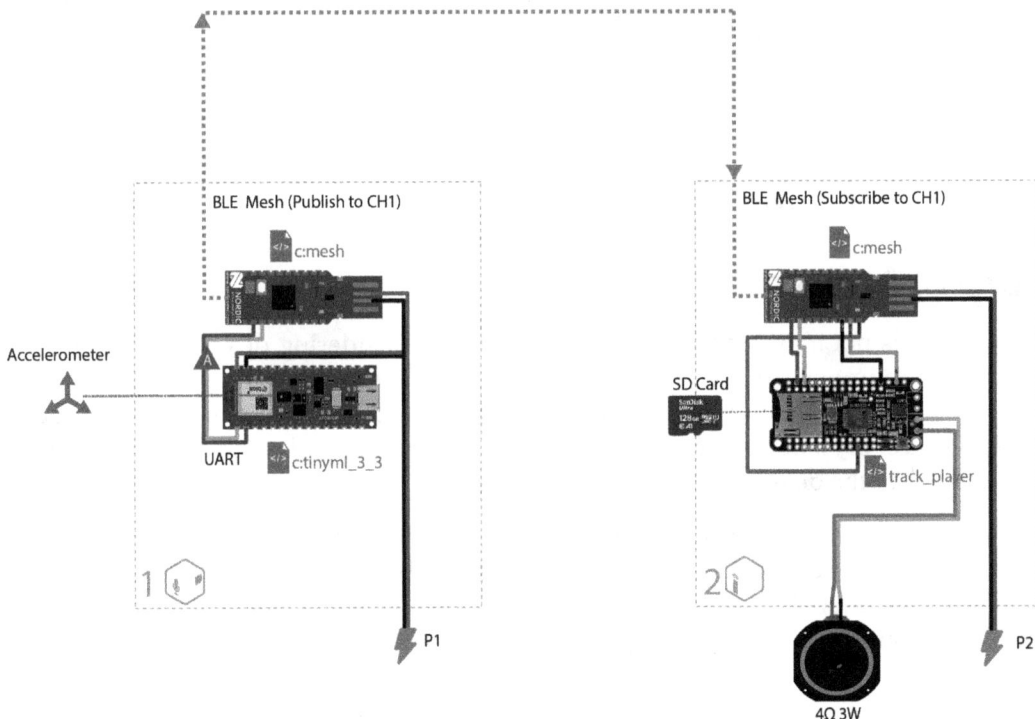

Figure 1.1: Connection diagram

Across this book, devices are portrayed as blocks with connection pins corresponding to their physical footprint. Connections are described with lines that start at a pin in the device transmitting information and end at a pin in the device receiving information. Refer to the following conventions:

- **Blocks**: Each device shows the following characteristics by its diagram block.
    - **Name**: Unique name of the device (e.g., Temperature Room 5).
    - **Type**: What the device is (e.g., Temperature Sensor).
    - **Technical characteristics**: Relevant device specs (e.g., 10mA @5V).
- **Connections**: Each connection shows its characteristics along its line.
    - **Data**: A reference to the data it is transporting (e.g., Raw Temperature Data).
    - **Protocol**: The protocol used in communication (e.g., I2C, UART, etc.).
    - **Direction**: Arrow showing what component is receiving the application data.
    - **Network**: If the connection involves a wireless network, the line is dotted, and its characteristics are explicitly stated (e.g., Channel, Frequency, Subscription, etc.).
- **Firmware**: If Firmware or a model is to be loaded onto a device, the device block explicitly shows its reference.
    - **Firmware**: Name of the executable to be loaded into the device (e.g., `Tiny_3-2.hex`).
    - **TinyML model**: Name of the model to be loaded on the microcontroller (e.g., `Temp_Anomaly_1`).

Step 8: Networking

Networking is not a topic you might think of when considering designing and building a TinyML application. As seen in the last section, networking is only necessary when the project needs to be split into multiple devices because of its size, complexity, or distribution across a space. Each device performs a specialized function and communicates its results with the rest of the devices using a network.

Low-energy mesh networks are best suited for applications requiring low power consumption and extensive coverage with a large number of small, interconnected devices. In contrast, traditional LAN networks are geared towards environments demanding high-speed data transfer, stability, and higher power consumption.

Comparison between a mesh and a LAN network

A low energy mesh network is a type of wireless communication network designed to connect devices with minimal power consumption in a reliable way. A **local area network (LAN)** is a network that connects computers and devices within a limited geographical area, such as a home, school, or office building, to share resources and information.

The characteristics of a mesh network are as follows:

- **Design principle**: A low energy mesh network is based on technology designed for short-range communication between devices. It employs a mesh networking architecture, allowing devices to communicate with each other directly or indirectly through other devices in the network, forming a mesh of interconnected nodes.

- **Purpose and use cases**: A low-energy mesh network primarily aims at low-power, low-bandwidth applications. It is ideal for **Internet of Things (IoT)** scenarios, smart business automation, and applications requiring extended coverage across multiple devices without a central router or extensive power consumption.

- **Power efficiency**: A low energy mesh network is highly power-efficient, making it suitable for battery-operated devices.

- **Range and speed**: While a low energy mesh network extends its range by allowing messages to hop between devices, its speed is relatively low compared to traditional LAN networks, as it is optimized for small data packets.

- **Scalability**: A low-energy mesh network can support thousands of nodes, facilitating large-scale device networks.

The characteristics of a LAN network are as follows:

- **Design principle**: Traditional LANs are usually based on Ethernet (wired) or Wi-Fi (wireless) technologies, which are designed for high-speed data transmission over relatively short distances.

- **Purpose and use cases**: LAN networks are suited for office, home, and industrial networks where high data throughput and reliable connectivity for computers, servers, and other network devices are required.

- **Power efficiency**: Power efficiency is less of a concern for traditional LANs, especially wired ones, as they often rely on continuous power sources.

- **Range and speed**: Traditional LANs offer higher data transfer speeds and a stable connection but are typically limited in range to the confines of a building or immediate geographic area without additional networking hardware like repeaters or bridges.

- **Scalability**: While LANs can support many devices, scalability is often constrained by the capacity of the central router or switch and the complexity of managing an extensive network.

Implementation strategy

The strategy consists of not having to select a single technology but leveraging the advantages of each type of network. Low energy mesh networks are usually utilized in the outer part of the Edge to communicate with sensors and actuators scattered around the area covered by the TinyML application. One of the low energy mesh nodes can be used as a gateway to have commands and status updates jump to a wider area network. Depending on the project, the wider area network can be a Wi-Fi connection or a wired LAN; if those networks are unavailable or difficult to access, an LTE-M network can reach the internet. A LoRA gateway is used to send out and receive data at long distances if a cellular connection is not an option because of cost or availability.

Notice that we are not creating a pipeline to send large amounts of data. There are small packets of data jumping networks and eventually reaching their destination. A little lag is acceptable because all we receive are status updates; the action takes place in the microcontrollers in real-time. Data is being acquired, classification is happening, anomalies are detected, and control commands are sent out to actuators on the spot. There is no need to call a cloud or remote system every time a decision needs to be made.

BLE mesh

The low-energy mesh network technology used in this book is **Bluetooth Low Energy Mesh Network (BLE Mesh)**. There are a couple of other excellent options, like ZigBee or Thread. Feel free to explore them all and select the one you feel most comfortable with for your projects.

The BLE mesh network employs a **Publish-Subscribe (Pub/Sub)** model to facilitate communication between devices within the network. This model is a fundamental part of BLE mesh's design, enabling efficient, scalable, and flexible message distribution without requiring direct device-to-device connections.

In the Pub/Sub model, network devices are configured as publishers, subscribers, or both. Publishers send messages to a specific topic without knowing which devices will receive them. Subscribers listen for messages published on topics they are interested in. In the context of BLE Mesh, a topic is often represented by a "group address" that subscribers can register to receive messages from.

When a device (publisher) has data to share, such as a sensor reading or a status update, it publishes this information on a predetermined topic. All devices (subscribers) that have subscribed to that topic automatically receive the published message. This mechanism allows for the decoupling of devices within the network, meaning that devices do not need to maintain information about other devices' network addresses. Instead, they communicate based on shared interests (topics), leading to a highly flexible and dynamically reconfigurable system.

The Pub/Sub model in BLE mesh is particularly advantageous for IoT and smart environments, where devices may frequently join or leave the network, and the system's configuration can change over time. It simplifies sending commands or disseminating information across a wide range of devices, from lighting systems and temperature sensors to alarms and automated machinery, enabling complex interactions and behaviors to be programmed with relative ease.

Each use case in this book contains a table specifying each device's publish and subscription configurations using the BLE mesh network. The source code includes a ReadMe document with detailed instructions on configuring the node.

Step 9: Power management

Power management in TinyML implementations is a critical aspect that ensures ML models can operate effectively on low-power, resource-constrained devices like microcontrollers and embedded systems. Given that TinyML applications are often deployed in battery-powered or energy-harvesting environments, such as IoT devices, wearables, and remote sensors, optimizing power consumption is essential to extend the operational lifetime of these devices and maintain functionality.

Power management in TinyML involves several strategies and techniques:

- **Efficient model design:** Designing lightweight ML models requiring less computation and memory. Techniques like model pruning, quantization, and knowledge distillation help reduce the model's complexity without significantly impacting its accuracy.

- **Duty cycling**: Implementing duty cycling by alternating between active and sleep modes is a common strategy. The device actively performs computations, such as data collection, inference, and communication, only during the active phase and enters a low-power sleep mode for the rest of the time.

- **Energy-aware algorithms:** Developing algorithms that are aware of the energy consumption and adapt their behavior based on the available power. For example, an algorithm might reduce the frequency of inferences or data transmissions under low battery conditions.

- **Hardware optimization:** Leveraging hardware features that consume little power, such as specialized low-power processing units for ML tasks, efficient sensor management, and energy-efficient communication protocols.

- **Selective sensing and processing:** Implementing strategies to selectively collect and process data based on predefined criteria or the detection of significant events, thus avoiding unnecessary computations and data transmissions.

- **Adaptive computing:** Dynamically adjusting the computational workload based on the task's complexity and the device's current energy state. This may involve choosing between different models or adjusting the model parameters to balance power consumption and performance.

Effective power management in TinyML implementations requires a holistic approach. This approach combines hardware and software optimizations to minimize energy consumption while delivering computational and inference capabilities. By doing so, TinyML applications can achieve long-term, autonomous operation, unlocking the potential for intelligent, connected devices everywhere, even in the most power-constrained environments.

Step 10: Materials and costs

In a TinyML implementation, a **bill of materials** (**BOM**) is a detailed inventory that lists all the components required to build and deploy a TinyML device or system. The BOM plays a crucial role in outlining the specific hardware and possibly software components needed to support ML functionalities for each one of the devices.

The BOM for a TinyML implementation typically includes microcontrollers, sensors, actuators, power sources (like batteries or solar panels), connectivity modules (such as Bluetooth or WiFi components for data transmission), and any additional components required for the device's physical assembly and operation. It may also detail specific component versions or models to ensure compatibility and performance.

Furthermore, the TinyML BOM can extend beyond hardware to include software licenses or services necessary for the device's operation, development tools, and ML model deployment. This comprehensive document is instrumental for project planning, cost estimation, procurement, and assembly processes, ensuring that all parts are accurately specified and accounted for. It facilitates the efficient and effective realization of TinyML projects by providing a clear and organized overview of all necessary materials and resources.

Conclusion

This chapter introduced the concept of TinyML and its significance as a subset of AI. It provided an explanation of applied TinyML and detailed the steps involved in developing an application. These steps include defining the problem, developing the concept, acquiring data, selecting features, designing the model, integrating it with a real application, selecting appropriate hardware, determining the need of network communication, understanding power requirements, and calculating the materials and costs associated with the project.

In the upcoming chapters, the reader will learn how to classify sounds, images, and movement; combine sensors to create new readings; perform regression using neural networks; and detect anomalies, all using TinyML.

CHAPTER 2
Sound Classification

Introduction

In this chapter, you will learn how to categorize and identify different types of sounds or audio signals automatically. Your system will be able to distinguish between various kinds of noise, music genres, human speech, animal sounds, environmental sounds, and more. Sound classification occurs in three main stages: acquisition, subtracting features from the soundwave, and running the soundwave features against a classification model. The output of this process is an array of numbers that indicates the probability of the sound being similar to one of the classes the model has been trained with.

However, before we can run inferences against real-time microphone input, we need to acquire data to train the model, select the best way to extract features from the type of sound we have captured, select the type and architecture of the model we will use to classify the data, and lastly, train the model iteratively until we get the performance and accuracy that we require.

Structure

This chapter covers the following topics:

- Acquiring data to train the model
- Balanced, diverse, and sufficient datasets

- Model
- Use case: Spectrogram based processing
- Use case: MEF based processing
- Use case: MFCC based processing

Objectives

By the end of this chapter, the reader will know how to acquire a balanced and sufficient data set for audio classification. The reader will also learn how to extract features from a raw soundwave. Additionally, the chapter discusses the architecture of a Neural Network specialized in sound classification. The reader will become familiar with all the steps and moving parts required to deploy a TinyML-based sound classification system in a real environment.

Acquiring data to train the model

Before capturing your data, you need to decide what your objectives are. In specific, you need to decide what are the different classes you want your model to recognize. Classification belongs to a category of machine learning models called **supervised learning**. Supervised learning implies that your model can only recognize known classes. For example, you cannot ask your model to recognize the sound of an animal that you do not have sound samples of.

There are many ways to obtain data to train your model. You can either use existing datasets or record your own. The former is more convenient if you know where to look for it; the internet is an excellent source of sound. Look for video platforms where people upload videos of everything imaginable. The main issue with using pre-recorded sounds you did not produce is that they might not reflect real sounds and noise situations your system will have to interact with. In other words, your model will work great in a controlled environment but fail in a real installation.

Since this book is about applied TinyML, and our objective is to create systems that run in real conditions (not only in controlled environments), it is recommended to capture your data in the location where you are going to install the system. Its advantages are the following: The white noise of the space is included in the training, the location of the microphones near the sound source could introduce unexpected noise (e.g. a refrigerator humming or the background sound of a crowded street), the soundwave might include atypical patterns, sounds or delays that you would not get from a studio produced sample that you downloaded from the internet.

There are great tools out there that make data acquisition a breeze. For this book, we used the Edge Impulse data acquisition client, which we can run from any smartphone. It captures, labels, and uploads all the samples for us. Refer to the following figure:

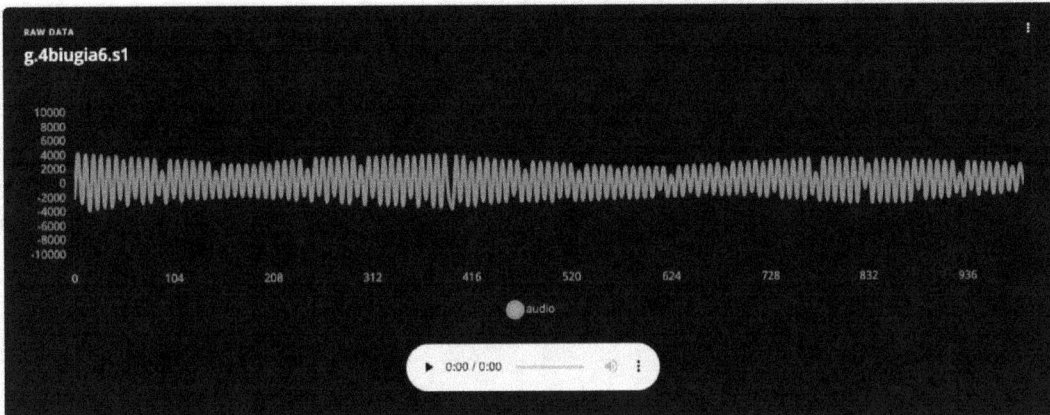

Figure 2.1: *Edge Impulse data visualization tool*

Balanced, diverse, and sufficient datasets

The main objective of a training dataset is to help the model generalize. Generalization is the characteristic that allows the model to reliably and accurately infer a class from unseen data.

A good training data set is balanced, diverse, and sufficient. Balanced means that all the classes are equally represented. Let us say you are trying to classify the sounds of a dog and a cat. If you train the model mostly with dog sounds, the model will know more nuances about the sounds dogs make. The model will indeed declare the sound belongs to a cat when it is obvious. When there is a sound that could be either one of them, it will lean towards declaring the sound as coming from a dog, as it might know that dogs make a similar sound and will not know that cats do it as well. A diverse dataset shows many instances of the same class that are different but maintain characteristics that define them as part of the same group. Using the dog and cat example, a diverse data set will include sound samples from many types of dogs and cats. A sufficient data set is large enough to allow the model to reach generalization. The rule of thumb is that more data is better. However, there is an inflection point of diminishing returns where more data would not make more difference. If you find yourself in that situation and still do not have the level of accuracy that you need after adding a substantial amount of data, you should reconsider your approach (maybe placing the microphones in a different place).

Extracting features from an acoustic signal

You can think of the features of an acoustic signal as a series of numbers that characterize a specific sound and allow the model to remember and find patterns in it. When a system runs in a real scenario, the microcontroller transforms the soundwave into numbers in real-time. Those numbers are fed into the model. The model will return a score of how similar the sound is to other sounds it was trained with. If the score is high enough, we can assume that the incoming sound is similar to the sound the model trained with.

Processing

The process of turning a soundwave into features consists of a series of sequential processing steps. The more specialized the features we are trying to extract, the more steps are required. There are 3 main sets of feature sets used in sound classification: Spectrogram, **Mel Filter Extraction (MFE)**, and **Mel Filter Cepstral Coefficients (MFCC)**. The steps used to obtain each one of the feature sets is shown in the following figure:

Processing

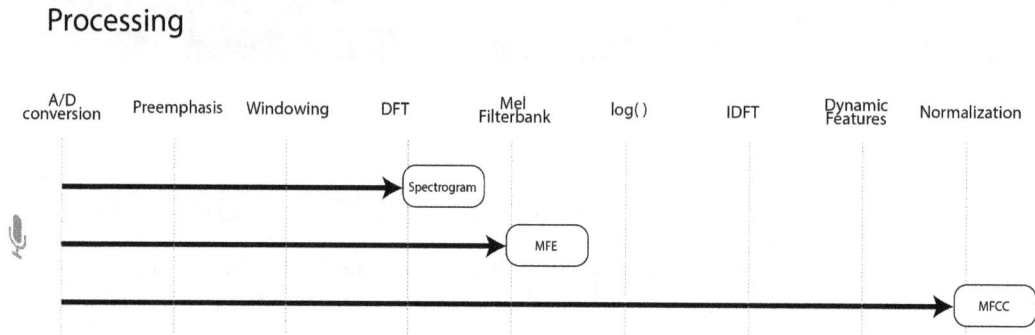

Figure 2.2: Processing steps

- **Analog to digital conversion**: This process is the act of turning an analog soundwave into a digital signal. The way it is done is that once every sixteen-thousandths of a second (that is, 16KHz), the microcontroller will read the voltage in one of its pins (the one connected to the microphone). Then, it will translate that voltage into a digital number stored in a memory register. If the register is 8 bits, the soundwave can only have 256 levels, zero being no sound and 256 being the loudest level. 16 bits is better, as every reading can be expressed in 65,536 levels.

  You may wonder why it is important to have more levels to express a soundwave. Think about a low-resolution image that you have downloaded from the internet. It is frustrating that you cannot see much detail even if you zoom in. It works the same with sound. If you capture a soundwave in **low resolution**, your model would not be able to recognize many details in your sound and might struggle to differentiate between two similar sounds. Having said this, remember we are in the universe of TinyML, where resources are incredibly constrained. Your use case might be fine with 8-bit soundwaves.

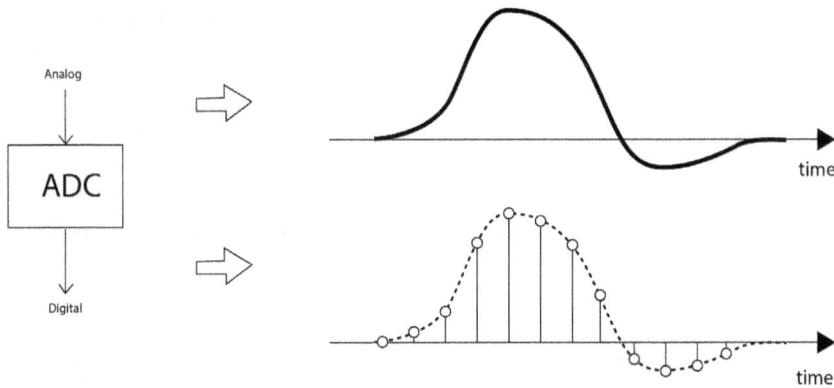

Figure 2.3: *Analog to digital conversion*

- **Pre-emphasis:** Due to the nature of sound waves, the lower tones tend to carry more energy, while the higher tones tend to carry less energy. Both are equally important. To avoid the model being biased towards tones with higher energy levels (that it can listen to more clearly), we modify the high tones to have a similar amount of energy. That is why this process is called **emphasis**. We emphasize the higher tones.

- **Windowing**: We have about 16 thousand samples per second. We group 400 of those readings to create a window of 25 milliseconds and then store them for further processing. Then, we advance 10 ms and perform the same operation again. This will give us about 100 windows per second of soundwave. Refer to the following figure:

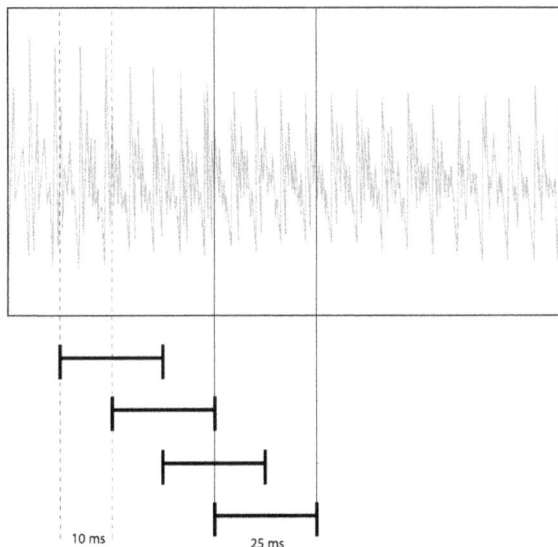

Figure 2.4: *Windowing*

- **Discrete Fourier Transform**: It transforms the time-based signal into the frequency distribution of the given window. The result of The **Discrete Fourier Transform (DFT)** provides a unique footprint of the sound that we are analyzing. The output of a DFT is also known as a spectrogram. If you align multiple spectrograms across time on the X-axis and align the frequencies on the Y-axis, you get a graph that represents the soundwave sample. If you are classifying sounds with a fixed pitch or a sound that has continuous frequencies (e.g. the sound of a machine, a musical instrument, or ambient noise), a spectrogram is enough to train the model.

> **Note: In this case, the features represent the magnitude of the sound at different frequencies over time.**

However, if you want to make a classification that emulates human perception (like animal sounds or voices) you might want to focus on eliminating data from your signal that is not relevant to the human ear. The following figure shows a sample of a spectrogram:

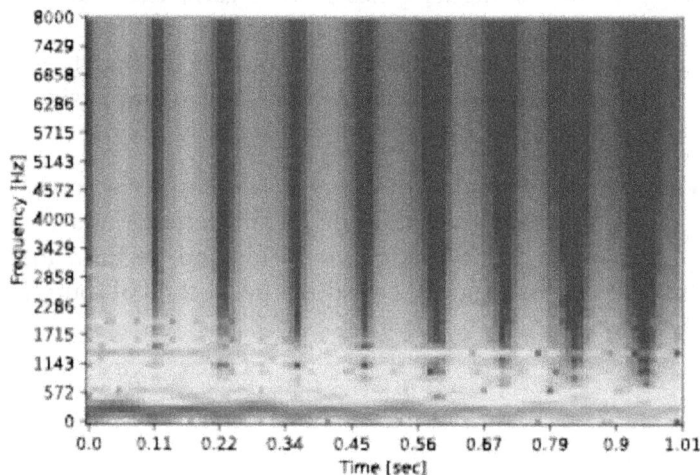

Figure 2.5: Spectrogram (source: Edge Impulse)

- **Mel filter bank**: It filters out information that human perception does not consider important. It does so by comparing the signal with something called the Mel scale. The Mel scale specifies what frequencies are ignored by the human ear at different levels. If you align all the different Mel scales one after the other, you create a bank of scales as shown in the following figure:

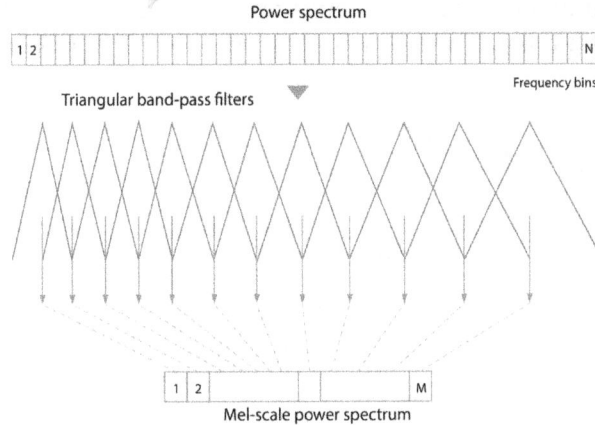

Figure 2.6: Mel filter bank

This step filters out all the data that the human ear does not consider relevant, according to the **Mel filter bank (MFB)**. The output of this step is like a spectrogram but oriented to human perception. It is incredibly useful to train models that focus on sounds that the human perception considers relevant. Among all the sounds that are of interest to humans, spoken word is the most important. As you might imagine, there is a way to obtain features that specialize exclusively in human language. *Figure 2.7* shows a spectrogram after filtering data not relevant to human language:

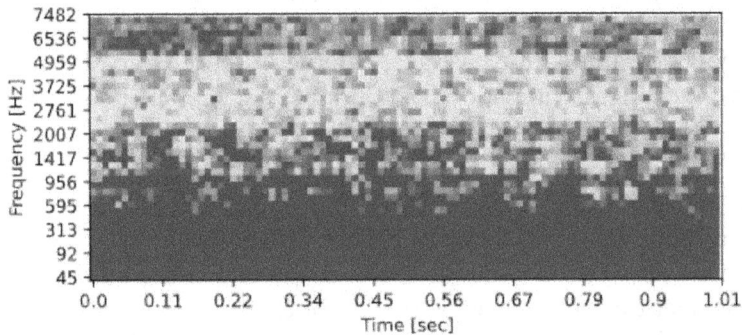

Figure 2.7: Spectrogram after the Mel filter bank (source: Edge Impulse)

- **Log function**: It removes the logarithmic nature of the MFB output that humans are less sensitive to.

- **Cepstrum inverse discrete fourier transformation (IDFT)**: It brings back the signal to the time domain with the signals already decomposed. By having the signals already separated, we can cherry-pick the signals we want to ignore (For example, signals that show pitch in a voice are irrelevant as we want to create a general model that disregards the pitch of the person) and select those that define voice recognition features. This step extracts 12 cepstral features and reconstructs the signal with them. The following figure shows a sample of the reconstructed signal:

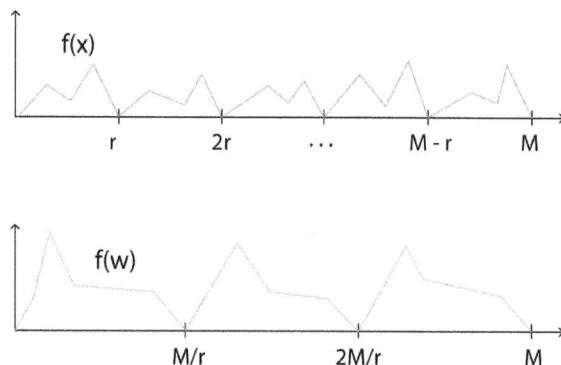

Figure 2.8: Decomposed signals after inverse discrete fourier transformation

- **Dynamic features**: This step focuses on obtaining information about context and pronunciation. It is done by adding a 13th feature to the cepstral features that define how much energy there is in the frame. Once we have the 13 features, we want to see how they change in time. We do this by differentiating the 13 features against time (first derivative). This helps us identify closures, gaps, and silences in the spoken language soundwave being analyzed. While the first derivative shows the rate of change of the features, the second derivative shows the rate of change of the change in the features. In an abstract way, this works as a mechanism to not only know how intonation changes (whether it is going up, down, or flat) but also how fast it changes. Intonation is a fundamental characteristic of any language.

The first and second derivatives can be explained as follows:

The signal carrying a spoken word takes on different shapes depending on the sound it represents. The shape of silence differs from that of a vowel, and so on. Mathematically, a model identifies the shape of a curve by analyzing changes in its slope over time. To reveal a curve's slope, we use its first derivative, a concept familiar from high school calculus. By deriving the 13 features and feeding them into the model, we effectively communicate the shape of the curve. The 13 derivatives are added to the features that we will send to the model.

Since derivatives express the rate of change, this second derivative no longer describes the shape of the curve itself but rather how the shape evolves over time. In the context of speech, if a word is always pronounced exactly the same way, its shape remains consistent. However, when the word is pronounced with variation, such as when asking a question, where pitch rises at the end, the shape remains similar but changes dynamically. The second derivative captures these nuances, providing insights into tone and speed of pronunciation, which can help the model detect sentiment or intention. The 13 second derivatives are added to the features that we will send to the model.

- Between the 13 cepstral features and the 26 dynamic features, we have 39 features. This group of 39 features is known as MFCC. The following figure shows the 13 cepstral features in time:

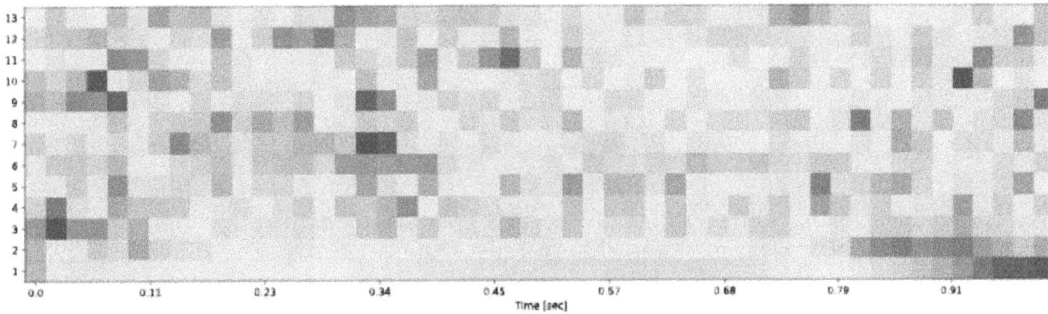

Figure 2.9: Cepstral features in time (source: Edge Impulse)

- **Cepstral mean and variance normalization**: This final step, as its name indicates, normalizes the characteristics of the sample to account for variations during the recording.

Selecting the right processing block for the job

Processing a soundwave delivers three different feature sets that can be fed into a deep Neural Network. The first and the most basic one, the spectrogram, is the simplest yet diverse of them all as it expresses sound as is. It retains the most information from the original sound wave.

Unless you are trying to classify a voice or a sound as **perceived by the human ear**, use the spectrogram. In the second place, we have the audio MFE. As described in the last section, this group of features is a human perception-oriented spectrogram. All the information in the soundwave that would be ignored by the human ear has been eliminated, and anything left has been emphasized. Use the audio MFE if you want the classifier to differentiate sounds like you would. The third set of features is the MFCC, which specializes in human language. Its features express not only an analysis of the word in terms of frequencies but also their context across different frames in time, intonation, word separation, silences, and pronunciation. Use the MFCC for any language-related classification (like wake words). *Figure 2.10* shows the decision process to select the right processing block:

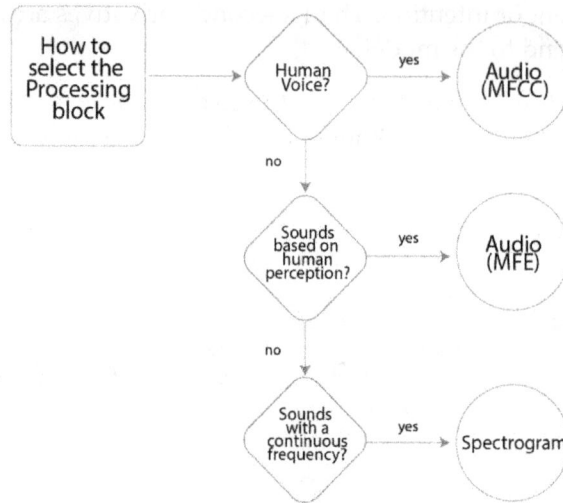

Figure 2.10: Selection of the process block

Model

The architecture of a machine learning model for sound classification typically uses convolutional layers as its core building blocks. A model can have many layers, each one with different filters, activations, and functions. *Arzo Mahmood* et al. in their 2021 paper called *Speech Recognition based on Convolutional Neural Networks and MFCC Algorithm*, proposed a simple yet powerful architecture with two convolutional layers, multiple dropouts, and one dense layer as shown in *Figure 2.11*. This architecture is widely used in TinyML projects that need to classify sound because of its simplicity, accuracy, and lightweight profile:

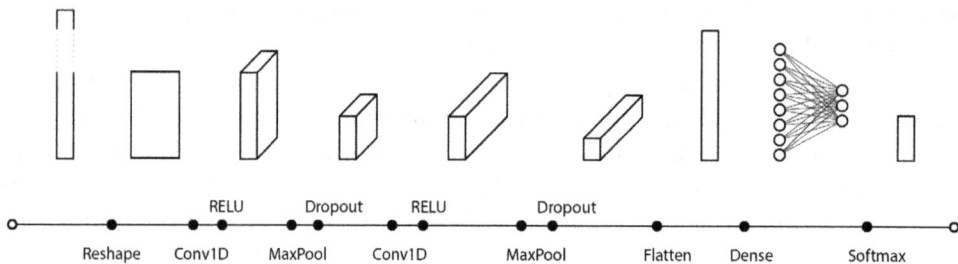

Figure 2.11: Architecture of a convolution neural network specialized in sound classification

The first layer takes the output from the processing stage and reshapes it from its original size to fit the Convolutional Neural Network input (shown in *Figure 2.12*). Assuming we are using a 128 x 50 spectrogram where every frame is 0.02 seconds with a stride of 0.01 seconds. 128 represents the number of frequency bands returned by the Fourier transform. 50 represents the number of frames in this sample.

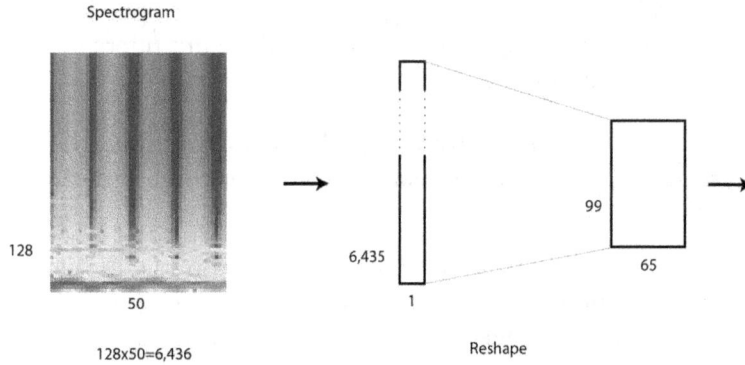

Figure 2.12: *Reshaping the spectrogram to fit the CNN input layer*

If we use an MFE, its dimensions should be 40x99. The 40 represents the number of filters in the filter bank. The 99 represents the number of frames in the sample. *Figure 2.13* shows a representation of the reshape layer:

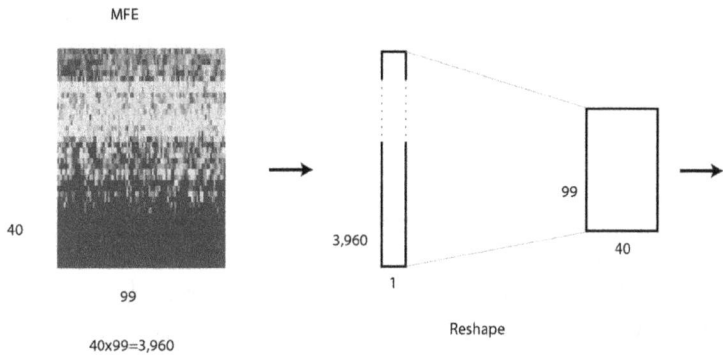

Figure 2.13: *Reshaping the MFE features to fit the CNN input layer*

If we use an MFCC, its dimensions are 13x50. The 13 represents the thirteen cepstral features. The 50 represents the number of frames in the sample as shown in *Figure 2.14*:

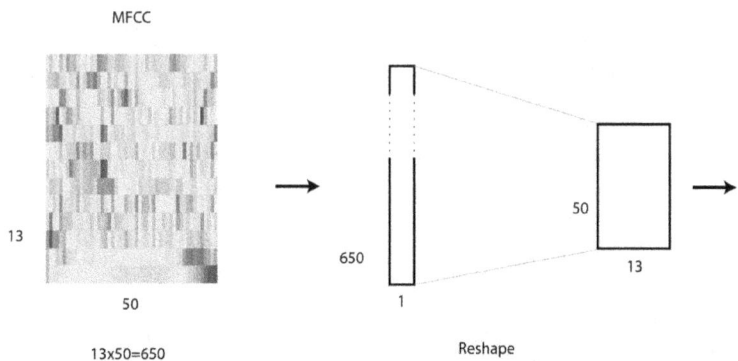

Figure 2.14: *Reshaping the MFCC features to fit the CNN input layer*

Now that we have all the processing stage features in the right shape, we run a 1D convolution with a kernel of 3 and step of 1 through the eight filters to discover different spatial characteristics of the input.

Note: This technique is borrowed from the CNNs convolutional layers from image classification. In them, the filters accentuate (or filter out) characteristics like horizontal lines, shapes, etc.

Spectrograms and MFCCs are visual representations of sounds. In this case, the shapes represent frequencies, silences, intonation, volume, etc. In other words, by turning sounds into images, we can use the image classification toolbox effectively to classify sounds as well. After the convolution, we run the output through an activation layer called **Rectified linear unit (ReLU)** that turns any negative number to zero. *Figure 2.15* shows a representation of the first convolutional layer:

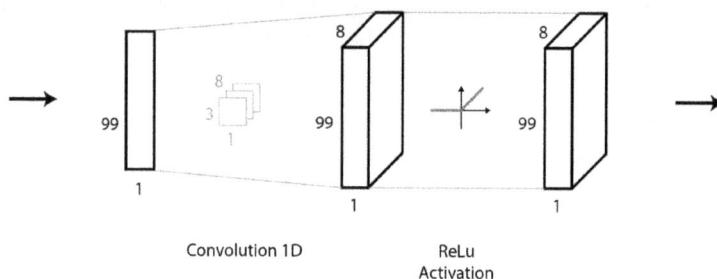

Convolution 1D   ReLu
                        Activation

Figure 2.15: First convolution layer

After that, we run the data through a max pooling layer with a stride of 2. This layer reduces the size of the array by selecting its most representative values. Immediately after, we run the data through a dropout function (0.25). What the dropout does is randomly remove features to avoid overfitting. Think about it as a way to force the network to look for alternatives on how to recognize a pattern. By doing so, you make the network more general and reliable. *Figure 2.16* shows a representation of the MaxPool and Dropout layers:

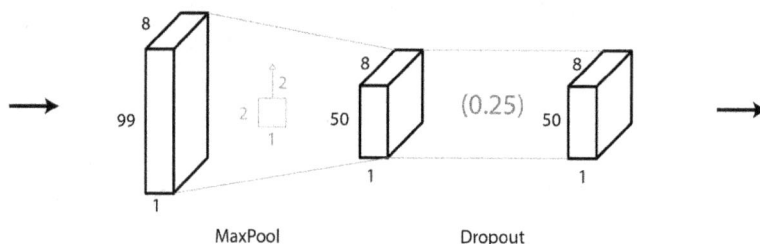

MaxPool   Dropout

Figure 2.16: MaxPool and Dropout layers

What happens after the dropout is a duplicate of the last four steps: We run the convolution again (now with 16 filters), the ReLU, MaxPool, and the dropout layer. In the end, we flatten the 3D matrix to obtain a vector of 400 features. *Figure 2.17* shows a representation of the Second Convolution, MaxPool and Dropout layers:

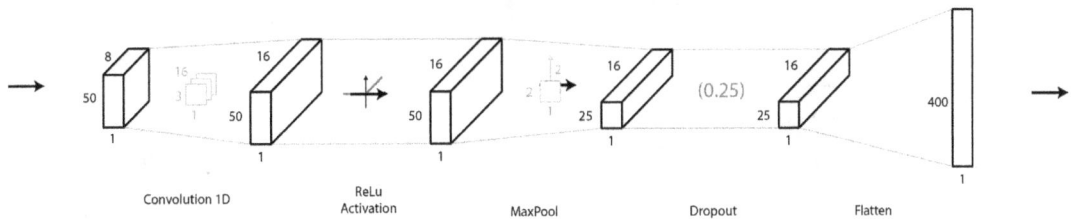

Figure 2.17: Second Convolution, MaxPool and Dropout layers

We connect each one of the 400 features in parallel to the input of a dense layer. This layer is used to iteratively create a function that returns a desired output giving an input. We create this function by running data through it several times, analyzing how far the result is from the desired output, modifying its coefficients to reduce the error, and trying repeatedly until the error is acceptable. With the help of the Softmax function, we turn the output of the dense layer into a probability distribution. *Figure 2.18* shows a representation of the Dense network and Softmax function:

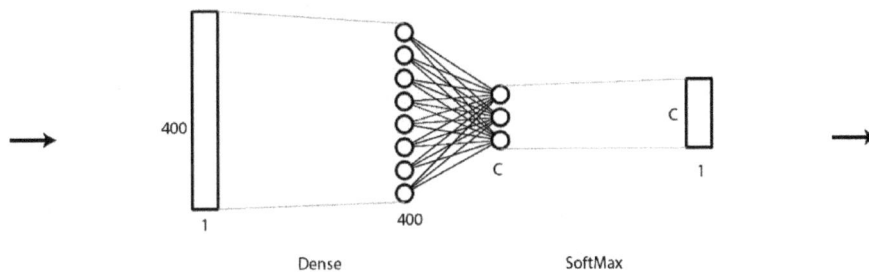

Figure 2.18: Dense network and Softmax function

This output distribution indicates the probability of an input belonging to a known class. The classes represent each one of the labels in the dataset that we used to train the model. If the probability is high enough (>90%), you can assume the model has successfully classified the sound as belonging to that class.

Training the model

The training process goes as follows: you have a set of data samples (training set) that you pass through a processing block to extract its features. Those features are fed to a model; the model improves by learning from its errors and modifying its weights to return a desired output giving a labeled input. All the training samples run through the model a predetermined number of times (epochs, also known as training cycles). In the end, you will have the first version of your trained model. *Figure 2.19* shows the iterative training process:

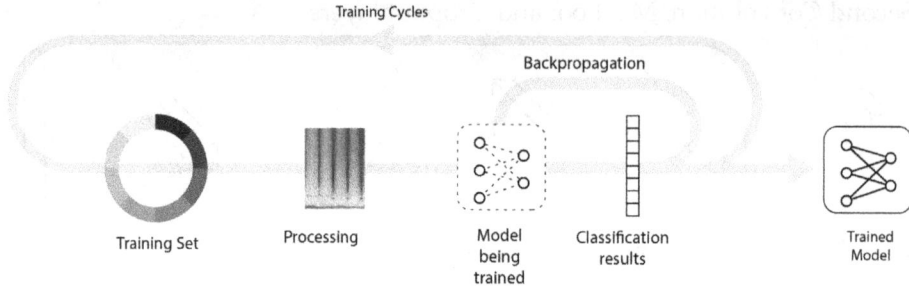

Figure 2.19: Training process

To know the performance of your new classification model, you run it through a set of samples that you separated from the training set (validation set). The validation set helps you get an unbiased evaluation and fine-tune the model. You can analyze the performance using a confusion matrix. The confusion matrix helps you calculate the model's precision, recall, specificity, and accuracy. *Figure 2.20* shows the validation dataset being processed and run through the trained model to return results that are validated with the help of the confusion matrix and accuracy metrics.

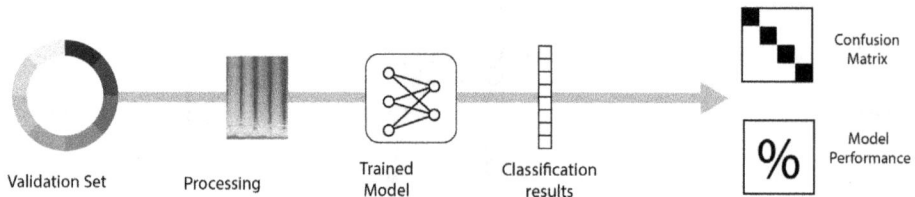

Figure 2.20: Validation process

Precision and recall can be explained with a simple example. Assume you must classify dogs from cats, and you are asked to be very precise. To do that, you have to be incredibly conservative and only choose those images where there is no doubt a dog is in the picture. By doing so, you might leave some dogs out of your selection because they look like cats. In this case, your precision is high, but your recall is very low. On the other hand, if you are asked to have a high recall, you will prioritize including every single dog at the expense of maybe including some cats in the results. Only the project's goals can determine whether you need higher precision or higher recall. Using another example, assume we need to identify the sound of a water leak to avoid costly damages. Our model must have very high recall at the expense of creating some false water leak alarms (false positives). On the other hand, let us say you are building a word-activated switch. It would aggravate the user to give a voice command and have the system do something else. In that instance, the model needs to prioritize precision over recall. Usually, the sweet spot is not on the extremes but somewhere in between.

You can determine precision, recall, and accuracy quantitatively with a results table called the confusion matrix. The confusion matrix is a key evaluation tool in classification tasks that provides a detailed breakdown of a model's performance by showing the number of correct and incorrect predictions across different classes. Refer to the following figure:

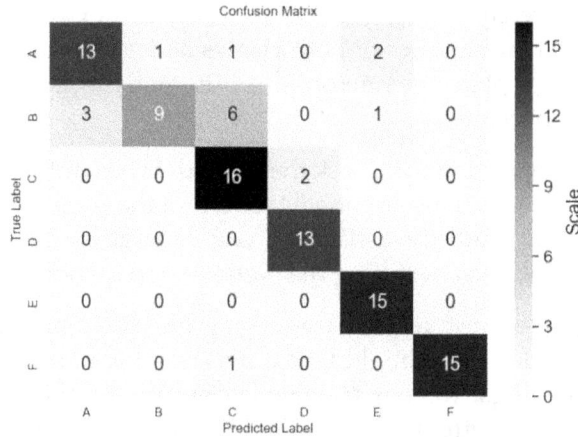

Figure 2.21: Example of confusion matrix

A confusion matrix works as follows: Columns represent predicted classes, and rows represent actual classes. Every cell in the table, contains a number. That number indicates how many times the model predicted a sample as belonging to the class represented by the column when it actually belonged to the class represented by the row. When the column and row are the same, the prediction is correct, as the predicted class is the same as the actual class; this is a **true positive (TP)**. When the model classifies a sample as belonging to a class but is incorrect, we have a **false positive (FP)**. When the model fails to classify a sample correctly, we have a **false negative (FN)** and when a model declares that a sample does not belong to a class correctly, we have a **true negative (TN)**.

You can manually calculate your model's accuracy, precision, sensitivity (also known as **recall**), negative predictive value, and specificity but it is better to automate that part. In the cases used in this book, we used the Edge Impulse classifier tool for that purpose.

How do you know your model is good enough if you only train it once? Maybe your accuracy is 90%, and you think it is good enough, but you would not know if you did not try different approaches. Training your model more than once, adjusting parameters, labels, processing blocks, layers, etc. in every iteration is the best way to converge to the optimal model. Refer to the following figure:

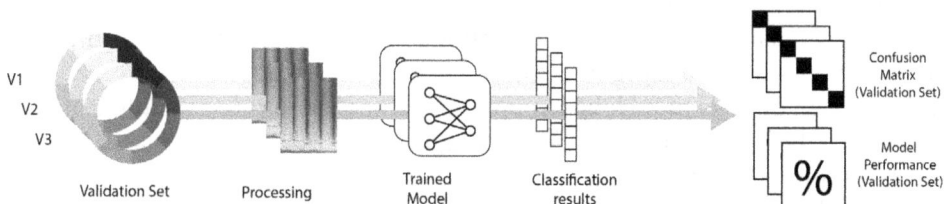

Figure 2.22: Iterative training process

Following is a list of things you might want to check in every training iteration to improve accuracy:

- Check the feature clustering graph. Are the clusters clearly defined? If they are not, then why? Play samples of both classes and try to understand why they are similar. You could place the microphone differently or isolate the external sound to achieve better results.

- Is your data diverse enough? Check that your data has different background noises for the model to learn to differentiate them from the common denominator, which is the sound you want to classify. Are you generating the sound from different sources? You might be overfitting the model if you do not.

- Are you using a few or too many training cycles? Too many training cycles would not kill your model, but it might take a significant amount of time that you could use to try new things. Too few training cycles might not let your model converge to a stable state. Pay attention to the console's output while you are training your model. You might be able to converge to the same result in a fraction of the time.

- Do you need to reduce your recall? You might be getting a lot of correct classifications at the expense of a lot of false positives. You should create a new class to focus on the similar sound you want to differentiate. By providing more data about the misclassified sound, you are helping the model understand the subtle differences in classifying it differently. You can always group many classes as *other* in your software after the classification.

- Is using data augmentation changing your results radically? If that is the case, your original data set might not be as diverse as you thought. Do not use data augmentation as a replacement to capture original data from where your system will run (assuming it is possible). Data augmentation might not be able to emulate the actual conditions your TinyML system might have to run under.

- Are you using the right data processing block? MFCCs are not better than spectrograms or MFEs just because they are more complex. Learn the differences and try them all.

- Is your data balanced? Pay attention to the columns in your confusion matrix that are not showing good results. Why is that? Figure out if your model gets enough quality data for the classes that are not doing well.

After running the training process multiple times, adjusting parameters, trying different process blocks, adjusting labels, troubleshooting poor classification results, improving the data set, etc., you will have more information to make an educated decision about which one of the trained models to pick based on your project needs. You should not just select the model with the highest accuracy. Pay attention to its precision and sensitivity (recall) metrics also; they should be aligned with the goals of the specific project you are working on. As a general rule, if the risk of misclassification is low, use the one with higher recall. If the risk of misclassification is high, use the one with higher precision.

Once you are satisfied with the accuracy, precision and sensitivity, we run the selected model through the testing dataset, which will give us the model's error rate after we have selected the final model. The difference between validation and testing is that because we used the validation set to select the final model, the model itself is biased by the validation set itself. The Test set offers a clean slate with never-seen data for the model to reveal its actual accuracy (given the existing dataset), as shown in the following figure:

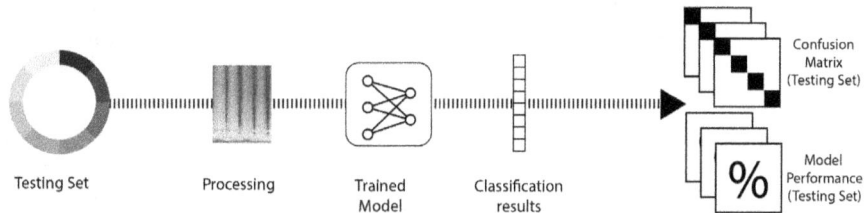

Figure 2.23: *Testing process*

Finally, we load the model to the microcontroller and test it in a real-life scenario. Just then, you will be able to know the true accuracy of the model. If you are not satisfied with the results, identify areas of improvement, implement changes, re-train the model, and test again. Refer to the following figure:

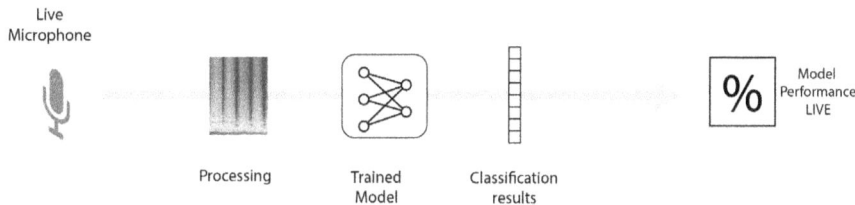

Figure 2.24: *Live process*

Use case: Spectrogram based processing

A musical tone is a sound characterized by a regular, repeating waveform with a stable pitch, amplitude, and timbre. It is typically continuous, periodic, and relatively simple compared to complex sounds or noise. This kind of signal is well-suited for spectrogram-based processing.

Classifying instrument notes

Problem definition: The stage designer of a music band has requested your help to build a series of stage props that change color depending on the note played by a specific instrument.

Solution: The proposed solution is a pitch classifier trained to recognize seven different notes of a grand piano (A3, B3, C3, D3, E3, F3, G3). The segment of the concert where the instrument will control the light props is a full song. The song is a sequence of low-tempo notes that play one after the other. The microphone will be placed near the piano before the concert starts. Sound classification will take place in the device while the music is being performed. Once a note has been recognized, the block will translate the note to a pre-defined hexadecimal color and will publish it as a message to a dedicated network channel, as shown in the following figure:

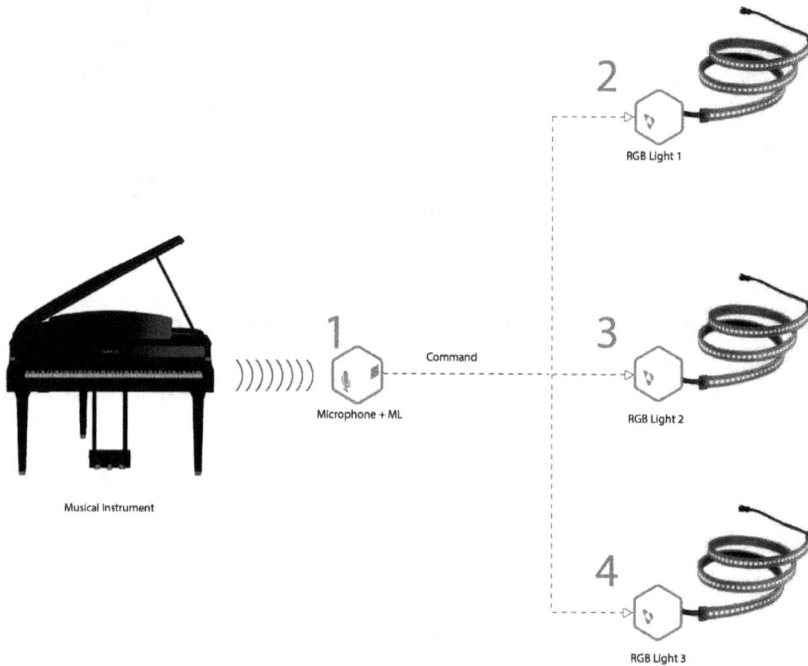

Figure 2.25: Solution concept showing data capture and control blocks

Each one of the blocks controlling the RGB lights blocks subscribed to the channel will receive the color and proceed to generate the signal to control each one of the independently addressable RGB lights in the NeoPixel strip connected to it.

While the light effect does not need to be extremely precise (a music note can be lost here and there), the effect of lights following the music is necessary. The designer would like changes to take no less than a second. This rate of change allows the blocks to communicate reliably with a low-energy wireless mesh network.

Data acquisition

In order to capture the training data set, each note in the instrument will be played under multiple environmental circumstances typical of a live performance venue. Training data will have the following elements: People and other instruments playing in the background and a silent room. The idea is to generalize the conditions under which the instrument is played while creating a model that will learn to recognize the specific sounds of the instrument and ignore everything else, as shown in the following figure:

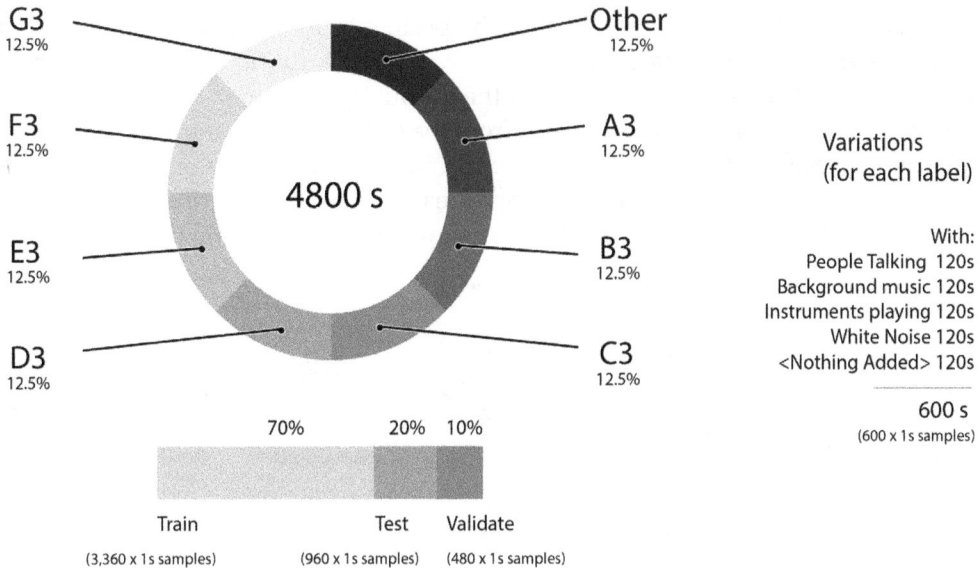

G3 12.5%

Other 12.5%

F3 12.5%

A3 12.5%

4800 s

E3 12.5%

B3 12.5%

D3 12.5%

C3 12.5%

Variations
(for each label)

With:
People Talking 120s
Background music 120s
Instruments playing 120s
White Noise 120s
<Nothing Added> 120s

600 s
(600 x 1s samples)

70%   20%   10%

Train   Test   Validate

(3,360 x 1s samples)   (960 x 1s samples)   (480 x 1s samples)

Figure 2.26: Data acquisition facts (classifying notes)

Processing

We use the spectrogram processing block to obtain the features from the musical instrument soundwave since it is a constant frequency sound. Notice how the different pitches are clustered, some closer than others. In *Figure 2.27*, the **Other** label is very distant from the musical instrument pitch clusters:

A: A3
B: B3
C: C3
D: D3
E: E3
F: F3
G: G3
X: OTHER

Figure 2.27: Cluster diagram of training set showing different pitches

Model

We are using the classification CNN, which specializes in sounds, as explained at the beginning of this chapter (*Figure 2.11*). It has two 1D convolution layers, two dropouts of 0.25 each, and one dense layer activated at the output by a Softmax function. To train this model with the 4,800 samples we acquired from the musical instrument, we ran 100 epochs at a learning rate of 0.005 with a batch size of 32. In earlier iterations of the training of this model, we used the MFE processor with poor results. Once we switched to spectrogram, the accuracy of the model went up to 96%, as shown in the following figure:

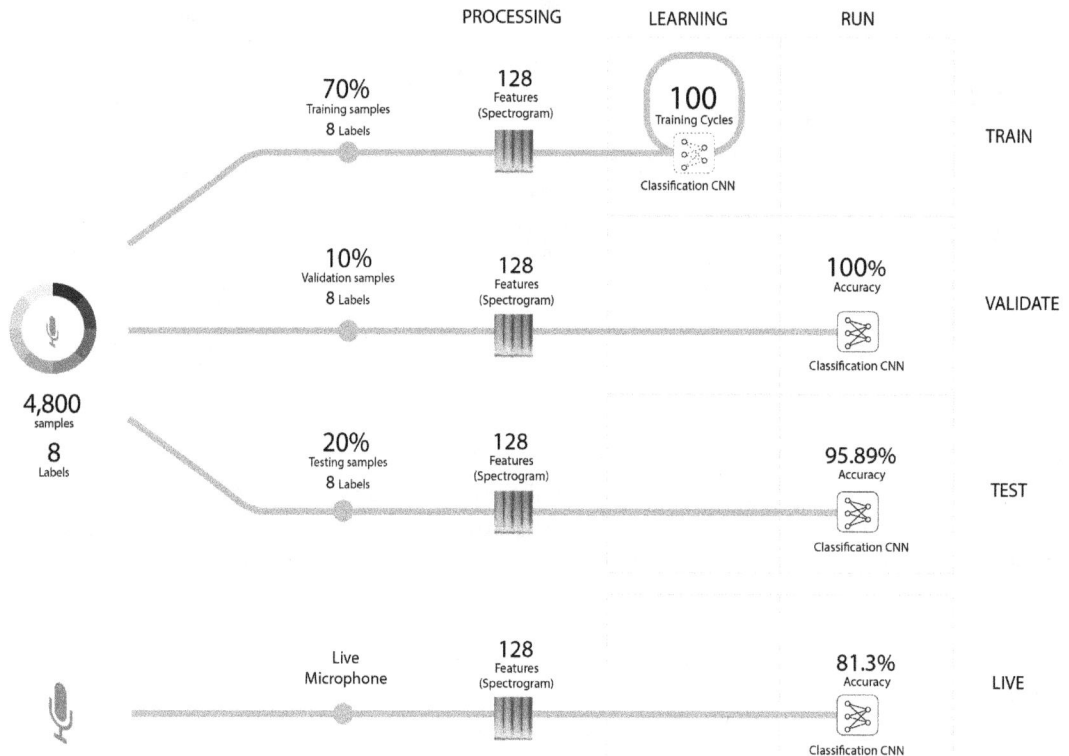

Figure 2.28: Training, validation, testing and live deployment statistics (classifying notes)

Edge Impulse estimated the Inference time for this model at 0.03 seconds. If we add the processing time (0.1 sec) plus additional firmware overhead, we will get to approximately 0.15 seconds to run one inference. That means we can run up to 6 inferences per second. This is important as the note needs to be approximately 1/6 of a second long to be detected. Additionally, it would be beneficial to the system's stability to require a series of similar consecutive classifications before declaring the formal identification of a sound pitch.

It is important to test all assumptions and real performance in real conditions. Once you test this model with a real instrument, you will be able to adjust the model and its parameters.

System implementation

The solution consists of two types of blocks. The first type (Block 1) is in charge of acquiring the sound and classifying it. The second type (Blocks 1,2 and 3) is in charge of controlling the lights. Refer to the following figure:

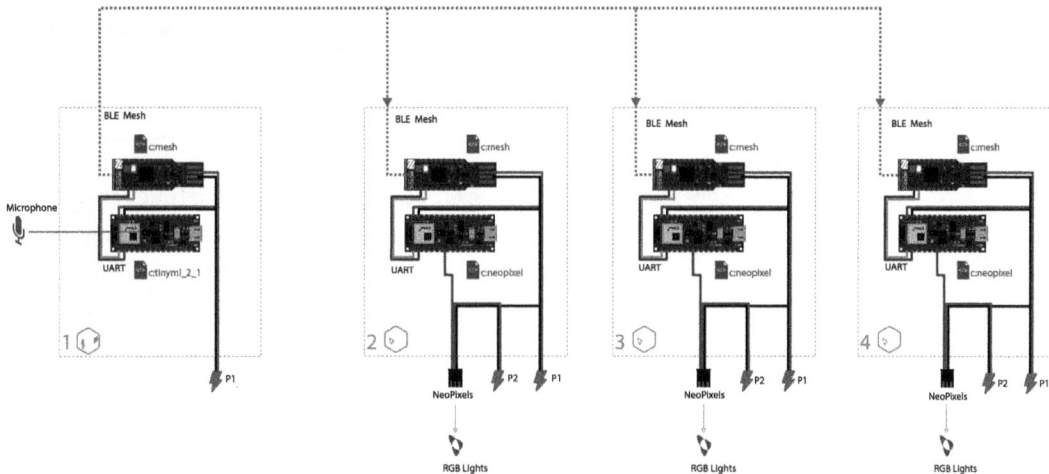

Figure 2.29: Connection diagram (Classifying notes)

Block 1 (acquisition block) uses two microcontrollers: The first is an Arduino Nano 33 BLE to capture the data from the microphone listening to the piano, process the data, and run the sound classification TinyML model. The second is an NRF52840 Dongle that receives color-changing commands from the Arduino and publishes them to a predetermined channel in the mesh network for other nodes to use.

Blocks 2, 3, and 4 (actuator blocks) are identical and use two microcontrollers each. The first is an NRF52840 Dongle that receives the messages from block 1 via the channel it is subscribed to in the mesh network. Once it receives and opens the message, it sends the color-changing command to the second microcontroller, the Arduino 33 BLE. The Arduino 33 BLE is specifically used to control the NeoPixel strip, as the timing needed is extremely precise. The Arduino communicates with the NeoPixels via its 1-wire interface (plus power).

Blocks 2, 3, and 4 require two power sources: one to feed the microcontrollers and the other to feed the NeoPixels. Given the power requirements of the bright LEDs in the NeoPixel lights, blocks 2, 3, and 4 need to be connected to a permanent power source. A 120vAC to 5VDC converter (not shown) is needed.

Source code

Refer to the following table:

c:tinyml_2_1	Code location: Arduino Nano 33 BLE @ Block 1
	Capture the sound, process it, and run the TinyML model with it. Pseudocode: 1. The microphone captures a soundwave from the musical instrument. Data is sent to the processing functions. 2. In the processing block, the soundwave is sliced in small windows, transformed to frequencies, converted to a spectrogram, and sent to the TinyML model to run. 3. The TinyML model runs the inference with the provided data and returns an array of results. Results are sent to the post processing functions. 4. The post processing functions resample the TinyML model output, remove outliers, and transform data to a color-changing command. Output is sent to the main script. 5. The main script prepares a message (A) with the color-changing command and sends it out to the network microcontroller along with the channel it needs to publish it to.

Table 2.1: Application logic (classifying notes)

Network

The blocks are connected via a wireless BLE mesh network which works with Publisher/Subscriber communication, a messaging pattern where senders (publishers) of messages do not directly send messages to specific receivers (subscribers). Instead, the messages are categorized into channels, and subscribers express interest in one or more channels. Subscribers then receive messages related to the channels they have subscribed to without needing to know the publishers of those messages. This decouples the producers of information from the consumers, allowing for greater scalability and flexibility.

The music venue is an open space that guarantees clear communication between devices. The messages published by Block 1 are not sound samples but color commands (less than

2 bytes of data). Blocks 2, 3, and 4 are subscribed to the same channel where Block 1 publishes the commands. Refer to the following table:

Block(s)	Action	Channel
1	Publishes to	CH1
2,3, and 4	Subscribes to	CH1

Table 2.2: Mesh network configuration (Classifying notes)

This architecture allows the set designer to add other components, like MidiPlayers, to publish signals to the channels that the light controllers are listening to so that they can also control the lights. Additionally, the architecture allows the addition of more lights to the show, if necessary, without adding overhead to the network or existing blocks.

Power analysis

Each type of Block has different power requirements. Block 1 runs real-time Neural Network inference and must communicate to the light controllers wirelessly. Block 2 must receive wireless messages and power the lights.

Here is block 1:

Power source	Device	Latent consumption	Active consumption	Notes
P1	Arduino Nano 33 BLE Sense	0.032A @5V	< 1A @5V	
P1	NRF52 Dongle	0.04mA @5v	3mA @5v	Active when publishing messages as a client.

Table 2.3: Power profile, Block 1

We need at least a 1A power source for Block 1 @5V. It cannot be battery-operated. Must connect to a permanent source of power (wall outlet).

Blocks 2, 3, and 4 are subscribed to the same channel where Block 1 publishes the commands:

Power source	Device	Latent consumption	Active consumption	Notes
P2	NRF52 Dongle	0.04mA @5v	0.3mA @5v	Active when receiving messages as a server.
P2	Arduino Nano 33 BLE	0.034mA @5V	< 1A @5V	Manages timing for NeoPixels
P3	Neopixels 60x	0.001mA @5v	1A @5V	Each NeoPixel draws 60mA at full brightness. 20mA is typical.

Table 2.4: Power profile, Blocks 2,3 and 4

We need a 2A power source for Blocks 2,3,4 (one for each). Given the power requirements of bright neopixels, this block must connect to a permanent source of power (wall outlet).

Bill of materials

The bill of materials for this project considers off-the-shelf components with general availability. Refer to the following table:

Description	QTY	Unit cost	Total
Arduino Nano 33 BLE Sense	1	$45	$45
Arduino Nano 33 BLE	3	$30	$90
NRF52840 Dongle	4	$12	$48
Neopixel Strip (60x)	3	$99	$297
Power Source 1A @5v	2	$10	$20

Table 2.5: Bill of materials (classifying notes)

The approximate cost of materials is $500.

Use case: MEF based processing

This use case demonstrates an application of the MEF based processing block that disregards any characteristic from the signal that is not significant to human voice perception.

Detecting noisy people in a business location

Problem definition: The owner of a popular restaurant is concerned that patrons waiting in line might be too noisy for the neighbors in the same building. The owner would like the manager to receive a visual cue when the noise caused by patrons waiting outside is too loud. The noise detector should ignore other street sounds, such as big trucks passing by.

Solution: The solution consists of a data acquisition block that captures sounds outside of the restaurant, processes and classifies them to decide whether patrons are speaking or being loud. In order to achieve this, the block needs to detect not only human conversations but also its loudness level. Once the block detects an event, it sends out a command to an alert light that will be visible to the restaurant manager for remediation actions to be taken. Refer to the following figure:

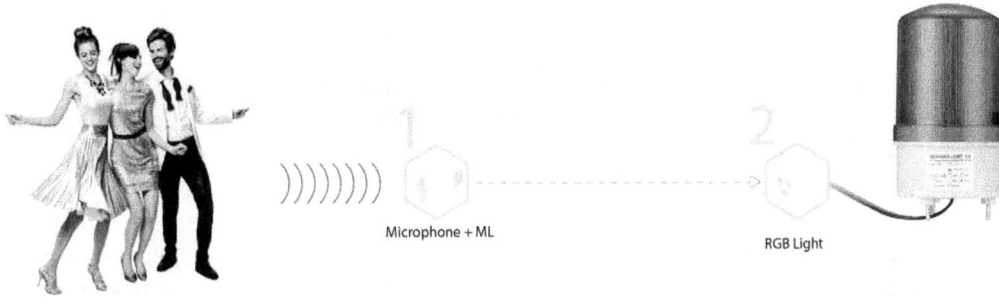

Figure 2.30: Solution concept showing the data acquisition block and the alerting component

Data acquisition

The data set is formed primarily by two classes: Noisy people and traffic noises. The original data set of noisy people was created from party and bar recordings found on the internet. The issue is that it does not reflect the actual sound of people being loud while waiting in line to get to this restaurant in particular. Luckily, we could go to the restaurant and record the sounds that we needed directly from the source to train the model. The model for the second class is trained with sound samples of cars passing by. The position of the microphone, the intensity of the sound, and the type of vehicles and their patterns were very different in the actual location. For this reason, we also captured samples of traffic sounds outside the restaurant. It is important to stress the fact that your model will be as good as the data that you provide. For the rest of the use case, we will use the first version of the data (the poorly captured data from online videos) for you to see the effects of it across the system. Refer to the following figure:

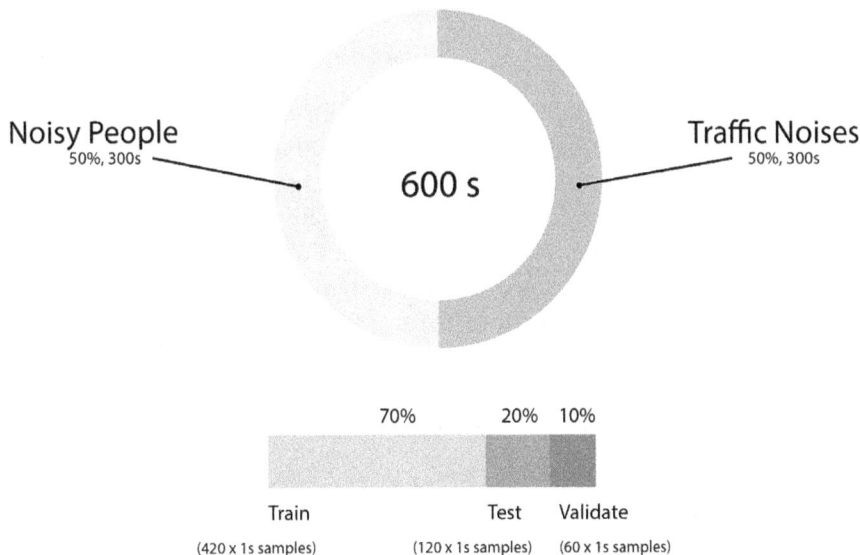

Figure 2.31: Data acquisition facts (Noise detection)

Processing

We are using the MEF processing block because human perception of noise needs to be detected. Notice how data is clustered in the feature clustering graph (*Figure 2.32*); however, both classes are present in most clusters. This is somewhat problematic as sounds of noisy people and street noise should differ.

Note: The data being used was captured from online videos of people at parties and cars recorded at street intersections. Because this data was originally created for different purposes under different conditions, it is causing the processing to perform poorly.

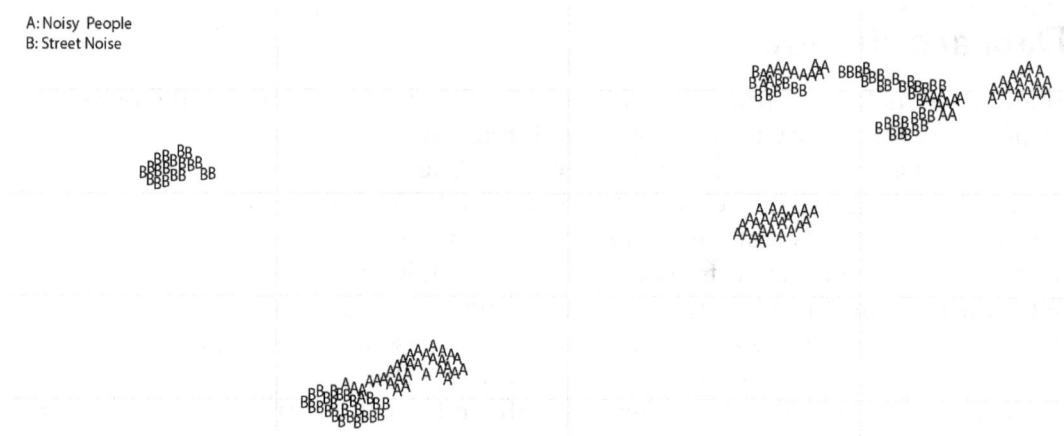

A: Noisy People
B: Street Noise

Figure 2.32: Cluster diagram of training set showing different noise types

Model

The CNN sound classifier model, specialized in sound, presented at the beginning of this chapter, is used to classify between loud people and street sounds. The model uses two convolutional layers with 8 and 16 filters (3x3) to recognize specific features, ReLU activation to eliminate negative values, two MaxPooling layers with a stride of two to compress the size of the sample, two dropout layers to reduce overfitting, and a dense layer at the end activated by a Softmax function to normalize the results into a probability distribution. To show the effect of bad data, we are training this model with poorly captured samples. What is interesting is that while the validation process shows an accuracy of 93.2%, it sharply drops when it runs against the test data set to 47.32%. After analyzing the confusion matrix, we realize that sounds from noisy people are often confused by street noise.

The solution to this problem is to capture better-quality data from the place where the system will be installed. Our tests showed that by doing so, we can get an accuracy north of 90% in live situations. Refer to the following figure:

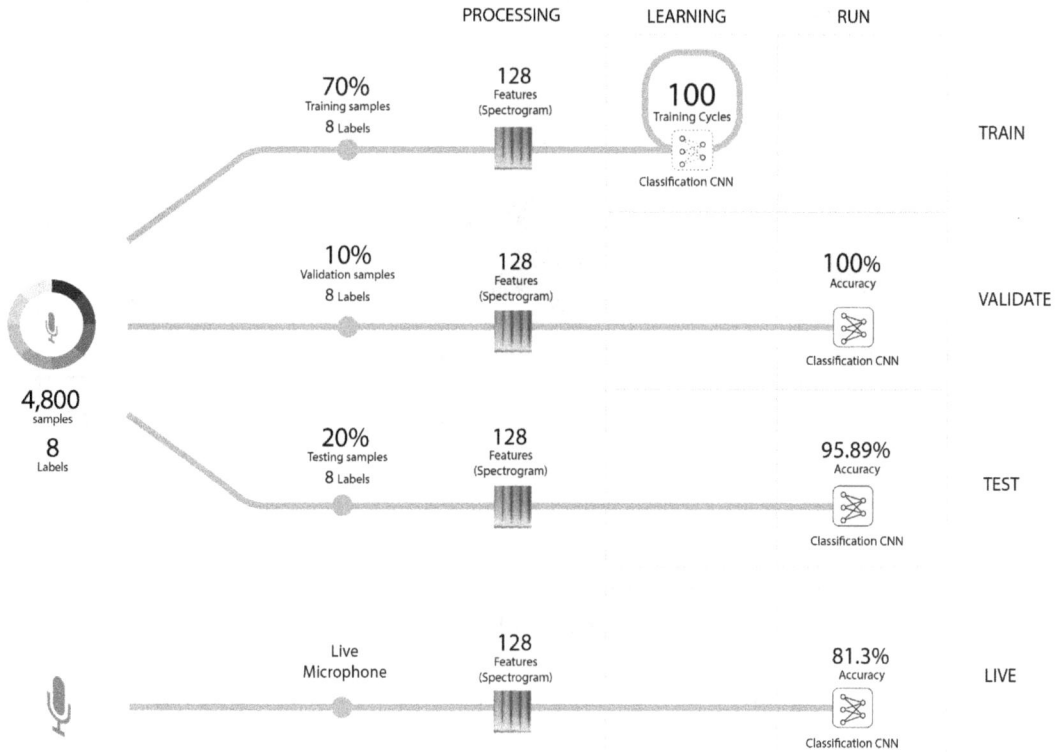

Figure 2.33: Training, validation, testing and live deployment statistics (noise detection)

The inference time is predicted to be about 0.2 seconds. Combining the processing and the inference time plus the overall overhead, the system will take about 0.5 seconds on each sample. Given the fact that noise levels caused by patrons will not change dramatically in a short amount of period, analyzing two samples per second is more than enough. The solution will be programmed to calculate a rolling average of the last 60 seconds before it declares a loud noise event.

System implementation

The solution consists of two types of blocks connected via a BLE mesh network. The first type are the acquisition blocks (Block 1 and Block 2) that are positioned in different parts of interest around the business location where noise events need to be detected. The second type is a central block (Block 3) that is subscribed to the acquisition blocks and keeps track of their state. If any block publishes a noise event, the central block activates a visual alert, as shown in the following figure:

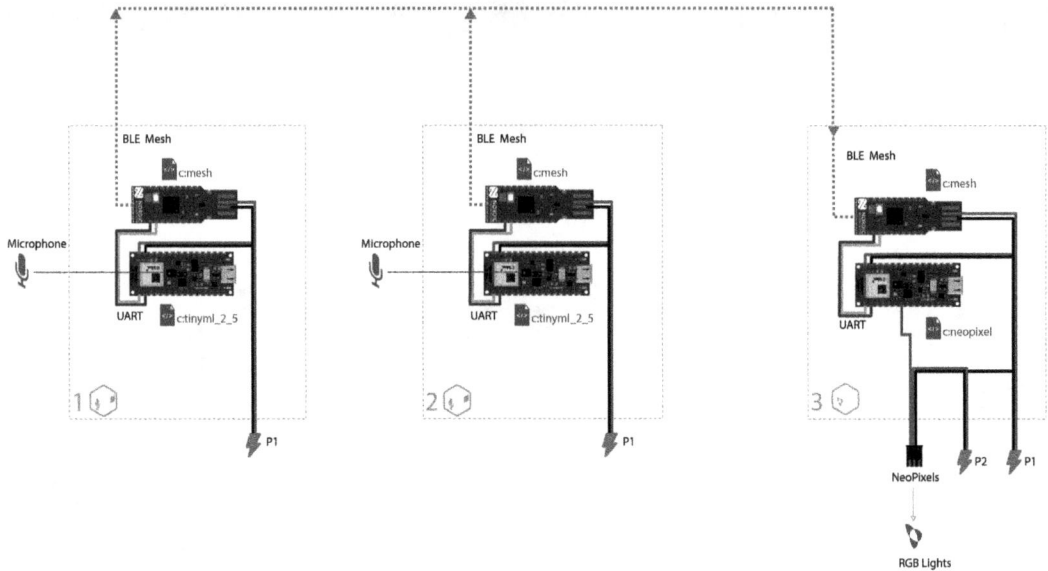

Figure 2.34: Connection diagram (Noise detection)

Blocks 1, and 2 (acquisition blocks) are identical. They use two microcontroller boards. The first is an Arduino Nano 33 BLE to capture the data from the microphone, process it, and run the TinyML model. The second is an NRF52840 Dongle to retrieve the inference results from the Arduino, buffer them and publish them to the mesh network for other nodes to use.

Block 3 (actuator block) also uses two microcontrollers. The first is an NRF52840 Dongle to receive messages from the network, and the second is an Arduino 33 BLE to translate the received information to a Hex color and send a command to the NeoPixels to transition to that color.

Source code

Refer to the following table:

c:edgeml_2_5	Code location: Arduino Nano 33 BLE @ Blocks 1,2
	Capturing outdoor sound, processing it, and running it through the TinyML model to detect noisy people Pseudocode: 1. The microphone captures environmental sounds from outside the buisness location. Data is sent to the Processing functions. 2. The soundwave is sliced in small windows, transformed to frequencies, converted to an MFE, flattened, and sent to the TinyML model to run. 3. The TinyML model runs the inference with the provided data and returns an array of results. Results are sent to the post-processing functions. 4. The post-processing functions detect people conversations, their duration and their loudness level. A combination of those three factors determine whether an alarm message should be issued. If that is the case, the main script is notified. 5. Main script gets the messages and sends them via UART to the network microcontroller.

Table 2.6: Pseudocode (noise detection)

Network

The three blocks use a BLE mesh network to send and receive messages. Each acquisition block publishes to a different channel. Block 3 subscribes to each one of the channels. This is necessary as Block 3 must be able to know what block sent the message to keep track of its state. By doing so, the color in the alert light can be different depending on the zone that the noise event has been detected. Refer to the following table:

Block(s)	Action	Channel
1 and 2	Publishes to	CH1, CH2
3	Subscribes to	CH1, CH2

Table 2.7: Network configuration (noise detection)

Power analysis

Since this is a permanent installation, it is recommended that all Blocks be connected to a permanent power source; however, if it is necessary and assuming there is enough daylight and we provide a large battery, the data acquisition blocks could be solar powered. We would need to make a couple of adjustments like reducing the inference frequency and number of messages that the blocks send to the central block.

For Blocks 1 and 2:

Power source	Device	Latent consumption	Active consumption	Notes
P1	Arduino Nano 33 BLE Sense	0.032mA @5V	<1A @5V	Active when running the TinyML model. The microphone needs to be always on.
P1	NRF52 Dongle	0.040mA @5v	3mA @5v	Active when publishing messages as a client.

Table 2.8: Power Profile, Blocks 1 and 2

We need at least a 1A power source for Block 1.

For Block 3:

Power source	Device	Latent consumption	Active consumption	Notes
P2	NRF52 Dongle	0.040mA @5v	0.3A @5v	Active when receiving messages as a server.
P2	Arduino Nano 33 BLE	0.034mA @5V	0.1mA @5V	Active when switching the light alert.

Table 2.9: Power profile, Block 3

We need a 1A power source for Block 3.

Bill of materials

The bill of materials for this project considers off-the-shelf components with general availability. Refer to the following table:

Description	QTY	Unit cost	Total
Arduino Nano 33 BLE Sense	2	$45	$90
NRF52840 Dongle	3	$12	$36
Arduino Nano 33 BLE	1	$30	$30
Power Source 1A @5v	3	$10	$40

Table 2.10: *Bill of materials (noise detection)*

The approximate cost of materials is $196.

Use case: MFCC based processing

In cases where the model needs to recognize human language, MFCC based processing is used to extract features relative to cadence, intonation and other characteristics that help the model differentiate and recognize words.

Voice activated switches

Problem definition: An adult care facility has found it incredibly useful for its patients to be able to give voice command instructions to turn on and off lights at night using a device like *Alexa*. The issue is that those devices require constant internet connection and are complicated to fix if they get misconfigured (which happens often). The facility manager is looking for a reliable stand-alone alternative solution that does not require an internet connection or subscriptions to a web service.

Solution: The spoken commands are captured by a microphone-enabled data acquisition block. The acquisition block's CNN recognizes two commands: **Lights on** and **Lights off**. Once a command has been recognized, the block sends a message to the switches to turn on or off, as shown in the following figure:

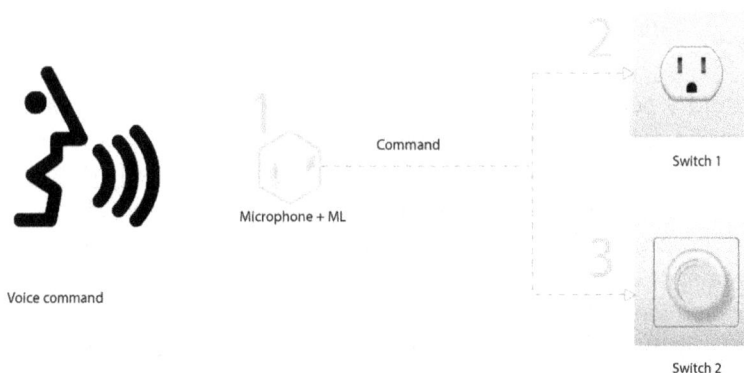

Figure 2.35: *Solution concept showing a simple setup for voice-activated switches*

Data acquisition

The training set consists of 4 classes. *Lights On, Lights Off, Noise* and *Unknown*. The samples for *Lights On* and *Lights Off* have been captured from 20 different volunteers. They have been asked to repeat the voice command at different speeds, intonation, and pitch. *Noise* in the background is typical of a home, like a loud TV, other people talking, music, and kitchen sounds, which are present during the recording of different samples. The samples in the *Noise* class contain the same background sounds but without the voice commands. The *Unknown* class is a group of random collections of sounds like horns, cars, animals, etc. Refer to the following figure:

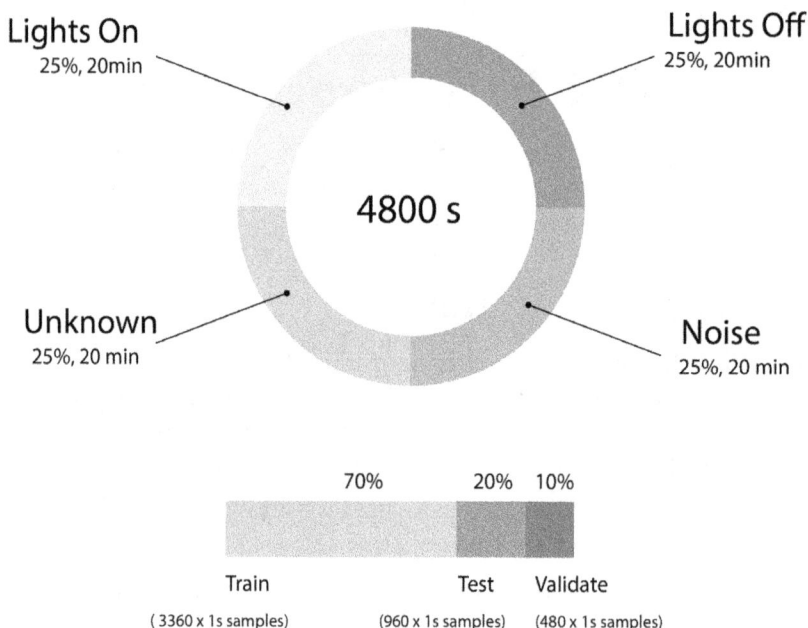

Lights On
25%, 20min

Lights Off
25%, 20min

4800 s

Unknown
25%, 20 min

Noise
25%, 20 min

70%   20%   10%

Train   Test   Validate

(3360 x 1s samples)   (960 x 1s samples)   (480 x 1s samples)

Figure 2.36: Data acquisition facts (Voice activation)

Processing

The processing block selected for this use case is the MFCC algorithm, as its cepstral and dynamic features have been specifically designed to characterize human language. Notice how both Lights off and Lights on voice command classes are clearly defined in the feature clustering graph. This kind of visualization is a 2D representation of the sound samples. In this type of graph, horizontal distance is more significant than vertical distance. Both clusters are spread horizontally and much closer vertically. You need to take into consideration that even if the TinyML model can recognize the cluster limits if the person giving the voice command has a specific way of talking that makes both commands sound more similar than the training data, we might be getting more false positives and false negatives. Refer to the following figure:

A: Lights off
B: Lights on
C: Noise
D: Unknown

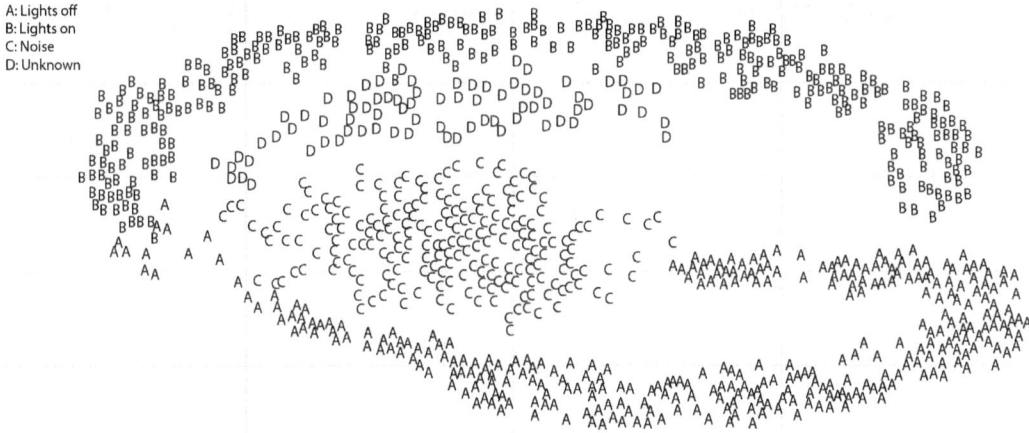

Figure 2.37: Cluster diagram showing clearly differentiated activation word groupings

The processing time is approximately 0.2 seconds. A long time is expected as we are using the MFCC, which is the specialized processing with the most steps.

Model

We use the classification model specialized in spoken language, that we introduced at the beginning of this chapter. It is important to mention that the original white paper that introduced this model (see reference at the end of this chapter) was focused on CNNs and MFCCs, which is an excellent fit for this use case. A reshaping function converts the data to a matrix of 13x50. The output of a 1D convolution layer with eight filters with a kernel size of 3 is activated by a ReLU function. Then, the features are input to a MaxPooling layer to select its most representative values, reducing its size by half in the process. A dropout function is applied to the features to reduce overfitting by randomly and temporarily removing features during training to create new paths to solve the same problem differently. Immediately after, we apply the second 1D convolution layer and similar MaxPooling and dropout functions. In the end, we find a fully connected layer that helps the model shape the function that relates input against labeled output. The final stage is a Softmax function that helps us normalize the output. The accuracy during the validation is 89.7%, but it drops to 73.58% during training. We need to be north of 90% to make this a viable product. The question is: Should the model adjust to every single mode of talking, or should the user adjust to a specific speed and intonation while giving the voice command? While the former is ideal, the latter is not that inconvenient and reflects the way people interact with devices similar to Alexa. Try to remember how you talk to a commercial voice-activated assistant. Do you always use the same speed and tone in your voice when doing so?

The following figure shows the split of the data to train, validate and test the model:

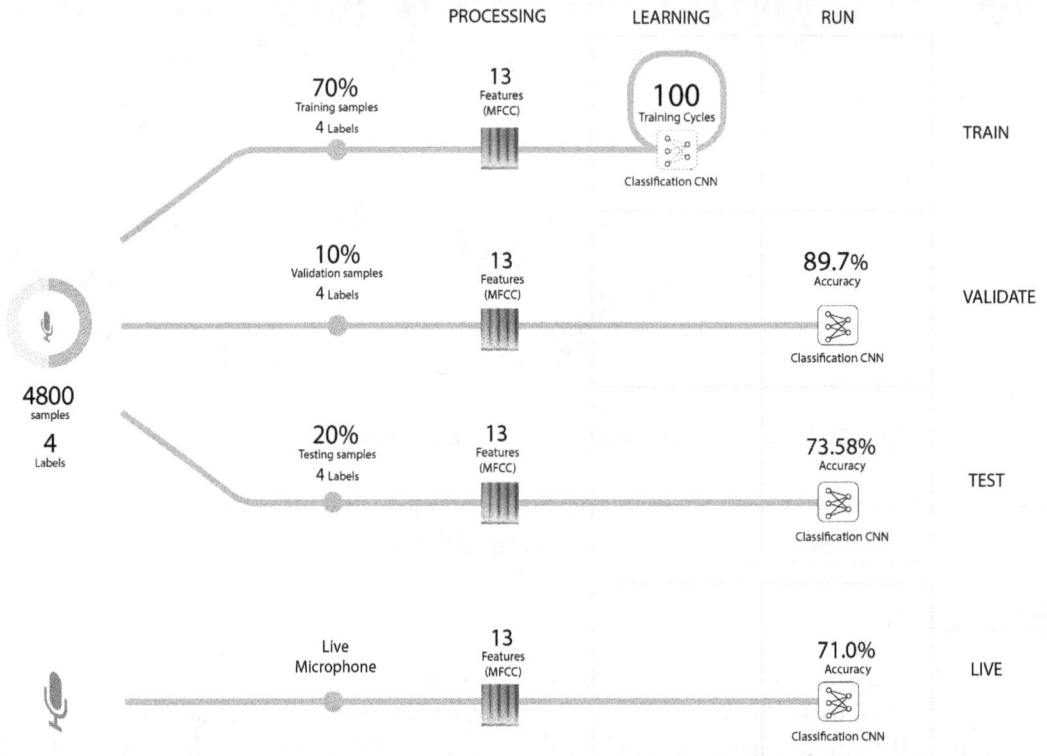

Figure 2.38: *Training, validation, testing and live deployment statistics (voice activation)*

The inference time to run a sample through the processing and inference stages is about 0.2 seconds. This is short enough for the model to run at least five samples per second. This allows the voice command to be repeated in case it does not work without causing a processing backlog.

System implementation

The implementation consists of a block that acquires the sound sample and issues the on or off commands and as many off-the-shelf Bluetooth enabled switches as the implementation requires. While this example assumes all the switches will go on or off at the same time, it would not be complicated to implement different activation words for each switch. Refer to the following figure:

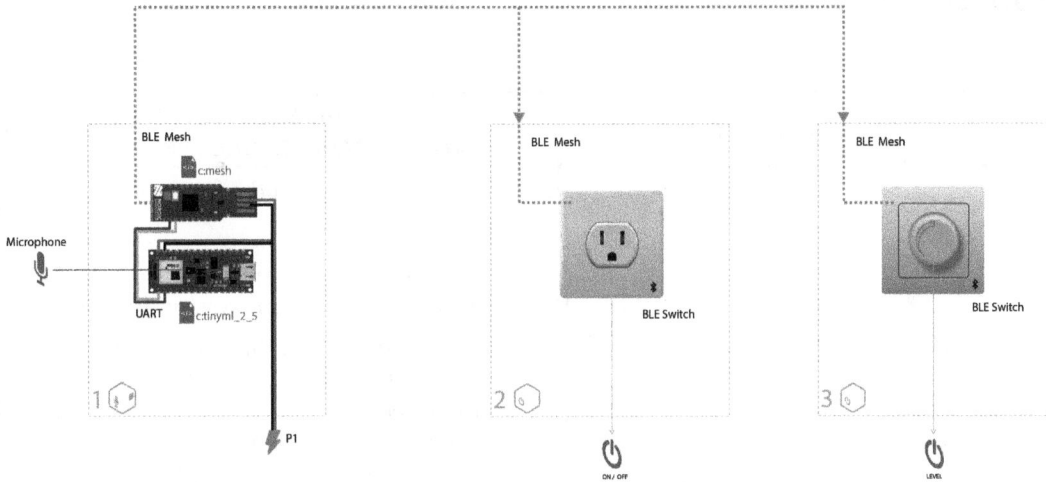

Figure 2.39: Connection diagram (Voice activation)

Block 1 (acquisition block) uses two microcontrollers: The first is an Arduino Nano 33 BLE Sense to capture the data from the microphone, process it and run the TinyML model. The second is a NRF52840 Dongle to retrieve the inference results from the Arduino, buffer them, and publish them to the mesh network for other nodes to use it.

Blocks 2 and 3 are off-the-shelf BLE mesh-enabled switches that handle the complexity and risk of handling higher voltages (120v, 220v). They follow the BLE-mesh network provisioning and configuration protocol like any other building block. They acquire their energy from the power line directly.

Block 1 actively listens to voice commands, and when a valid one is detected, it sends an on or off command to blocks 2 and 3. Block 1 keeps track of the state of the switches but can also ask the actuator blocks for their current state in case it needs to double check.

Source code

Refer to the following table:

c:edgeml_2_6	Code location: Arduino Nano 33 BLE @ Block 1
	Capturing voice commands Pseudocode 1. The microphone captures room sounds. Data is sent to the processing functions. 2. The soundwave is sliced in small windows, transformed to frequencies, converted to MFCC features, flattened, and sent to the TinyML model to run. 3. The TinyML model runs the inference with the provided data and returns an array of results. Results are sent to the post-processing functions. 4. If a known voice command is recognized, a message is prepared, and state is saved. 5. The main script gets the message and sends it via UART to the network microcontroller.

Table 2.11: Application logic (voice activation)

Network

The blocks communicate using a BLE mesh network. This use case underscores the importance of using the Standard Models established by the BLE Mesh Specification. The switches and the acquisition block do not have the same manufacturer and are still able to communicate between them thanks to the standard messages. The generic OnOff Server/Client model is used in this use case. Refer to the following table:

Block(s)	Action	Channel
1	Publishes to	CH1
2,3	Subscribes to	CH1

Table 2.12: Network configuration (voice activation)

Power analysis

We are controlling high voltage (120-220v) with low voltage (5v-3.3v). The Wireless mesh network provides an air gap implementation that decouples the data acquisition and the

TinyML model performed in low voltage from the electric switches. It is recommended to use off-the-shelf Bluetooth-controlled electric switches from well-known brands instead of trying to implement your own.

For block 1:

Power source	Device	Latent consumption	Active consumption	Notes
P1	Arduino Nano 33 BLE Sense	0.032mA @5V	<1A @5V	Active when running the TinyML model. The microphone needs to be always on.
P1	NRF52 Dongle	0.040mA @5v	3mA @5v	Active when publishing messages as a client.

Table 2.13: Power profile

We need at least a 1A power source for Block 1.

Bill of materials

The bill of materials for this project considers off-the-shelf components with general availability. Refer to the following table:

Description	QTY	Unit cost	Total
Arduino Nano 33 BLE Sense	1	$45	$45
NRF52840 Dongle	1	$12	$12
120v Switch	1	$20	$20
Smart Light	1	$10	$10

Table 2.14: Bill of materials (voice activation)

The approximate cost of materials is $87.

Conclusion

Sound classification opens the door to previously impossible use cases, but implementing a successful system requires a comprehensive understanding of various aspects: the types of sounds that can be classified, how to create a training set, feature extraction from sound samples, the types of features and their applications, the inner workings of a convolutional network specialized in sound classification, troubleshooting models, and calculating execution time. Additionally, it is crucial to consider factors surrounding the model, such as power consumption, communication between elements, and the overall cost of implementation.

In the next chapter, we use the techniques learned in this chapter to analyze a different type of signal to classify movement, in this case accelerometer and gyroscope signals.

References

- https://www.researchgate.net/publication/348432098_Speech_recognition_based_on_Convolutional_neural_networks_and_MFCC_algorithm/link/5ffed38aa6fdccdcb84de010/download

- https://studio.edgeimpulse.com/

- https://gilberttanner.com/blog/arduino-nano-33-ble-sense-overview/

- https://medium.com/@MuhyEddin/feature-extraction-is-one-of-the-most-important-steps-in-developing-any-machine-learning-or-deep-94cf33a5dd46

- Sound classification use case 1: **https://studio.edgeimpulse.com/public/289478/live**

- Sound classification use case 2: **https://studio.edgeimpulse.com/public/291172/live**

- Sound classification use case 3: **https://studio.edgeimpulse.com/public/277828/live**

Join our book's Discord space

Join the book's Discord Workspace for Latest updates, Offers, Tech happenings around the world, New Release and Sessions with the Authors:

https://discord.bpbonline.com

CHAPTER 3

Movement Classification

Introduction

Movement classification refers to the process of using algorithms to automatically recognize and categorize different types of physical movements based on sensor data, typically from accelerometers or gyroscopes. Movement classification involves capturing motion data, such as changes in acceleration or orientation, and using machine learning models to classify these patterns into predefined categories, like walking, running, jumping, or other complex movements. Movement classification is widely used in areas such as activity recognition for fitness trackers, fall detection in healthcare, gesture control in smart devices, and even robotics, where machines must interpret human motion or autonomously analyze their own movement. The goal is to create models that can accurately predict the type of movement based on patterns learned from the data.

Structure

The chapter covers the following topics:

- Capturing training data from accelerometers
- Extracting features from accelerometers
- Creating the classification model
- Use case: Correct usage detection

- Use case: Free fall detection
- Use case: Movement profiling

Objectives

In this chapter, you will explore the essential data required for movement classification and the techniques for extracting meaningful features from that information. You will learn how to train a movement classification model using the processed data and implement a real-world example of a movement classification model. Each step will guide you through the process of turning raw sensor data into a functional machine learning model capable of accurately recognizing and classifying various types of movement.

Capturing training data from accelerometers

The basic principle of capturing movement data and using it to train a model is simple: You attach an array of accelerometers to a body that is performing a movement that you want to learn from, you capture many samples of the same movement under different conditions and you use that set to train a model, then, you load the trained model into a microcontroller and send real-time accelerometer readings to it, after that, the microcontroller reads and processes the movement signals and recognizes when a move is made. In order to train a model to recognize specific movements, you first need to capture the movement data. This process involves recording movement through accelerometers and then labeling the data for supervised learning. However, there are several challenges in capturing movement data. One challenge is isolating the specific movement from other unrelated movements. This can be done in a controlled environment when the movement can be triggered on command, but in many cases, it is not easy to isolate the movement, especially when it is unpredictable or very short.

Labeling the accelerometer time series data can also be complicated, especially when the events are unpredictable and continuous. For example, when trying to capture data for a model that recognizes reckless driving, it is not easy to label sudden stops or careless lane changes in real time. One approach is to use a dashboard camera in the car to record the entire ride and then label the accelerometer data in post-production.

Additionally, capturing movement on command may not reflect natural movement accurately. Even seemingly easy-to-capture movement events, like recording how a tool is used by an operator, can differ when captured in a controlled session versus regular day-to-day usage. In conclusion, it is important to capture movement data in actual conditions, even though it may be more challenging to do so.

Extracting features from accelerometers

You can compress movement data from a sample of three-axis accelerometer time series into 39 features. Each axis (x, y, z) uses 13 features. For each axis, 8 features describe spectral power, while the remaining 5 are root mean square, kurtosis, spectral kurtosis, skewness, and spectral skewness.

The 8 spectral power features describe the power per hertz for each of the following frequency bands:

1.95 - 5.86 Hz, 5.86 - 9.77 Hz, 9.77 - 13.67 Hz, 13.67 - 17.58 Hz, 17.58 - 21.48 Hz, 21.48 - 25.39 Hz, 25.39 - 29.3 Hz, 29.3 - 33.2 Hz

Spectral power

The following figure illustrates the distribution of power (energy released over time) across frequencies that characterizes a sample movement:

Spectral power (log)

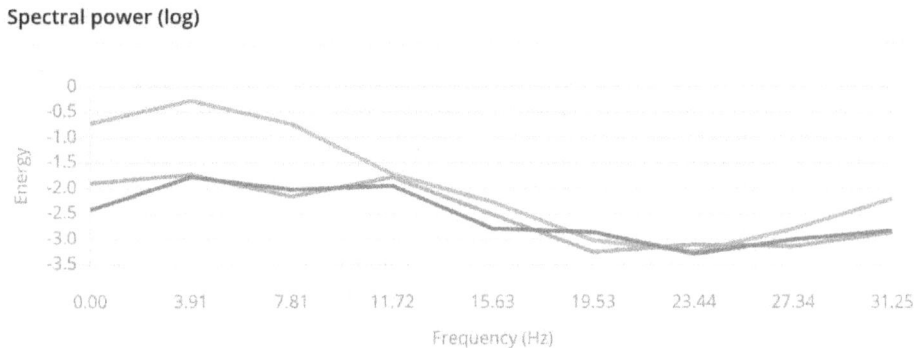

Figure 3.1: Example of energy levels per frequency (red:x, green:y, blue:z)

The reason the bands span up to 33.2 Hz is because the acquisition frequency is twice that of its highest frequency (66.5 Hz). According to the **Nyquist-Shannon** sampling theorem, your capture rate needs to be at least twice as much as the largest frequency you want to capture. In other words, you can only capture and fully reconstruct frequencies (with the help of DTF) that are half or less of your capture rate. The highest frequency that you can capture is called the **bandwidth**. We are splitting the bandwidth into eight equal parts, each 3.91 Hz wide. We could have partitioned it into any arbitrary number of parts. If we did that, we would just need to adjust the neural network input layer to have as many inputs for the spectral power features as partitions. The goal is to calculate the power contained in every band. If we had no partitions, we could tell the neural network the whole power content of the signal, but we are doing that already with the feature called root mean square by calculating the area under the curve, which is proportional to the power. In this case, we want to be more specific. Showing a distribution of power across the frequencies helps us understand and characterize the signal much better by knowing at what frequencies the body is moving most significantly. To do this, we multiply the readings by themselves (hence the square) to avoid negative numbers that would cancel the signal when averaging it. We are doing the same as we did with the whole signal to calculate RMS, but in this case, for the decomposed signals specific to the partitioned frequencies. If we leave it at that, the signals will not be aligned. Higher frequency bands will show incorrectly as if they had more power, even though they have lower levels. The reason is that, because of the high frequency, the energy is squeezed horizontally and shown as a taller vertical column because the base of the column is smaller *(Figure 3.2)*. In order to normalize this, we divide the power of every band by its frequency. Now, we have a normalized characterization of power for each band that we can feed into the network. Refer to the following figure:

Note: RMS at higher frequencies shows taller because the base of the partitions is smaller although the power in the sample is the same.

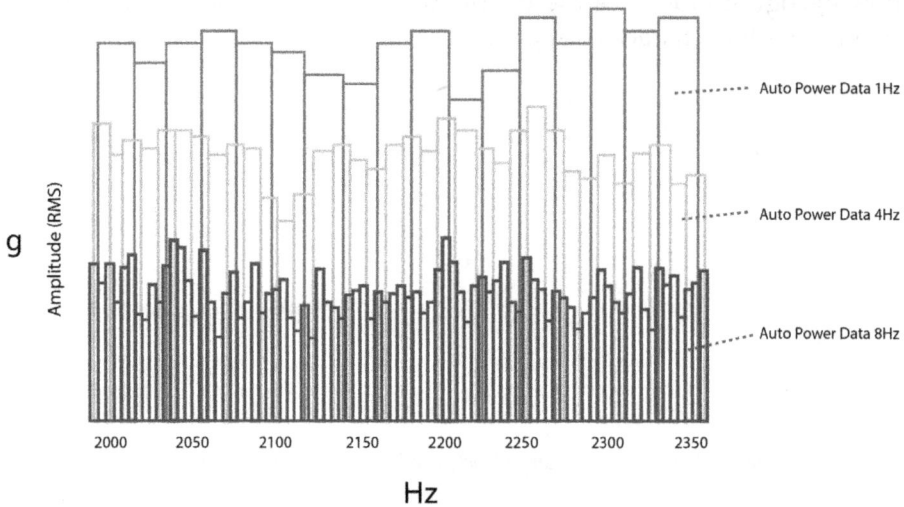

Figure 3.2: RMS at different frequencies

Kurtosis

Kurtosis indicates the tailedness of the distribution, while skewness shows whether the curve leans to the left or right in relation to a normal distribution.

Kurtosis can be interpreted as the degree of outliers in your data. If your data has many outliers, it means that your accelerometers are capturing a lot of sudden and instantaneous jerky movements. It is important to determine whether these movements are noise or part of the phenomena you want to capture.

The different types of kurtosis and their shape characteristics are illustrated in *Figure 3.3*. Positive kurtosis is taller than the normal distribution with thinner tails, while negative kurtosis is shorter than the normal distribution with thicker tails.

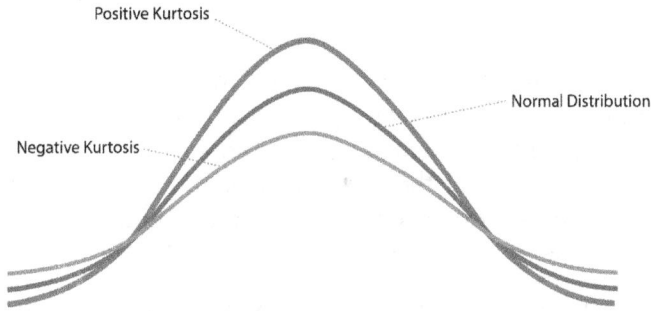

Figure 3.3*: Positive kurtosis, zero kurtosis and negative kurtosis*

Spectral kurtosis, similar to tailedness in the time domain, pertains to the presence of outlier frequencies in your data in the frequency domain. An outlier frequency signifies an occurrence that is not frequent, but when it does occur, it exhibits a significantly different frequency than usual. To illustrate spectral kurtosis, consider a salesperson who typically sells one item per month but occasionally sells three items in a single day. The frequency between these events is notably different, but such instances are infrequent. If these uncommon days occur almost never (once in a lifetime), it results in negative kurtosis, also known as a thin tail. If these occurrences are uncertain but are expected to happen occasionally, it results in zero kurtosis, as even normal distributions include outliers. However, if they start happening more frequently than normal, it results in positive kurtosis, also known as a thick tail. When applied to accelerometer data, although the time scale is measured in milliseconds instead of months and years, the underlying concept remains the same.

The following heatmap *(Figure 3.4)* displays spectral kurtosis with respect to frequency and window length. A positive spectral kurtosis for a given frequency and level indicates that outliers are more common under those conditions.

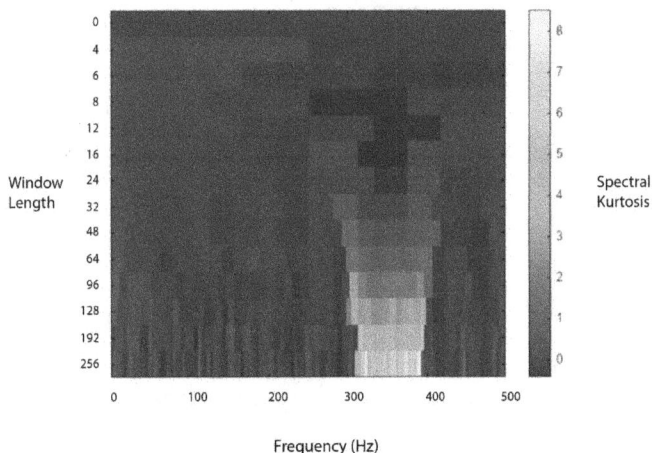

Figure 3.4*: Spectral kurtosis heatmap (frequency versus level)*

Skewness

To understand the physical meaning of skewness in terms of movement, consider the range of movement of an object. In a normal distribution, most of the samples belong to the middle section of the movement range, with fewer samples at the extremes. Now, imagine a scenario where most of the movement belongs to the top of the range. This illustrates negative skewness. Conversely, if most of the samples belong to the lower range of the movement, then you have a positive skew.

The following figure shows normal distributions with negative and positive skews:

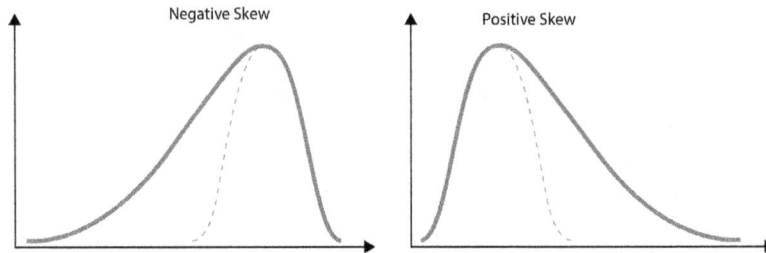

Figure 3.5: Negative versus positive skew

The concept of spectral skewness differs from regular skewness. It indicates that the distribution of frequencies tends to lean more towards either the low or high frequencies while leaving the median frequency behind. This can be interpreted as the body making either repetitive fast movements (such as high vibration) or repetitive slow movements (like swinging), with most of the movements occurring at a middle frequency.

It is easy to understand the skewness of a frequency distribution by examining its frequency diagram, as shown in the following figure:

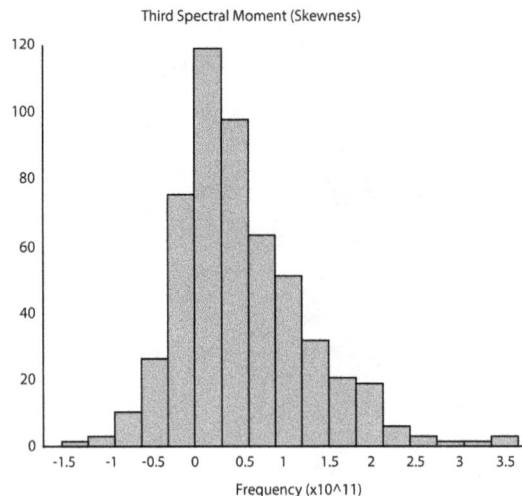

Figure 3.6: Positive skew in a frequency distribution

Creating the classification model

The architecture of the TinyML model for classifying movement includes an input layer with 39 neurons, two hidden dense layers of sizes 20 and 10 activated by a ReLU function, and an output layer with as many classes as needed for the events being classified.

The first layer is a fully connected dense layer where all 39 features are connected to the hidden layer of 20 neurons. L1 regularization function (with delta=0.00001), also known as **Lasso Regression**, helps prevent overfitting in cases where there are a large number of features by eliminating unimportant features. This is important because models with a large number of features tend to overfit (7).

The ReLU activation is used to introduce non-linearity into the neural network. The reason for needing non-linearity in movement is that it is necessary to show not only how fast the position is changing, but also how fast the rate at which the position is changing is changing (this is not a typo). A linear function can only show a rate of change, but to show the rate of change of a rate of change, a nonlinear function is necessary.

The following figure illustrates the input layer, the dense layer and the regularization and ReLU functions:

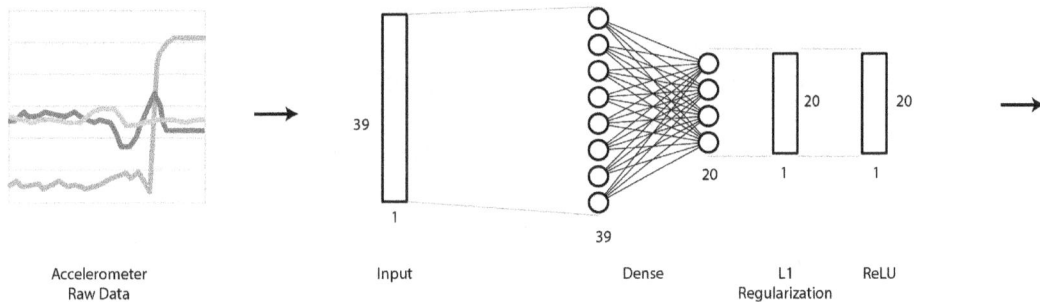

Figure 3.7: *Input, dense layer, L1 regularization function and ReLU activation function*

The second dense layer compresses the 20 outputs of the ReLU function by connecting them to a 10-neuron layer. After this, the output undergoes L1 regularization (with delta=0.0001) and is then passed through a second ReLU activation function. Multiple ReLU activation functions help in creating a more accurate regression curve, allowing the model to generalize better.

Figure 3.8 shows the second dense layer and the regularization and ReLU functions:

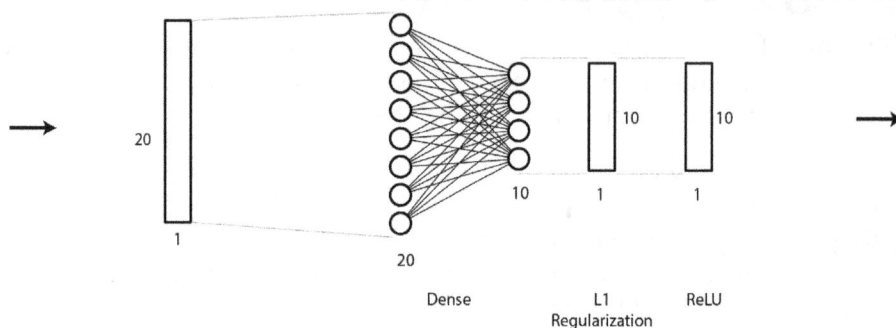

Figure 3.8: Dense layer, L1 regularization function and ReLU function

The final layer in the network is the classification layer. It takes the output from the second layer and converts it into a set of numbers, with each number representing a specific class. A high number indicates that the object might belong to that class. These numbers are not normalized, so they are passed through the SoftMax activation function, which normalizes the results and turns them into a probabilistic distribution. This distribution serves as the output of the model.

Figure 3.9 illustrates the classification layer receiving the output of the second ReLU and producing a set of results normalized by the SoftMax function. Here, C represents the number of classes. A post-processing algorithm identifies the largest number in the set and declares the classification result based on specific conditions. These conditions include determining whether there is a clear winner and whether a series of consecutive classification events all indicate the same winner. This process is crucial for ensuring result stability.

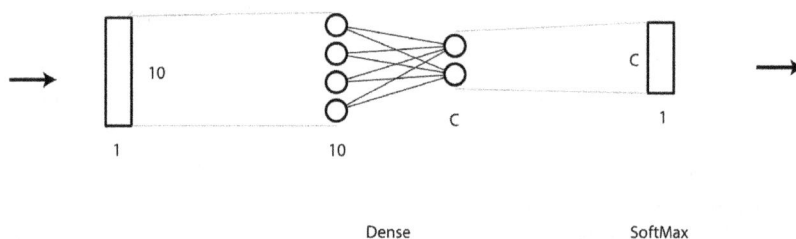

Figure 3.9: Dense classification layer and Softmax function

Use case: Correct usage detection

This use case demonstrates how movement classification can be applied to distinguish between normal vibrations and rotations versus those that signal a malfunction or improper use of the equipment. By analyzing sensor data from accelerometers and gyroscopes, the system can identify patterns that correspond to expected operational behavior and detect anomalies that may indicate wear, structural issues, or misuse.

Tool usage tracker

Problem definition: A toolmaker has asked for assistance in designing a TinyML model that can detect whether a person is using a tool correctly. They plan to integrate this model into various power tools. The initial focus is on a handheld power drill. The model should be able to identify both correct and incorrect tool operation in all directions (vertical, horizontal, inclined, etc.). The toolmaker wants the model to alert the operator if the angle at which the drill bit penetrates the material remains consistent.

Solution: The proposed solution involves a small microcontroller mounted on the handheld power tool. This microcontroller runs a TinyML model that can recognize whether the drill is being used properly. The correct movement is a straight motion, while any oscillatory movement that is not aligned with the drill bit is considered incorrect. The microcontroller mounted on the power tool provides a visual indication to the operator by projecting a red light onto the work surface using a directional LED. Additionally, there is a secondary microcontroller responsible for publishing drill events to a mesh network.

The following figure shows a conceptual diagram of the proposed solution:

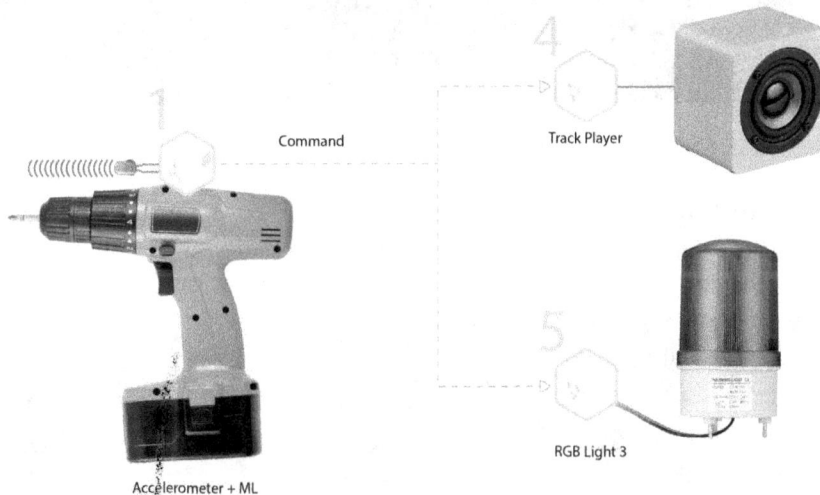

Figure 3.10: *Solution concept (Tool usage tracker)*

An auditory alarm and a visual indicator are connected to the drill messages in a wireless mesh network. If an incorrect usage message is received, a sound is played through the speaker, and the alert light flashes an intermittent visual signal. The solution should function properly regardless of the angle at which the tool is used.

Data acquisition

We have chosen a handheld power drill for this specific purpose. Drill bits are designed to cut material in the same direction as their longitudinal axis. Trying to cut a material in any other direction will cause damage to the drill bit and the internal parts of the power drill. A common incorrect use of the tool is attempting to enlarge an already drilled hole by moving the drill around the hole in a cone shape. Another common incorrect use is trying to move the drill in a zig-zag shape to cut material. To gather the dataset, we drilled approximately 600 holes into three different materials (wood, paper, and aluminum). Each material was drilled in four different directions: horizontal (90°), bottom-up (360°), top-down (180°), and inclined (45°). Half of the holes were drilled at a constant angle aligned to the direction of the drill bit (labeled as correct drilling), and the other half of the holes were drilled using cone and zig-zag motions while advancing the drill bit into the material with a moving angle not constantly aligned to the normal of the surface.

The following figures show samples of acceleration along the three axes when the drill is used correctly and incorrectly:

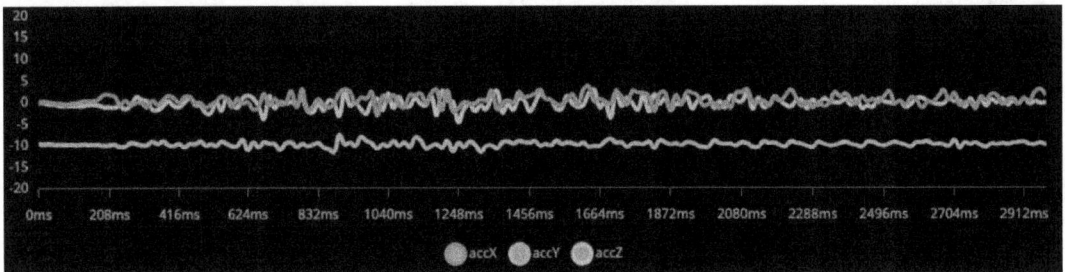

Figure 3.11: Sample of acceleration readings during correct drilling

- **Correct drilling**: This graph illustrates a material being perforated vertically. The negative acceleration (accY) represents the gravitational pull aligned to the drill bit, and the jagged lines are caused by the drill's vibration.

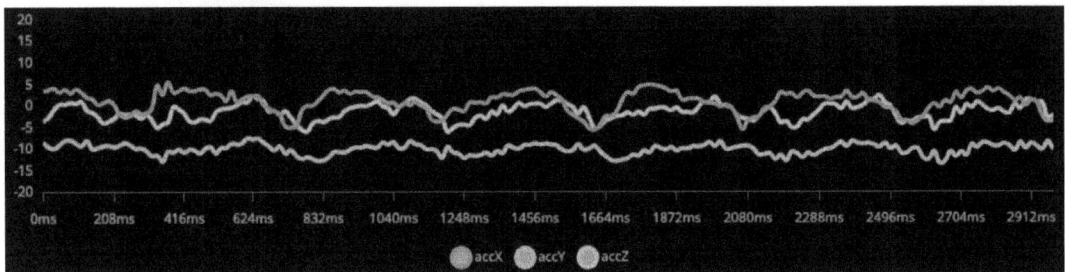

Figure 3.12: Sample of acceleration readings during incorrect drilling

- **Incorrect drilling**: The accelerometer (accY) indicates the negative acceleration due to gravitational pull, while accX and accZ show the oscillatory movement in a cone shape on the XZ plane, perpendicular to the drill axis, with a period of about 500 ms or a frequency of 2Hz.

The following figure shows the characteristics of the training dataset, which includes samples of both correct and incorrect drilling instances in various materials:

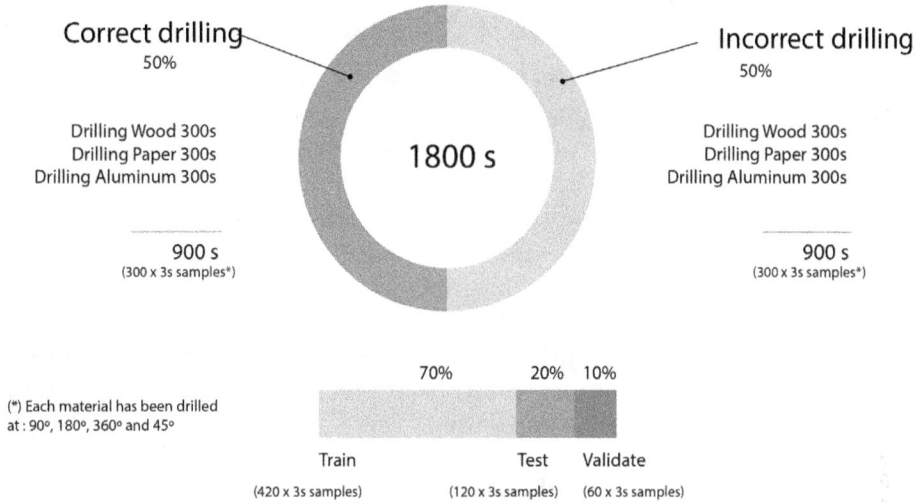

Figure 3.13: Training, testing and validation dataset (Tool usage tracker)

Processing

Data from three input axes is captured at a frequency of 62.5Hz. It is then trimmed in 2000 ms windows and sent to the spectral analysis block to extract 13 features per axis. Out of the 39 features, the most important ones for this use case are the spectral power at 1.95 - 5.86 Hz in the X and Z axes. These features characterize the power from events that occur approximately every 500 ms to 100 ms on the XZ plane, which is about the same frequency at which the operator moves the drill in a cone shape and zigzag perpendicular to the drill bit. Movements on the XZ plane should not occur during drilling.

The most important features in this use case are the ones that differentiate the two classes. Both classes are clearly defined in the clustering diagram (*Figure 3.14*). It is evident that the incorrect class is slightly more spread out as it characterizes different incorrect movements. Some movements are very close to the correct movement but are still distinguishable.

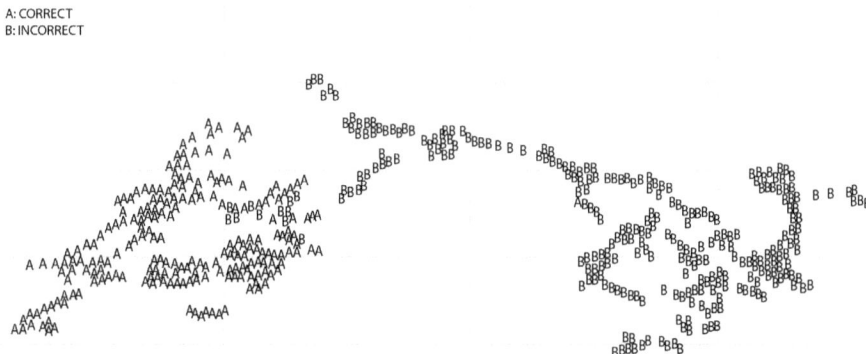

Figure 3.14: Clustering diagram showing correct and incorrect classes

Model

During the training process, 1800 seconds of training data are used to generate 4,160 training windows. Each training window has a size of 2000 ms and is incremented by 200 ms. These windows undergo processing to obtain 39 features, which are then fed into a three-layer dense neural network for training. An error score is calculated at the output, and the weights in the neural network are adjusted using backpropagation at a learning rate of 0.0005 for every iteration. This process is repeated 30 times to complete an epoch. After training, the model is evaluated using a validation dataset, resulting in an accuracy of 95.6% and a loss of 0.09. To further improve accuracy, adjustments can be made to the learning rate, number of training cycles, the architecture of the neural network, and the training data. It is also recommended to try different processing blocks and to store different versions of the model for comparison.

The following figure shows how training data is distributed and used across the different stages (training, validation, and testing), the steps that each stage goes through, and the relevant results at the end of each stage:

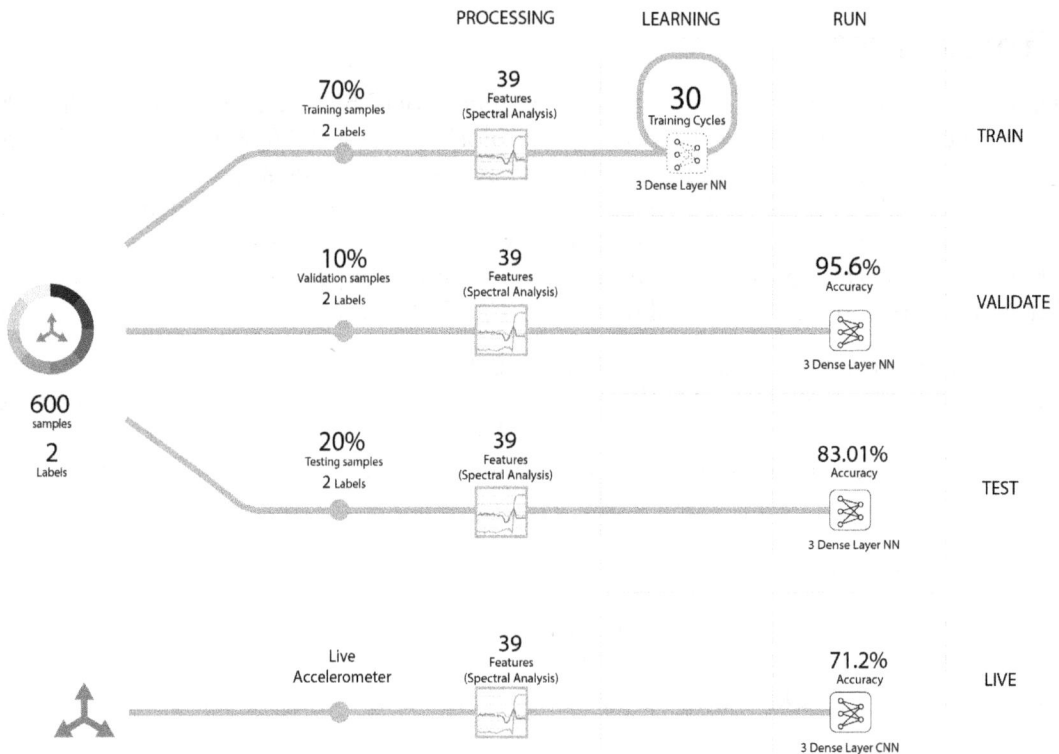

Figure 3.15: Training, validation and testing metrics (Tool usage tracker)

System implementation

The following figure shows a connection diagram with the three main building blocks and the connections between them. Additionally, it displays their inputs, outputs, and power sources:

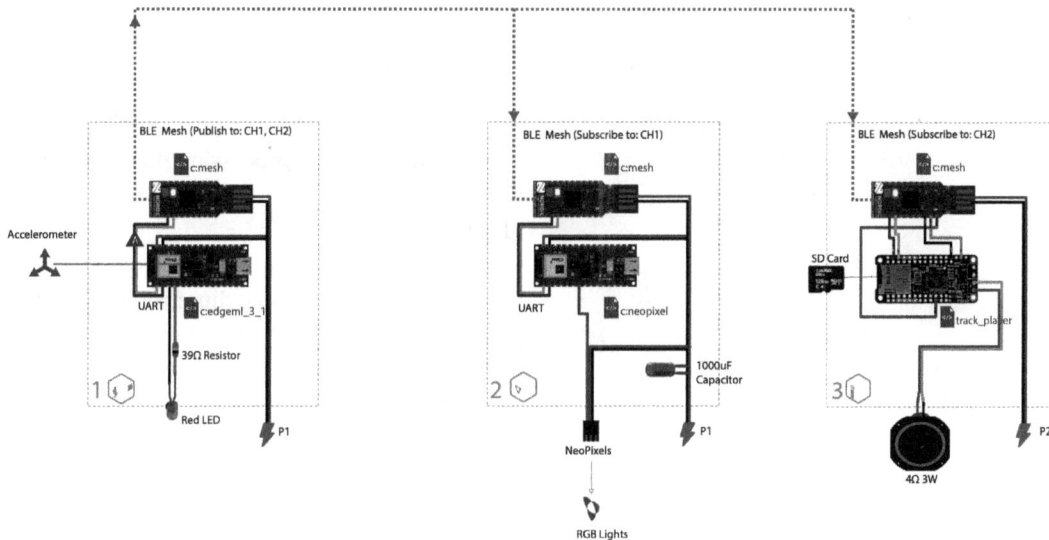

Figure 3.16: *Connection diagram (Tool usage tracker)*

Block 1 (Acquisition block) utilizes two microcontrollers. The first one is an Arduino Nano 33 BLE Sense that captures data from its three accelerometers, processes it, and runs the movement classification TinyML model. A red LED is connected to the GPIOs of this microcontroller to signal the operator about incorrect use. When an incorrect movement is detected for over five consecutive windows, two messages are prepared to be sent to the network. The first message contains the command that activates the alert light in block two, and the second message contains the command that activates the sound alarm in block three. These messages are sent to the second microcontroller (NRF52840 Dongle), which publishes them to the mesh network.

Block 2 (Actuator block) uses an NRF52840 Dongle to receive messages from block one via the mesh network. Incoming messages are sent to the Arduino 33 BLE, which is responsible for activating the alert light using the NeoPixel protocol.

Block 3 (Actuator block) also uses an NRF52840 Dongle to receive messages from block one. A signal is sent to the Adafruit feather with the track player wing to play an alert soundtrack stored on its SD card.

Source code

The trained model and the logic that captures the data from the tool vibrations, processes it, feeds it to the model, verifies and validates the output is loaded to the Block 1. In the following table, the pseudocode explains step by step how data is handed to different parts of the firmware and its resulting command sent out to the network for the visual alert and audible alert to act on it:

c:edgeml_3_1	Code location: Arduino Nano 33 BLE @ Block 1
	Capturing the data, processing it and running the TinyML model. Pseudocode 1. Three accelerometers capture movement in three dimensions. Data is sent to the processing functions. 2. In the processing block, the accelerometer data is sliced in small windows, transformed to frequencies, converted to spectral features, and sent to the TinyML model to run. 3. The TinyML model runs the inference with the provided data and returns an array of results. Results are sent to the post processing functions. 4. The post processing function waits for a series of positive identifications of an incorrect movement before it notifies the user via the local LED. 5. The main script prepares a message (A) to the light alert and another message (B) to the track player. It sends messages to the network microcontroller along with the channels they need to be published to.

Table 3.1: Pseudocode for block 1 (Tool usage tracker)

Network

The blocks communicate wirelessly using a BLE-Mesh network that operates under a pub/sub paradigm. Channel configuration is performed during the initial setup. *Table 3.2* shows Block 1 publishing the color and intensity commands on channel 1, to which Block 2 (the light actuator) is subscribed. Additionally, Block 1 also publishes the sound command on channel 2, to which Block 3 (the track player) is subscribed.

Block(s)	Action	Channel
1	Publishes to	CH1
1	Publishes to	CH2
2	Subscribes to	CH1
3	Subscribes to	CH2

Table 3.2: BLE Mesh network configuration (Tool usage tracker)

Power analysis

The power profile of each block is shown in the following table:

Block 1: Data capture, inference and feedback

Power source	Device	Latent consumption	Active consumption	Notes
P1	Arduino Nano 33 BLE Sense	0.032A @5V	< 1A @5V	
P1	NRF52 Dongle	0.04mA @5v	3mA @5v	Active when publishing messages as a *Client*.

Table 3.3: Power profile for block 1 (Tool usage tracker)

Ideally, we should be able to tap into the power tool battery for energy.

Block 2: Visual alert

Power source	Device	Latent consumption	Active consumption	Notes
P2	NRF52 Dongle	0.04mA @5v	0.3mA @5v	Active when receiving messages as a *server*.
P2	Arduino Nano 33 BLE	0.034mA @5V	< 1A @5V	Manages timing for NeoPixels
P3	NeoPixels 60x	0.001mA @5v	1A @5V	Each NeoPixel draws 60mA at full brightness. 20mA is typical.

Table 3.4: Power profile for block 2 (Tool usage tracker)

We need a 2A power source for block 2. Given the power requirements of bright NeoPixels, this block must connect to a permanent source of power (wall outlet).

Block 3: Audio alert

Power source	Device	Latent consumption	Active consumption	Notes
P2	NRF52 Dongle	0.040mA @5v	0.3A @5v	Active when receiving messages as a server.
P2	Adafruit NRF52840 Feather+track player	0.034mA @5V	0.6A @5V	Active when playing a track.

Table 3.5: Power profile for block 3 (Tool usage tracker)

We need a 1A power source for blocks 4 and 5 (one for each). The current requirements of a 4 Ohm 3W speaker at 5v are 0.6A.

Bill of materials

An approximate cost and quantity of the materials needed to build the prototype in this use case is presented in the following table:

Description	QTY	Unit cost	Total
Arduino Nano 33 BLE Sense	1	$45	$45
Arduino Nano 33 BLE	2	$30	$60
Adafruit NRF52840 Feather	1	$45	$45
Adafruit Music Maker FeatherWing	1	$25	$25
NRF52840 Dongle	3	$12	$36
Neopixel Strip (60x)	1	$99	$99
Power Source 1A @5v	3	$30	$20

Table 3.6: Bill of materials (Tool usage tracker)

Approximate cost of materials is $330.

Use case: Free fall detection

Detecting free-fall events has numerous safety applications across various fields, including industrial monitoring, wearable technology, and accident prevention. Free fall, characterized by the sudden acceleration of an object due to gravity, can be identified using movement classification techniques that analyze sensor data from accelerometers and gyroscopes.

Worker fall detection

This use case focuses on the classification of sudden and abrupt movements such as a rapid vertical drop followed by immobility, to create an end-to-end solution for detecting falls.

Problem definition: A major construction company is looking to implement a system that can detect if a worker has tripped or fallen at the construction site. This system should enable quick response and provide medical assistance from the on-site medical team. All workers are required to wear a vest and a helmet that can accommodate a small device running a TinyML model. The solution needs to be battery-powered (lasting at least a full day) and capable of wireless communication with the foreman's office to alert them in the event of a fall. The system should be able to support hundreds of devices, one for each construction worker.

Solution: The proposed solution involves using a microcontroller to run a movement classification model. This model will receive data from an array of accelerometers that are mounted on a wearable device, such as a vest, pin, hat, or wristband. The TinyML classification model will be able to detect when the device is in free-fall and will immediately send a message to the network to report the event. When a free-fall message is received, a sound alarm and a light alert, both connected to the wearable device, will be activated.

The following figure shows the proposed solution and the connections between its components:

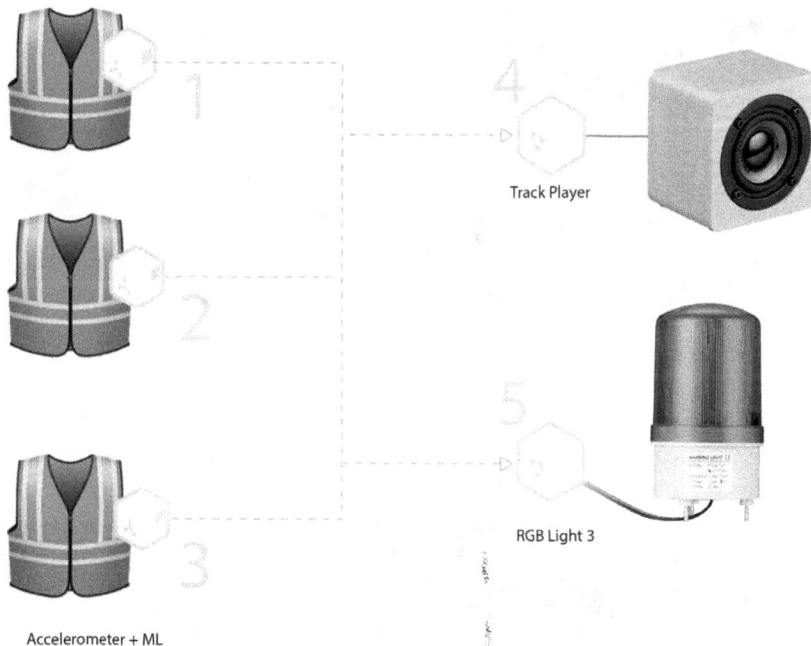

Figure 3.17: *Solution concept (Worker fall detection)*

Data acquisition

To collect the free-falling training data set, we utilized a data capture device equipped with the Edge Impulse data capture client and a set of accelerometers (three axes) attached to various bodies of different shapes and weights, and allowed them to free fall in a controlled environment. Additionally, we engaged a professional dancer (with an accelerometer attached to her body) to simulate free falls in a studio. Not surprisingly, we discovered that acceleration is independent of mass. However, certain forces, such as rotation during a free fall, generate centrifugal acceleration, which is also detected by the accelerometers. When a static body lies on a flat surface, the accelerometer reading will show two components being equal to zero, but one of them will show a reading close to the gravitational acceleration of 9.81m/s^2, which is the acceleration due to gravity on planet Earth. All the readings go to zero when that body is in free fall. This is a specific characteristic of the accelerometer's physical implementation; it does not mean the acceleration disappears. However, it is useful for detecting free fall, as the neural network we are using will observe the shape of the curve transitioning from gravitational acceleration to zero in the axis pointing to the center of the earth. The labels for this supervised learning data set are: Free fall simple, free fall spinning, free fall throw, and Static.

The following series of figures shows samples representing different free-fall scenarios: simple free fall, throw free fall, and spinning free fall. Additionally, a graph of a static object is presented for comparison:

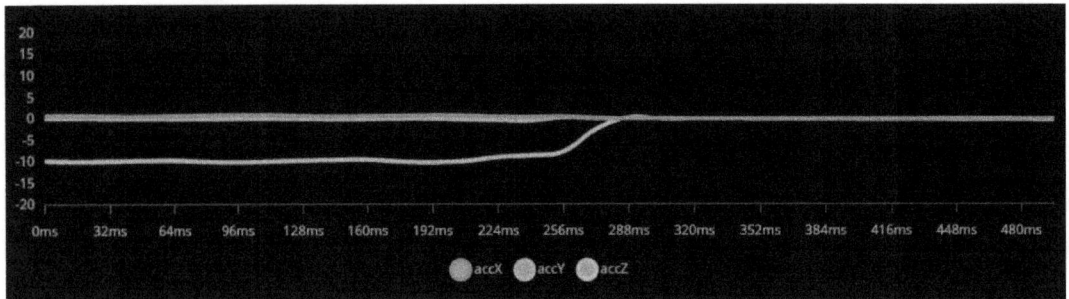

Figure 3.18: Simple (vertical) free fall

- **Sample of free fall simple**: The acceleration in the Z direction (accZ) shows as -9.81m/s^2, representing the gravitational acceleration of the Earth. It is important to note how the Z acceleration approaches zero during free fall.

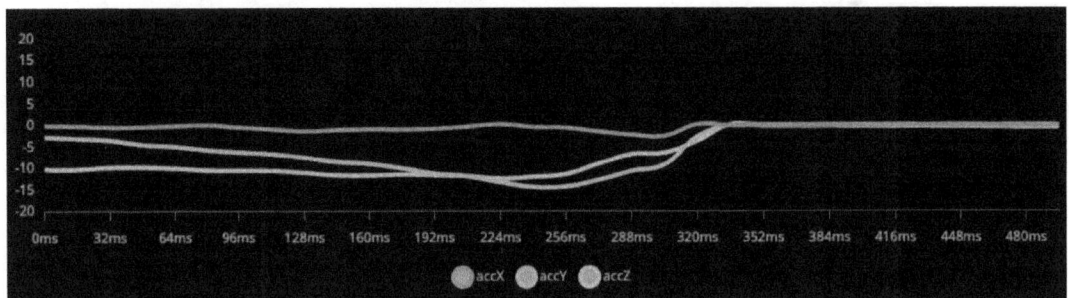

Figure 3.19: Parabolic throw and free fall

Sample of free fall throw (parabolic trajectory with horizontal and vertical components due to gravitational pull). Notice how accY shows the acceleration and deceleration that characterizes the throw, independent of the free fall component on accZ.

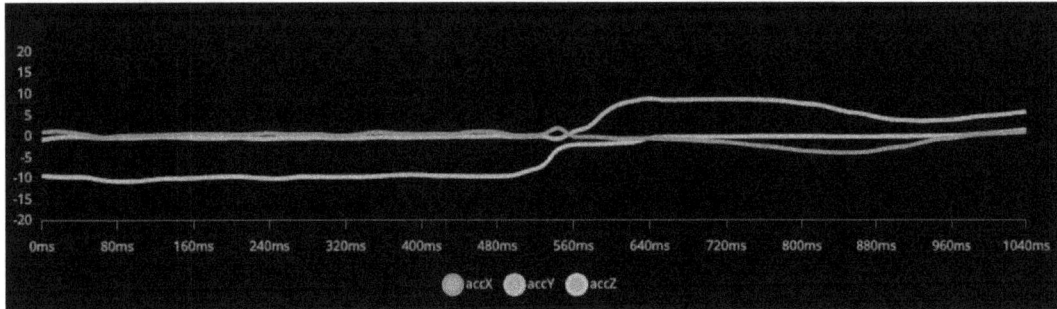

Figure 3.20: Spinning free fall

- **Sample of free fall spinning**: The Y-axis acceleration (accY) is influenced by the body's rotation, while the Z-axis acceleration represents free fall independently.

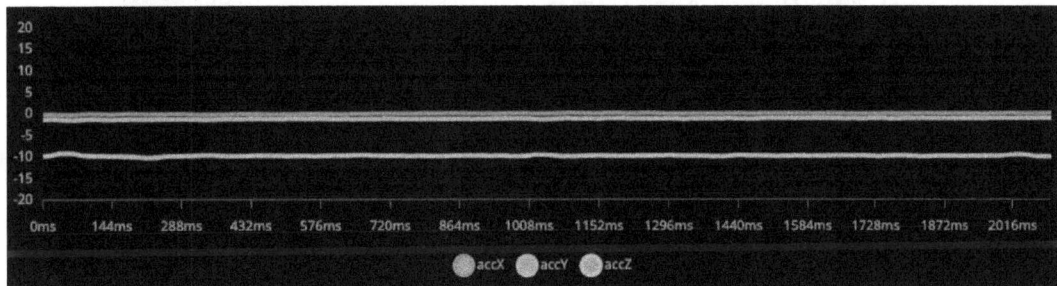

Figure 3.21: Static body (no free fall)

- **Sample of static body**: The accX and accY are zero, while the accZ shows a constant gravitational pull.

Figure 3.22 shows the configuration of the training, testing, and validation datasets. The datasets are divided into two classes: *Freefall* and *Other*. Each class consists of different subgroups of data. In the Freefall class, we captured 30 seconds of vertical freefall, 30 seconds of throw freefall, and 30 seconds of spinning freefall. In the *Other* class, the dataset includes any movement that is not free fall, such as standing, walking, and running (30 seconds each). The entire dataset is then split into three parts: 70% for the training dataset, 20% for the testing dataset, and 10% for the validation dataset.

Freefall
50%

Other
50%

Vertical Freefall 30s
Throw Freefall 30s
Spinning Freefall 30s

180 s

Standing 30s
Walking 30s
Running 30s

90 s
(180 x 0.5s samples*)

90 s
(180 x 0.5s samples*)

70%   20%   10%

Train   Test   Validate

(126 x 0.5s samples)   (36 x 0.5s samples)   (18 x 0.5s samples)

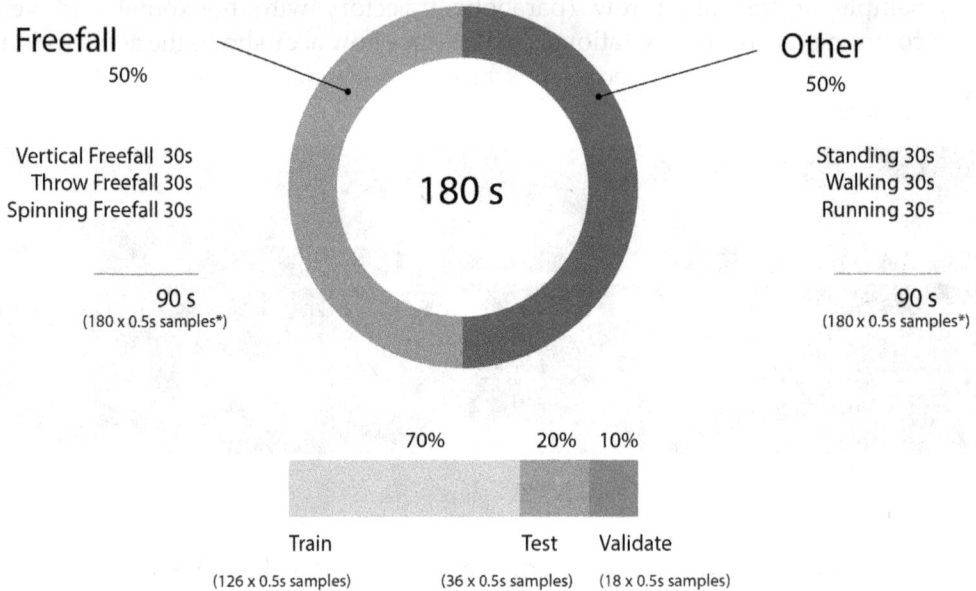

Figure 3.22: Training, testing and validation datasets (Worker fall detection)

Processing

The raw accelerometer data is used to generate 39 features from each window. During a free fall event, there is an abrupt change from a stationary state with gravitational pull in one axis to another stationary state where all acceleration readings drop to zero. It is crucial to note that acceleration does not actually disappear during a free fall event; the zero acceleration readings result from the sensor's electronic and mechanical components lacking a reference point during free fall. The neural network identifies a free fall event when all readings reach zero. This transition from one stationary state to another occurs within a small window of about 30ms. Given that our samples are 500ms long and our processing block takes chunks of about 100ms to extract the 39 features, there's a high likelihood that many of those chunks will indicate a stationary event rather than the switch from a static state to a free fall state, which is what we aim to detect with our model. To address this, the processing window needs to cover the entire event. We adjust the processing window to 500ms and run the processing block to obtain the following cluster diagram. The lower cluster, which shows both classes together, includes freefall, walking, and running samples. This makes sense, as walking and running movements are similar to an inverted pendulum with a free fall component. Nevertheless, as you will see, the model can differentiate between them without a problem.

Figure 3.23 shows similar movements clustered together. Notice how all the freefall events are grouped together, while the *Other* category forms three distinct clusters. This is because the *Other* category includes standing, walking, and running events, which are quite different. However, they are grouped under the same class for the purposes of this use case.

A: FREE FALL
B: OTHER

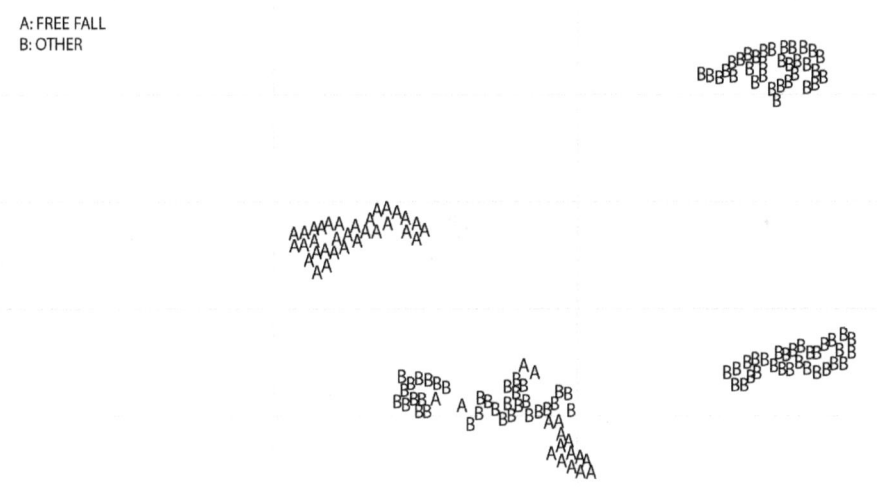

Figure 3.23: *Cluster diagram of Freefall versus other events*

Model

The features obtained from the processing block are input to the three dense layer model at a learning rate of 0.001 for 40 epochs. This yielded an accuracy of 96.4% and a loss of 0.16, which was reached in epoch 33. We experimented with running the training for 60 epochs, but nothing changed; the same accuracy was reached on Epoch 33. It is important to always check if you're using enough training cycles or if you could have used less. When we modified the learning rate to 0.002 (faster), the accuracy converged to 96% in half of the training cycles, around 16. From this, we can learn that the quality of the data and the model architecture have a greater impact on accuracy than the number of epochs and the learning rate. The training cycles and learning rate are directly connected to the resources and time needed to train the model.

The following figure shows how training data is distributed and used across the different stages (training, validation, and testing), the steps that each stage goes through, and the relevant results at the end of each stage:

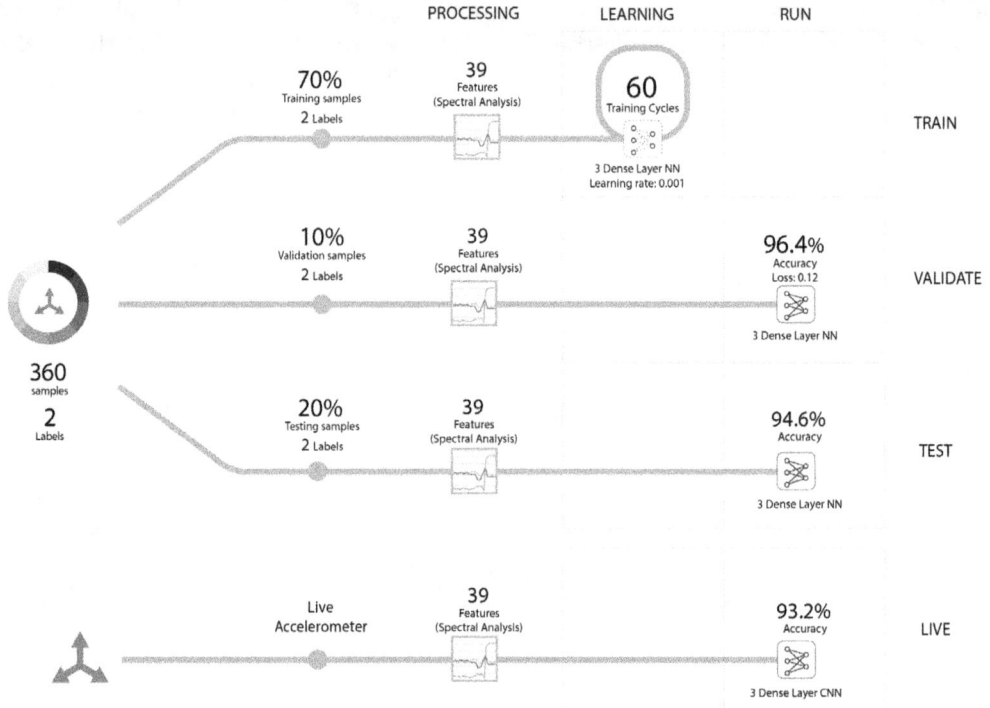

Figure 3.24: *Training, validation, testing and deployment stages (Worker fall detection)*

System implementation

The following figure shows a connection diagram with the three main building blocks and the connections between them. Additionally, it displays their inputs, outputs, and power sources:

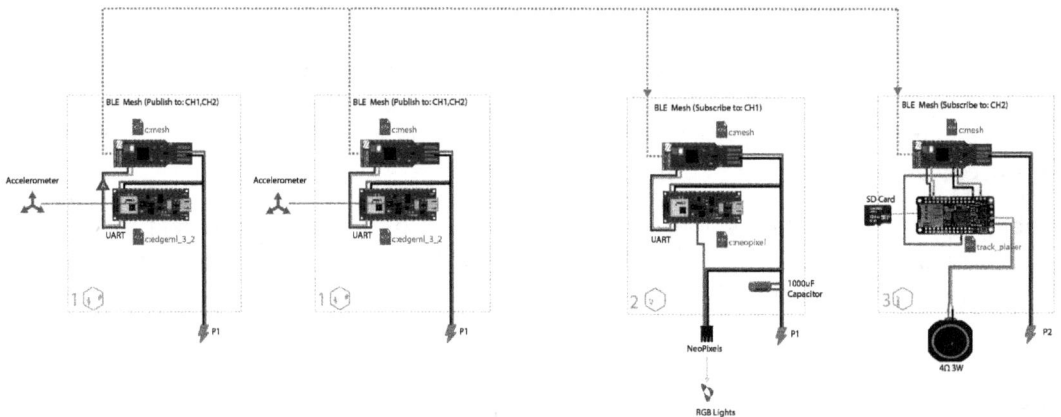

Figure 3.25: *Connection diagram (Worker fall detection)*

Block 1, the acquisition block, utilizes two microcontrollers. The first microcontroller is an Arduino Nano 33 BLE Sense, which captures free fall motion using its three accelerometers (X, Y, Z). The accelerometer data is then sent to an embedded processing block and fed into a TinyML model running on the Arduino microcontroller. The classification process takes approximately 1ms and uses 1.4k of RAM. If a free fall is detected, the Arduino sends an event to the NRF52840 Dongle. The dongle then prepares two messages: one for the light alert to turn on and another for the sound alarm to go off, and sends out the messages via the mesh network.

Block 2, the actuator block, uses an NRF52840 Dongle to receive messages from Block 1 via the mesh network. It subscribes to the channel where Block 1 sends messages to light alerts. Upon receiving a message, it sends the message payload to the Arduino controlling the NeoPixel lights. The Arduino reads the payload, which contains a command to set the alert lights for a predetermined period.

Block 3, another actuator block, also relies on an NRF52840 Dongle to receive messages from Block 1. In this case, the message instructs what track to play and for how long. The dongle then sends the command to the feather connected to the track player wing, which plays a preselected alarm track via the 4 Ohm 3W speakers connected to its output.

Source code

The trained model and the logic that detects the free falls, is loaded to the block 1. In the following table, the pseudocode explains step by step how data is handed to different parts of the firmware and the resulting messages sent out to the network to alert of the incident:

c:edgeml_3_2	Code location: Arduino Nano 33 BLE @ Block 1
	Capturing and classifying free falling events. Pseudocode 1. The accelerometer captures the movement in three dimensions (X,Y,Z) and sends it to the processing block. 2. In the processing block, the movement data is sliced into small windows, turned into 39 features, and sent to the TinyML model to run. 3. The TinyML model runs the inference with the provided data and returns an array of results. Results are sent to the post-processing functions. 4. The post processing functions wait for at least two free fall consecutive events to be reported to issue a free fall notice to the main script.

c:edgeml_3_2	Code location: Arduino Nano 33 BLE @ Block 1
	5. The main script prepares a message to the light alert block specifying color and duration. It also prepares a message for the sound alert block specifying what track to play and how long to play it. It sends both messages to the network block to publish them to the mesh network.

Table 3.7: Pseudocode (Worker fall detection)

Network

The blocks communicate wirelessly using a BLE-Mesh network that operates under a pub/sub paradigm. Channel configuration is performed during the initial setup. *Table 3.8* shows multiple instances of Block 1 (each representing a free-fall sensor) publishing the free-fall events to channel 1, to which Block 2 (the visual alert) is subscribed. Additionally, Block 3 (the audio alert) is also subscribed to the free-fall events.

Block(s)	Action	Channel
1	Publishes to	CH1
1	Publishes to	CH2
2	Subscribes to	CH1
3	Subscribes to	CH2

Table 3.8: BLE Mesh network configuration (Worker fall detection)

Power analysis

The power profile of each block is shown in the following table:

Block 1

Power source	Device	Latent consumption	Active consumption	Notes
P1	Arduino Nano 33 BLE Sense	0.032A @5V	< 1A @5V	
P1	NRF52 Dongle	0.04mA @5v	3mA @5v	Active when publishing messages as a *client*.

Table 3.9: Power profile for block 1 (Worker fall detection)

This block must be battery-operated as it will be embedded into a wearable.

Block 2

Power source	Device	Latent consumption	Active consumption	Notes
P2	NRF52 Dongle	0.04mA @5v	0.3mA @5v	Active when receiving messages as a *server*.
P2	Arduino Nano 33 BLE	0.034mA @5V	< 1A @5V	Manages timing for NeoPixels.
P3	NeoPixels 60x	0.001mA @5v	1A @5V	Each NeoPixel draws 60mA at full brightness. 20mA is typical.

Table 3.10: Power profile for block 2 (Worker fall detection)

We need a 2A power source for block 2. Given the power requirements of bright NeoPixels, this block must connect to a permanent power source (wall outlet).

Block 3

Power source	Device	Latent consumption	Active consumption	Notes
P2	NRF52 Dongle	0.040mA @5v	0.3A @5v	Active when receiving messages as a *server*.
P2	Adafruit NRF52840 Feather+ track player	0.034mA @5V	0.6A @5V	Active when playing a track.

Table 3.11: Power profile for block 3 (Worker fall detection)

We need a 1A power source for Block 3. The current requirements of a 4 Ohm 3W speaker at 5v are 0.6A.

Bill of materials

An approximate cost and quantity of the materials needed to build the prototype in this use case is presented in the following table:

Description	QTY	Unit cost	Total
Arduino Nano 33 BLE Sense	1	$45	$45
Arduino Nano 33 BLE	3	$30	$90
Adafruit NRF52840 Feather	1	$45	$45
Adafruit Music Maker FeatherWing	1	$25	$25
NRF52840 Dongle	4	$12	$48
Neopixel Strip (60x)	1	$99	$99
Power Source 1A @5v	4	$30	$120

Table 3.12: Bill of materials (Worker fall detection)

Approximate cost of materials is $472.

Use case: Movement profiling

Movement classification enables the detection of specific motion patterns that serve as indicators of particular behaviors. By analyzing data from sensors such as accelerometers and gyroscopes, machine learning models can identify and differentiate between various types of movement, from subtle gestures to more complex activities.

Car driving style tracker

This use case focuses on the classification of vehicle movement, including acceleration, braking, cornering, and speed changes, to build an end-to-end solution for monitoring driving behavior and performance in real-time.

Problem definition: An insurance company is conducting an experiment to determine whether providing real-time feedback to drivers can reduce the risk of accidents. The company is willing to offer a significant discount on their insurance policy to drivers who are willing to use a device that provides real-time feedback on their driving style. The device will be equipped with a small speaker mounted on the dashboard, which will emit a beep if the driving behavior is considered dangerous or outside the normal limits.

Solution: The proposed solution involves using a microcontroller running a TinyML model equipped with embedded accelerometers to detect driving events and their intensity. The microcontroller communicates serially with a track player that produces discrete beeps when the driver is not operating the car carefully. The beeps can be heard by the driver in a nonintrusive and non-distracting manner.

The following figure shows a conceptual diagram of the proposed solution:

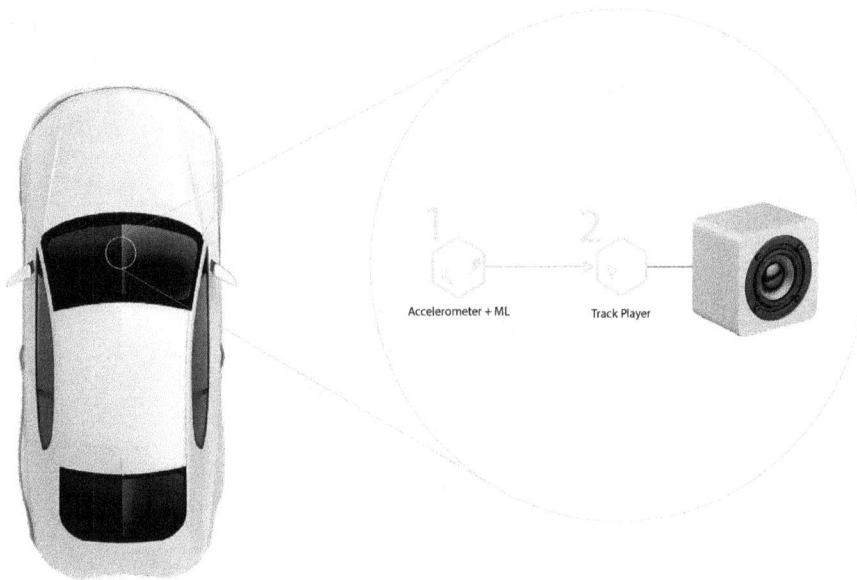

Figure 3.26: *Solution concept (Car driving style tracker)*

Data acquisition

The objective of this use case is to determine whether the car is being driven recklessly. To gather the training data, we have installed a device with a set of three accelerometers on the dashboard of the test car. The Y-axis is aligned with the direction of the car. A negative reading on the Y-axis indicates acceleration, while a positive reading indicates deceleration. The X-axis is perpendicular to the car's direction and parallel to the road surface. A negative reading on the X-axis represents the centrifugal forces resulting from a right turn, while a positive reading indicates a left turn. The Z-axis is normal to the driving surface and aligned with the earth's gravitational acceleration of 9.81m/s^2. When a car is in motion, it is subject to various forces, some of which may be stronger than the gravitational pull (1G). For instance, if you are traveling at approximately 15 km/h and need to make a sudden stop to avoid hitting someone, you will experience the equivalent of about 1G but in the Y-axis. This is safe but not a pleasant experience, and it should not occur frequently if you are a good driver. The device records accelerometer data when the car is moving and stops when the car is parked and turned off.

Figure 3.27 shows the characteristics of the training dataset, which includes samples of different instances of sudden stops and normal driving. The dataset is divided in three parts: Training dataset (70%), test dataset (20%) and validation (10%).

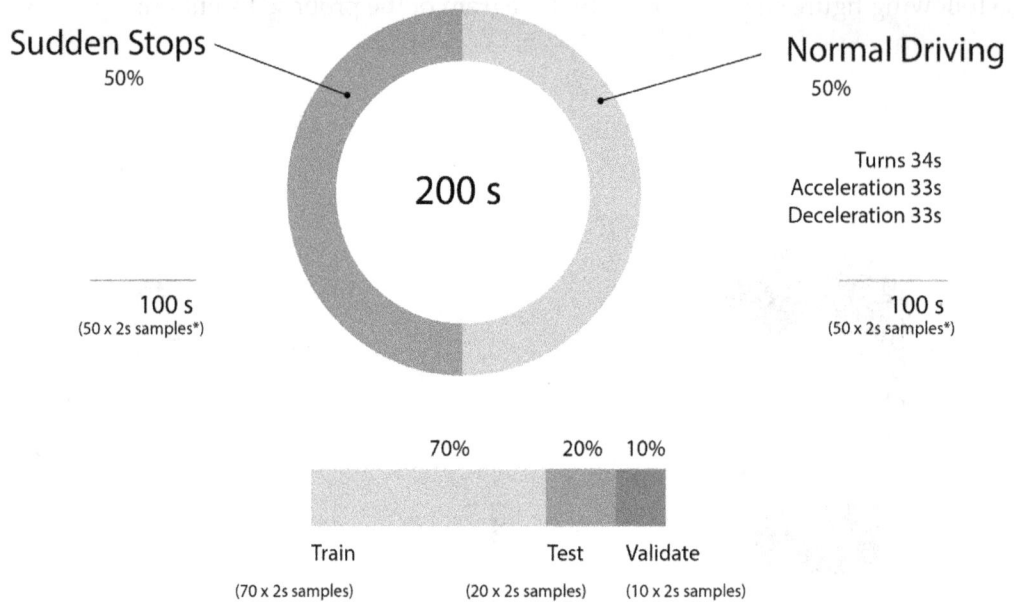

Figure 3.27: Training, testing and validation dataset(Car driving style tracker)

If you are a reckless driver, you might take more risks such as running amber lights, not allowing others to merge into your lane, or trying to weave between cars. While most of the time the driver may get away with it, occasionally they will have to make a sudden stop to avoid a collision. Initially, we tried to classify driving behaviors like changing lanes, speeding up, and slowing down to identify different driving styles. However, we discovered that sudden stops are a common factor across all driving styles that indicate dangerous driving. As a result, we created a binary dataset with 50% of the samples representing sudden stops and the other 50% representing regular driving maneuvers that do not exceed 0.5G (such as normal turns, acceleration, and deceleration).

Processing

A sudden stop at 15 km/h is a short-lived event lasting between 500 and 1000ms on average. When a vehicle is traveling at lower speeds, the deceleration peak lasts longer compared to higher speeds. Therefore, this model is not suitable for detecting real crashes at higher speeds.

A processing window of 2000 ms is sufficient to display a sudden stop event. The processing block analyzes 39 features from the three accelerometer time series. Notably, for this specific use case, the most important features are the spectral power for the Y axis. In essence, the model analyzes the energy released on the Y-axis to detect a sudden deceleration event. Refer to the following figure:

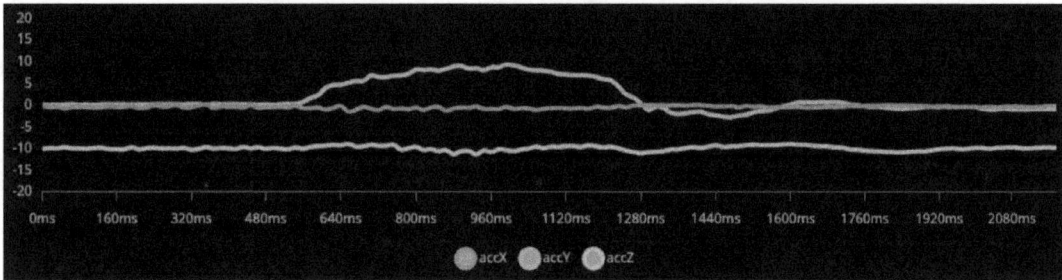

Figure 3.28: Sample of a sudden stop

Notice how the accelerations in the X and Z directions are constant, while the acceleration in the Y direction shows a deceleration that peaks at about 10 m/s^2.

Figure 3.29 clearly indicates a distinct separation of both classes. The vertical spread demonstrates the diversity of the dataset, but it is important to note that the close horizontal separation also reflects how similar the regular driving events are to the sudden stop events.

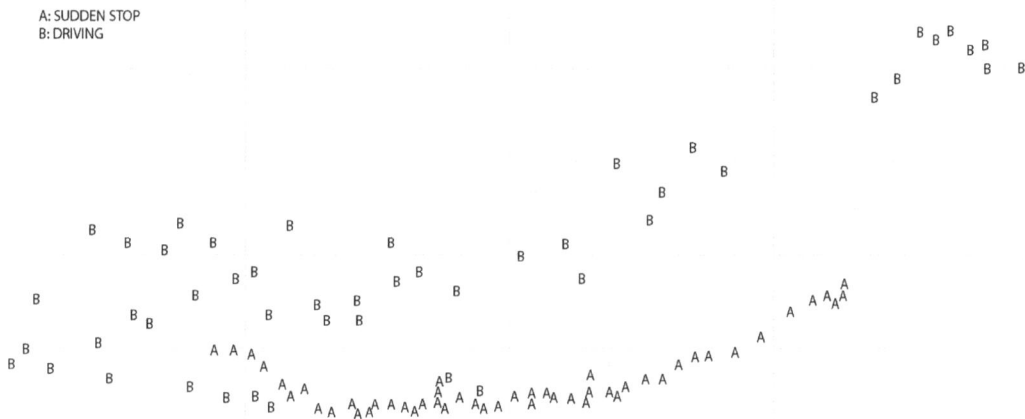

Figure 3.29: Cluster diagram showing separation between sudden stop events and normal driving events

Model

We process 100 samples, extracting 39 features. These features are then input into a three-layer neural network for 30 training cycles at a learning rate of 0.0005.

The first layer is a fully connected layer with 20 neurons, receiving input from all 39 features. The output undergoes L1 regularization and is activated by a ReLU function before being sent to the second dense layer. The second layer consists of ten neurons, also with L1 regularization and ReLU activation. The final dense layer has two neurons, one for each class, and is activated by a SoftMax function to produce a probability distribution for the inference result.

The model takes 1 ms to run on a Cortex M4 processor operating at 80MHz.

The following figure shows how training data is distributed across the different stages (training, validation and testing), the steps that each stage goes through, and the relevant results at the end of each stage:

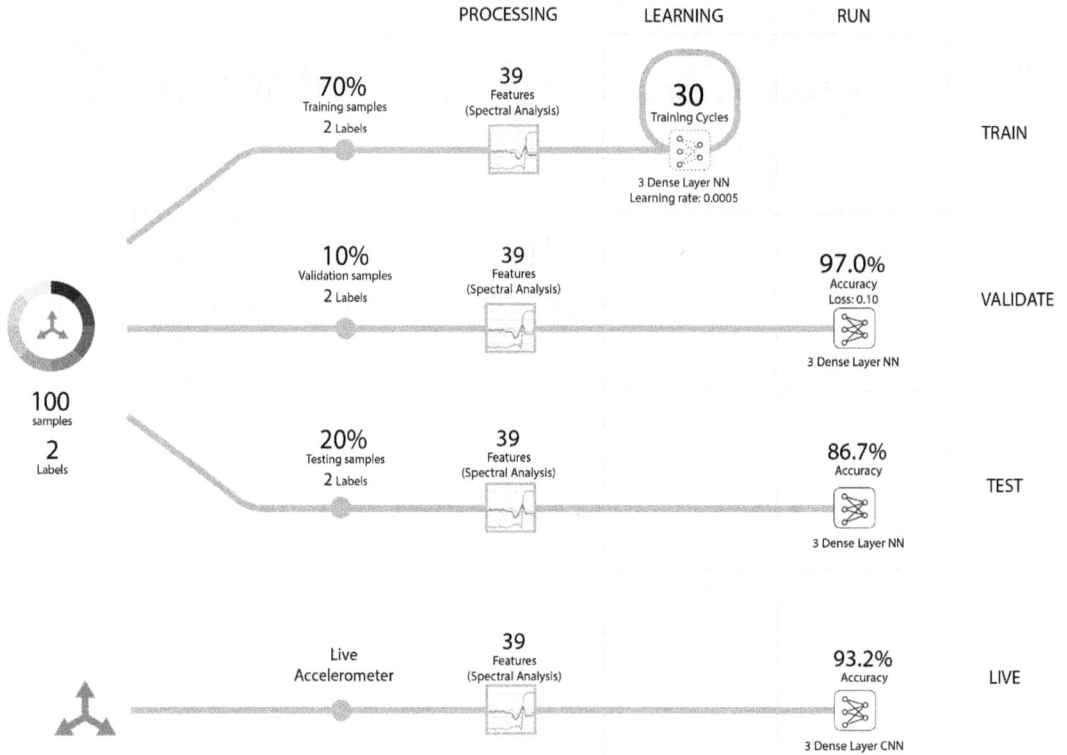

Figure 3.30: *Training, validation, testing and deployment stages (Car driving style tracker)*

System implementation

The following figure shows a connection diagram between its two building blocks. Additionally, it displays their inputs, outputs and power sources:

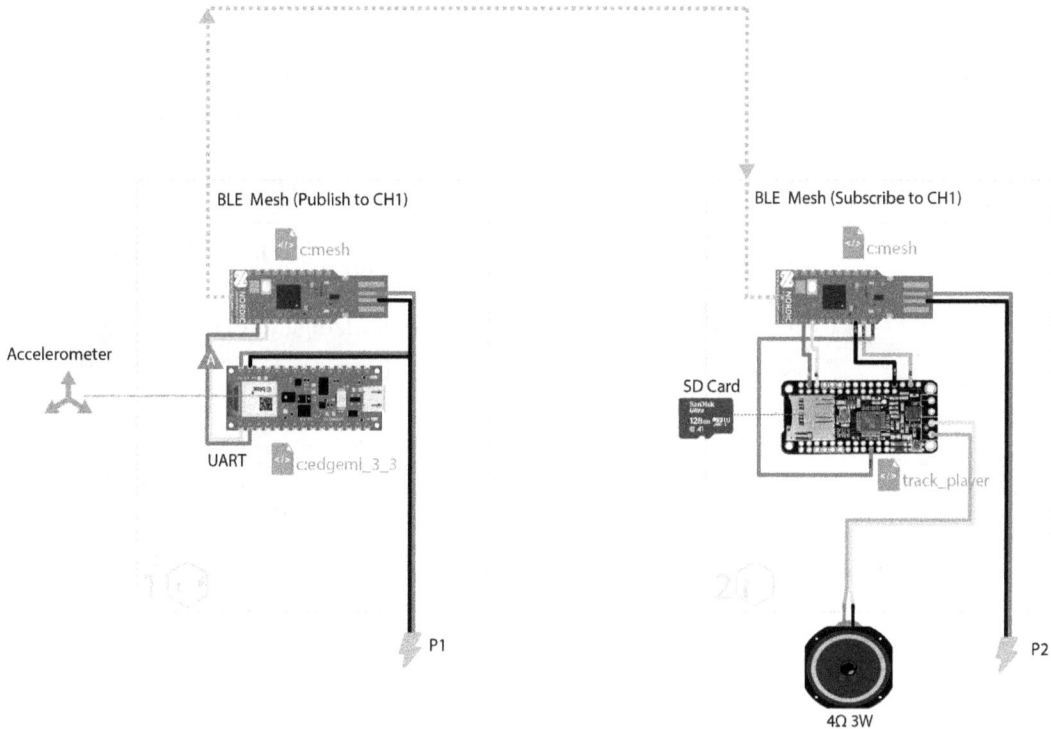

Figure 3.31: Connection diagram (Driving style tracker)

Block 1 (Acquisition block) utilizes two microcontrollers. The first microcontroller is an Arduino 33 BLE Sense, which is equipped with embedded accelerometers to capture, process, and analyze the car's movement through its M4 ARM processor. The output of the analysis is then received by a local script, which prepares a track player command to be sent to the second microcontroller board, an NRF52840 Dongle. This command is then published to a local mesh network for Block 2 to pick up. While having a mesh network inside a car may seem like unnecessary over-engineering, it opens up numerous possibilities, such as custom car dashboards, real-time communication with the cloud, and black box record-keeping.

Block 2 (Actuator block) also utilizes the same track player components as other use cases in this book. It includes an NRF52840 dongle to subscribe and receive sudden stop messages from Block 1. Additionally, it incorporates an Adafruit wing and a track player feather connected to a 4 Ohm 3W speaker. This setup provides auditory feedback to the car driver. The auditory feedback is a subtle beep, similar to other auditory cues that the car provides to alert the driver about events requiring attention, such as fastening a seatbelt, turning on lights, and detecting cars in blind spots.

Source code

The trained model and the logic that processes the data from the data captured by the accelerometers mounted in the car is loaded to the block 1. In *Table 3.13*, the pseudocode explains step by step how data in captured, processed, handled to the model, its results analyzed by the post-processing stage and communicated to its peripheral block (block 2).

c:edgeml_3_3	Code location: Arduino Nano 33 BLE @ Block 1
	Recognizing sudden stop events Pseudocode 1. The three accelerometers (X,Y,Z) capture the car movement and send it to the processing functions. 2. The processing block extracts 39 spectral features from each sample. It feeds them to the TinyML model 3. The TinyML model recognizes sudden stops while the car is moving and outputs results to the postprocessing functions. 4. The post processing function runs a series of checks before declaring an actual sudden stop. A command to play a sound in the track player is prepared and sent to the local main script. 5. The local main script communicates the event to the microcontroller in charge of network communication.

Table 3.13: Pseudocode for block 1 (Car driving style tracker)

Network

The blocks communicate wirelessly using a BLE-Mesh network that operates under a pub/sub paradigm. The following table shows one to one communication between blocks via the channel 1. Block 1 publishes commands to the track player to play feedback sounds to the driver:

Block(s)	Action	Channel
1	Publishes to	CH1
2	Subscribes to	CH1

Table 3.14: Mesh network configuration (Car driving style tracker)

Power analysis

The power profile of each block is shown in the following table:

Block 1

Power source	Device	Latent consumption	Active consumption	Notes
P1	Arduino Nano 33 BLE Sense	0.032A @5V	< 1A @5V	
P1	NRF52 Dongle	0.04mA @5v	3mA @5v	Active when publishing messages as a *client*.

Table 3.15: Power profile for block 1 (Car driving style tracker)

A model running inference every second will consume about 0.5Amps. While the block can run on batteries, it would be ideal to power it from a car power source. That way, the system would become a fixture in the car same as any other electronic component on the dashboard.

Block 2

Power source	Device	Latent consumption	Active consumption	Notes
P2	NRF52 Dongle	0.040mA @5v	0.3A @5v	Active when receiving messages as a *server*.
P2	Adafruit NRF52840 Feather+ track player	0.034mA @5V	0.6A @5V	Active when playing a track.

Table 3.16: Power profile for block 2 (Car driving style tracker)

We need a 1A power source for Block 2. The current requirements of a 4 Ohm 3W speaker at 5v are 0.6A. Same as Block 1, this block should be powered by a car power source.

Bill of materials

An approximate cost and quantity of the materials needed to build the prototype in this use case is presented in the following table:

Description	QTY	Unit cost	Total
Arduino Nano 33 BLE Sense	1	$45	$45
Adafruit NRF52840 Feather	1	$45	$45
Adafruit Music Maker FeatherWing	1	$25	$25
NRF52840 Dongle	3	$12	$36
Power Source 1A @5v	2	$30	$60

Table 3.17: Bill of materials (Car driving style tracker)

Approximate cost of materials is $211.

Conclusion

Movement classification is incredibly useful to detect events that were impossible to detect with traditional sensors. Movement classification and small battery-operated ML models that run independently are a great fit with systems that cannot afford a permanent connection to the internet because they are remote or in constant movement. The relative low cost of implementation mainly due to a reduction in size and moving parts enables solutions with hundreds of classifiers (e.g.: worker fall detection) all of them independently detecting events. Technologies like low energy mesh networks and LTE-M, share low energy and low data design principles with movement classification implementations enabling more complex solutions.

In the next chapter, we will explore image classification, a fundamental task in computer vision that enables machines to recognize and categorize objects within images. The reader will learn how **Convolutional Neural Networks** (**CNNs**), which have been applied to sound and movement classification in previous sections, were originally designed for image recognition.

References

- https://www.quora.com/Why-is-the-Nyquist-Shannon-sampling-rate-exactly-2-times-the-maximum-frequency-Where-is-the-proof-for-that-constant-2

- https://github.com/jeandeducla/ML-Time-Series

- https://towardsdatascience.com/over-fitting-and-regularization-64d16100f45c

- https://www.adafruit.com/product/3436 Music Maker FeatherWing w/ Amp - MP3 OGG WAV MIDI Synth Player - Stereo 3W Amplifier

- https://community.sw.siemens.com/s/article/what-is-a-power-spectral-density-psd

- Nerijus Kudarauskas (2007) Analysis of emergency braking of a vehicle, Transport, 22:3, 154-159, DOI: 10.1080/16484142.2007.9638118

- https://doi.org/10.1080/16484142.2007.9638118

- https://towardsdatascience.com/intuitions-on-l1-and-l2-regularisation-235f2db4c261

- https://crlab.cs.columbia.edu/humanoids_2018_proceedings/media/files/0065.pdf

- Movement classification use case 1: **https://studio.edgeimpulse.com/public/289478/live**

- Movement classification use case 2: **https://studio.edgeimpulse.com/public/300899/live**

- Movement classification use case 3: **https://studio.edgeimpulse.com/public/301063/live**

Join our book's Discord space

Join the book's Discord Workspace for Latest updates, Offers, Tech happenings around the world, New Release and Sessions with the Authors:

https://discord.bpbonline.com

CHAPTER 4
Image Classification

Introduction

Image classification is one of the most popular applications in TinyML. It provides the ability to detect and count objects of practically any type. Just as a thermometer can sense temperature, a camera working together with an image classification model can sense the presence of specific objects and the occurrence of certain events. This opens the possibility of creating a new generation of sensors that provide invaluable and never-seen-before data to a system for further analysis, decision-making, and actuation. Running image classification in the same device that is capturing the image is a perfect match for applications that guarantee privacy, as pixels are never sent out to any external system. Furthermore, the stand-alone nature of the model allows us to eliminate dependencies related to internet connection and cloud infrastructure.

Structure

The chapter covers the following topics:

- Capturing training data for image classification
- Extracting features for the images
- Image classification model
- Use case: Gesture detection

- Use case: Face detection
- Use case: Object recognition

Objectives

This chapter guides the reader through the end-to-end process of implementing image classification in a constrained environment. It begins by demonstrating how to capture the training data, followed by identifying the key features and explaining how to extract them automatically. Next, the chapter discusses the inner workings of a neural network specialized in image classification. The implementation details are then covered step by step, starting with the electronic components, the pseudocode for the firmware logic, the network configuration, and the power requirements. Finally, the chapter concludes with an overview of the bill of materials.

Capturing training data for image classification

Training an object recognition model can be challenging and time-consuming, as it requires both a large, diverse dataset to accurately learn and distinguish features, and significant computational power to achieve a stable and reliable model. Fortunately, it is possible to reuse already trained Neural Networks by replacing their specialized layers with new ones that classify different objects. Such a process is called **Transfer Learning**, and it allows you to train a model for your needs with a reduced set of images, as you are only training the specialized layers instead of the whole network from scratch. In most cases, you only need a smartphone to capture around 100 images per class (a class is a type of object you want to recognize). Tools like Edge Impulse provide a web-based client that will automatically help you snap a picture and upload it to their cloud. You can also use any camera to collect the images and load them directly to any computer performing processing and training.

Extracting features from the images

The process of extracting features from an image might be familiar to anybody who has ever worked with an image on a computer. The first step is to crop the image to a square shape (1:1); this might feel unnecessary as all cameras return a rectangular image however, resizing to a square shape helps simplify the computation, creates consistency in the input, and enables the reutilization of pre-trained models. The second step is to resize the image to a smaller size (e.g., 96x96, 160x160, or 320x320 pixels). While some detail and texture data are lost in the image size reduction, the shape and contours of the image should still be clearly delineated. Neural Networks mainly learn how to recognize objects by their contours. As you can see in the following example, you can still recognize a flamingo even in the 96x96 image, as shown here:

320x320   160x160   96x96

Figure 4.1: *Different versions of the same image at different sizes*

The following (optional) step is to decide whether color is essential for the use case classification. If it is (e.g., you want to classify birds by their color), you need to send a color image to the neural network. The number of features in a color image is the total number of pixels times the number of channels. A color image has three channels (Red, Green, and Blue). However, in most cases where color is irrelevant, you can reduce the number of features by turning the image to grayscale. In that case, the number of features is the total number of pixels in the image. Each pixel expresses its brightness with a number from 0 to 255 (8bits).

The relationship between the number of channels, dimensions, and the total number of features in images is shown in the following table:

Image type	Channels	Dimensions	Total pixels or features
Color image	3	320x320	307,200
Color image	3	160x160	76,800
Color image	3	96x96	27,648
Grayscale image	1	320x320	102,400
Grayscale image	1	160x160	25,600
Grayscale image	1	96x96	9,216

Table 4.1: *Relationship between number of channels, dimensions and number of features*

The final step is to send the array of numbers containing the series of pixel levels to the neural network's input layer. The neural network will have as many inputs as pixels in the image. For that reason, it is important to resize all images to a predetermined size during the processing stage.

Image classification model

The array of pixel information sent from the processing Block is known as a Feature Map. If you want to obtain a specific characteristic from that map (like horizontal lines or color in specific), you pass the Feature Map through a filter. After passing the data through the filter, you obtain a Modified Feature Map highlighting the characteristics that such filter specializes in. This is similar to what happens when you wear polarized sunglasses; your eyes get a modified version of the light that would reach your eyes. It is called polarized because you only receive the light aligned in one direction, filtering out everything else. In the same way, the first layers of the model filter out basic shapes like lines, curves, or corners of a shape using filters specialized in lines, curves, and corners.

The effect of the **Convolution Kernel filter** on an input image where the edges are emphasized is clearly shown in the before and after in the following figure:

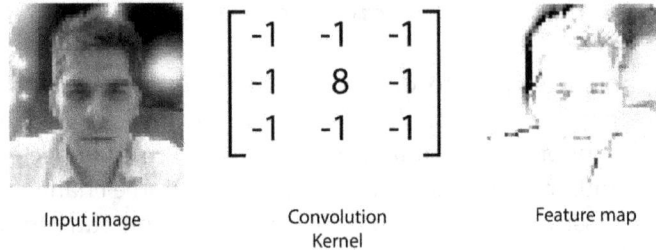

Input image   Convolution Kernel   Feature map

Figure 4.2: Example of the effects of a convolution kernel filter

Once that is done, you pass the Modified Feature Map through another set of filters. Such filters are specialized in more complex characteristics built from the basic ones and so on. A good example is a filter dedicated to squares. We would be unable to detect squares if we did not filter for lines first, as squares are made of lines. The result is a new but even more specialized Modified Feature Map at every step. You can guess what happens next: we run such a map through another set of specialized filters; in this case, the filters detect basic objects. This progression is effective because the earlier layers of the network focus on identifying basic features like edges and lines, which are essential for constructing more complex shapes that the later layers analyze to detect basic objects. The next step is to create a layer that detects objects made from a combination of objects (like a car or a face).

The progression from detecting low-level features to medium and high-level features is shown in the following figure:

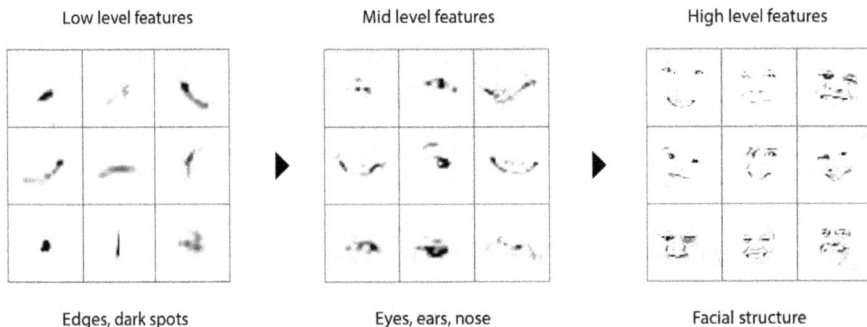

Low level features   Mid level features   High level features

Edges, dark spots   Eyes, ears, nose   Facial structure

Figure 4.3: Low level, mid-level and high-level features

The process of applying a filter to a Feature Map is called **convolution**. A convolution runs the filter through all sections of the Feature Map in a way similar to a long multiplication to generate a new Modified Feature Map.

Pooling is used to detect variations in position and rotation to improve detection capabilities. This allows the model to detect specific characteristics without being centered or rotated. Normalization standardizes pixel values by scaling them to a consistent range, typically between 0 and 1. This helps the model process and compare pixel data more efficiently, enhancing its ability to learn patterns and improve overall performance. Dropout is used to ignore some neurons randomly and temporarily to force the network to learn different ways to infer the same object, avoiding overfitting.

Multiple activation functions, specifically ReLU, introduce non-linearity to the model at every step. Think about introducing non-linearity as a way to help the model represent natural objects and actual events more accurately. We need this because we live in a non-linear world where almost nothing behaves like a predictable straight line.

So far, we can extract features, normalize them, and make them non-linear. What is next is to classify them. We connect the specialized Feature Map to a dense layer to do that. In other words, every feature in the map is assigned an input neuron. Every neuron will be connected to the next layer in the same way, and a random weight will be given to each one of those connections. Using backpropagation, we run all the samples already labeled through the entire pipeline (feature extraction and classification) to obtain an error score that tells us how far we are from inferring the object correctly. This will hint at what weights we need to modify to reduce the error in the next run. We do this repeatedly with all the training sets as many times for a couple of dozen training cycles. If we see the error going down, we are on the right path; we keep running training cycles until the error no longer changes. At that point, we had reached a stable version of the model. We should have separated a small group of samples from the training data set that we will use to validate the model. Because the model has never seen the validation samples, it will give us a good idea of the real accuracy of the model.

So far, we have described a classic Convolutional Neural Network used to classify images. However, those models usually have several megabytes in size and are very expensive to train. They would not fit in a highly constrained system like a microcontroller. Also, investing many resources to create a model for every use case would not make sense. There are many different techniques to reduce the cost of training a model, its size, and processing requirements. The first is called Transfer Learning. As you have learned, basic filters extract characteristics like lines and curves, but more advanced filters extract shapes, objects, and specific classes. The trick here is to reuse the layers that recognize basic geometric characteristics and shapes and focus only on training the model on the last specialized layers. Since we are only training the last layers, we can have a smaller training set (of about 100 images) per class instead of millions of images. The technique to reduce size and memory requirements in the model is called depth wise-separable convolution. DSC reduces the complexity of a convolution by splitting the operation into two more simple convolutions. One is called depthwise convolution, and the other is called pointwise convolution. The first performs lightweight filtering by applying a single filter per input channel. The second one is responsible for building new features by computing linear combinations by running 1x1 convolutions across each one of the input channels. The result is the same number of features that a regular convolution would have returned, except that doing it with DSC is nine times faster (it uses about 11% of the computational power of a traditional convolution layer). The first model that proposed this architecture was MobileNetV1, created by Google. This was incredibly important as it placed image classification within reach of microcontroller-based applications.

Eventually, MobileNetV2 was released with further optimizations, namely inverted residuals and linear bottlenecks. They work together to optimize memory efficiency, which is also incredibly limited in microcontrollers.

Use case: Gesture detection

Gesture recognition is the process of recognizing dynamic or static body movements, particularly hand signs or motions, through computer vision. The system interprets meaning from body language or hand positions, allowing it to understand gestures that convey intent or information. This technology is commonly used in applications that require interaction or semantic understanding, such as interpreting sign language, recognizing commands, or detecting actions like waving.

Using hand signs to unlock a door

Problem definition: A lock maker is designing a new contactless product that unlocks a door when the user shows a sequence of hand signs to the camera. If the sequence is correct, the lock moves the latch to a position that lets the user open the door. The camera and the door lock cannot be wired directly as the door needs to run freely from the door frame. For that reason, a wireless connection between the camera and the lock is necessary.

Solution: A camera embedded in the wall will capture a continuous flow of images of people standing in front of the door. A model connected to the camera input in the same device will detect whether the person is doing a hand sign. If a hand sign is recognized, the microcontroller will classify it, store the event in memory, and wait for the next hand sign to be performed. The sequence of hand signs events is stored in a buffer in the same order they were detected. The microcontroller has been programmed in advance to recognize a pre-determined sequence of hand-sign events. If there is a match between the captured and pre-determined sequences, the lock declares a matching event and will publish a message to the second Block, commanding the lock to change its status to unlocked. The microcontroller attached to the lock will receive the message and send a positive signal to the NPN transistor. This will cause current to flow through the solenoid, generating a magnetic field that will move the metal core to a displaced position, compressing the spring around it.

The flow of information from hand signs, camera capture, on-device classification and wireless communication to the actuator device is shown in the concept following figure:

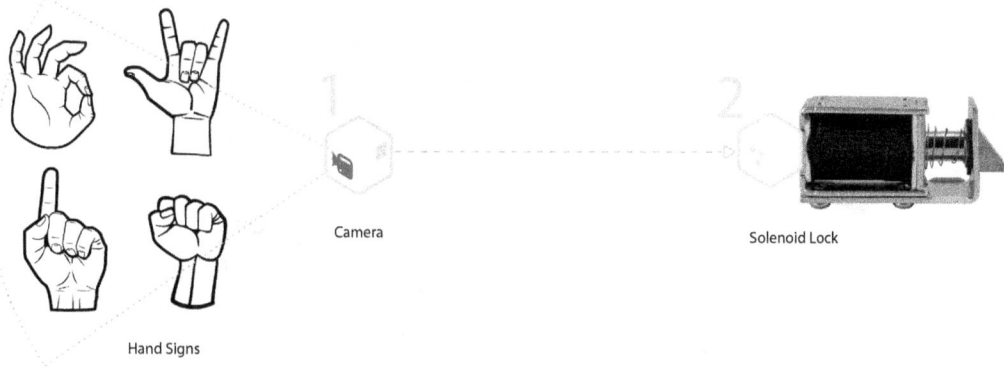

Figure 4.4: *Concept diagram (gesture detection)*

The metal core is directly connected to the bolt of the door. The bolt is retracted from the frame by moving the core and will no longer Block the door from opening. The lock stays retracted as long as the solenoid's magnetic field is active. However, if power is lost or the microcontroller stops sending signals, the spring mechanism will automatically push the bolt back into the locked position, ensuring security. However, the microcontroller will stop sending the signal after a couple of seconds, causing the transistor to close the gate, stopping the current flow through the solenoid, causing the magnetic field to disappear, and making the bolt go back to its original position thanks to the decompression of the spring.

Data acquisition

The model will be trained to recognize seven different hand signs: Fist, horn, index, ok, pinky, thumb, and two. A hand sign is performed by a three-dimensional object (the human hand). The same hand sign looks different from different angles. In many instances, two different hand signs look the same depending on the angle from which they are being observed. For example, the horn sign looks very similar to the index sign if observed from the thumb side. Because the model will be trained on flat pictures that only show two dimensions, the third dimension is often flattened and, in some cases, hidden. For this reason, we had to devise the convention that the model would be limited to recognizing hand signs that show the palm facing forward. We captured 60 images of each class under the same light conditions to control for everything but the shape of the hand. This helped us recognize that the pinky hand sign is the most difficult to identify as it is similar to the horn. We recommend not using the pinky hand sign for a live prototype.

The following figure illustrates the balanced composition of the training set, featuring pictures of the seven different hand gestures that the model will recognize:

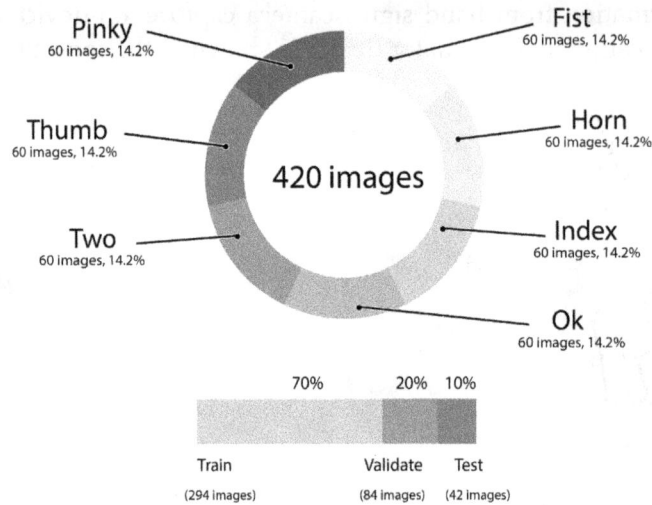

Figure 4.5: Training set (gesture detection)

All samples show a left hand; however, using augmentation, the picture was flipped and shown as a right hand. Augmentation helps the model generalize better by showing multiple variations of the same class.

Processing

The images coming from the camera are trimmed to a square ratio and downsized to 48x48 pixels. During the validation process, we discovered that the model shows better accuracy if we use the color version of the image. This gives a total of 48x48x3 = 6,912 features that will be sent to the input layer of the model. Notice in *Figure 4.6* how clusters of different hand signs are clearly defined. However, the index and the two hand signs are very close. This is caused by the fact that the two hand signs have the same shape as the index, except that it has an extra finger. In the top part of the graph, you can see the same situation between the pinky and the horn signs, which have similar shapes. The ok and the fist signs are clearly defined and separate from any other class as they are very specific and characteristic.

Figure 4.6 Cluster diagram (gesture detection)

Model

The model has been trained with 420 images to achieve an accuracy of 90.2%. The model was trained with half of the images in its first version but only achieved 60% accuracy. This shows the importance of having enough quality data in the training set. Another factor that affected the accuracy to a great degree is the Learning Rate. In the first version, we used 0.05, but it never converged. Instead, the error validation error oscillated from 0.3 to 0.08 even when we increased the number of training cycles to 120. It took us up to 8 iterations to adjust hyperparameters to achieve more than 90% accuracy in the validation. The inference time in an Arduino Nicla Vision (Cortex M7 480MHZ) is 22ms. This allows approximately 45 frames per second. The post-processing stage will create a count based on the results higher than 0.8 scores in each frame and declare an identification if a class is present in more than 90% of the frames for every given second as shown in the following figure:

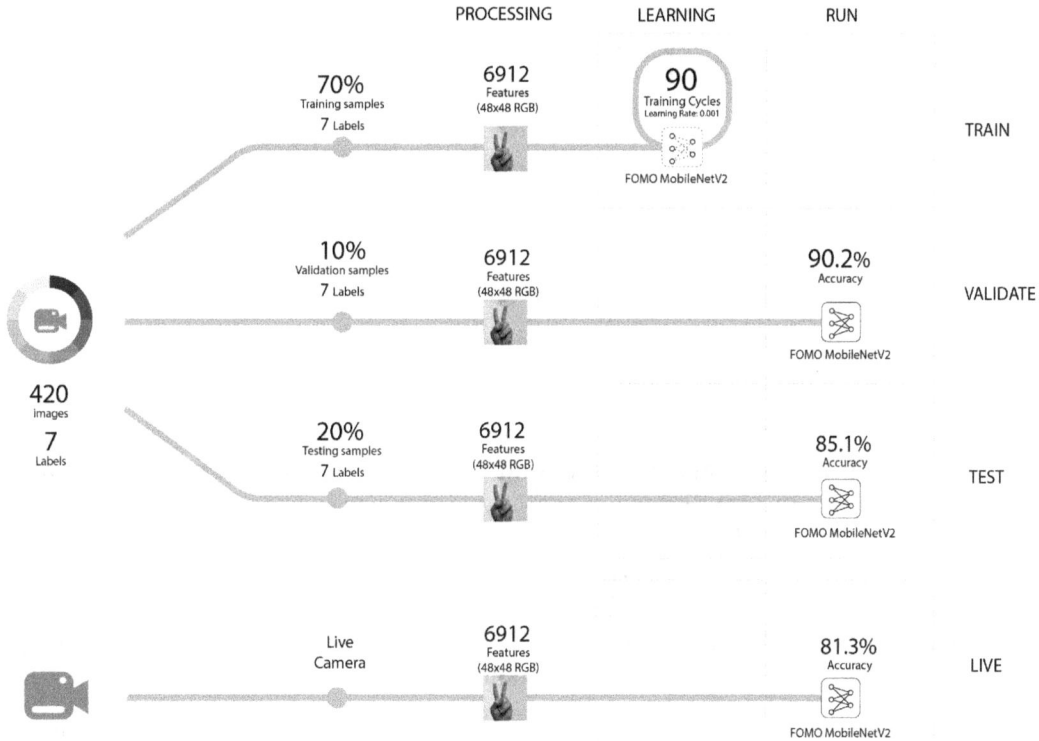

Figure 4.7: *Training, validation, testing and production model metrics (Gesture detection)*

System implementation

As shown in the following figure, the application consists of two building blocks:

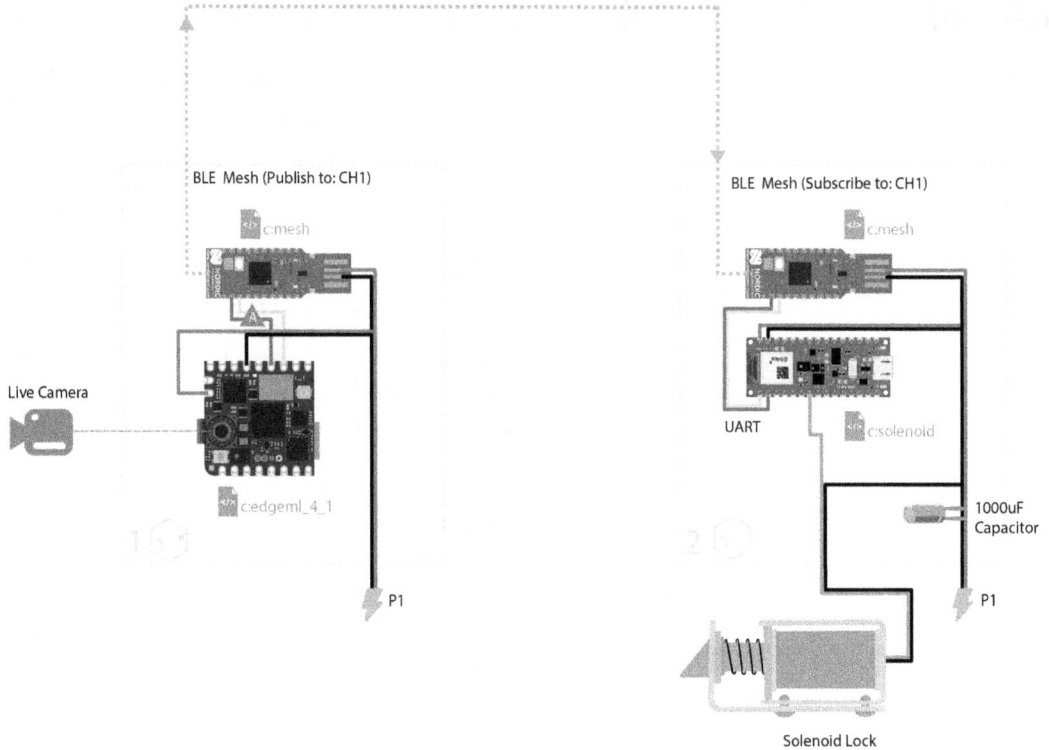

Figure 4.8: Connection diagram (Gesture detection)

- The first one is an acquisition block containing two microcontroller boards. The first is an Arduino Nicla Vision with a Cortex M7 480MHZ MCU performing the image capture and running the TinyML model. If a hand sign is positively identified, it stores it in a buffer that keeps track of the order of events. It has been programmed in advance with a small array of authorized sequences. The program continuously monitors if the buffer of events contains one of the authorized sequences. If that is the case, the Arduino Nicla Vision sends a message with an **Open-Door** command to the second microcontroller board, an NRF52840 Dongle in charge of networking. The Dongle sends the command out in a Mesh Network message by publishing it to a channel dedicated to door commands.

- The second block, which is subscribed to the channel dedicated to door commands, receives the message from Block 1 via its NRF52840Dongle and sends it down to the Arduino Nano 33 for further processing. The Arduino Nano knows how to handle an **Open Door** command. It outputs a 1 in the pin connected to an NPN transistor's base. The transistor operates like a gate that allows low-current pins to control high-current components. Specifically, the pin is controlling a lock that requires up to 0.65Amps to generate a magnetic field with enough force to compress the spring that is restricting the movement of the iron core of the solenoid, moving the lock to an open position that will allow the user to push the door and open it. The lock displacement will only last one second before the microcontroller switches the pin to 0, sending the lock back to its closed position.

Source code

The logic in block 1 is presented as a step by step numbered process in the following table:

c:edgeml_4_1	Code location: Arduino Nano 33 BLE @ Block 1
	Capturing the data, processing it and running the EdgeML model. Pseudocode 1. A camera captures images of people standing before the door. Images are sent to the Processing functions. 2. In the Processing Block, the image is resized and reshaped. Resulting pixels are sent to the model. 3. The EdgeML model runs the inference with the provided data and returns an array of results. Results are sent to the post-processing functions. 4. The Post Processing function validates that the hand sign is present in front of the camera by analyzing multiple frames. Once a hand sign is identified, the event is stored in a buffer. The program compares buffer contents with authorization sequences. If it finds a match it sends command payload to the local main script for further handling. 5. Local Main Script communicates with network MCU the command.

Table 4.2: Block 1 logic (Gesture detection)

Network

We are using a BLE-Mesh Network with elements using pub-sub protocol to send and receive messages.

Block(s)	Action	Channel
1	Publishes to	CH1
2	Subscribes to	CH1

Table 4.3: Network configuration (Gesture detection)

Power analysis

The power requirements per block is as follows:

Block 1:

Power source	Device	Latent consumption	Active consumption	Notes
P1	Arduino Nicla Vision	0.032A @5V	< 1A @5V	
P1	NRF52 Dongle	0.04mA @5v	3mA @5v	Active when publishing messages as a client.

Table 4.4: Power requirements for Block 1 (Gesture detection)

While the camera could run on a battery for a while, since this Block is going to become a permanent fixture, it would be best if we feed it from a permanent power source.

Block 2:

Power source	Device	Latent consumption	Active consumption	Notes
P2	NRF52 Dongle	0.04mA @5v	0.3mA @5v	Active when receiving messages as a Server.
P2	Arduino Nano 33 BLE	0.034mA @5V	< 1A @5V	Activates Solenoid Lock

Table 4.5: Power requirements for Block 2 (Gesture detection)

We need a 1A power source for Block 2. Given the power requirements of the Solenoid, this Block must connect to a permanent power source (wall outlet).

Bill of materials

The bill of materials offers an approximation of the cost of the project:

Description	QTY	Unit cost	Total
Arduino Nicla Vision	1	$85	$85
Arduino Nano 33 BLE	1	$30	$30
NRF52840 Dongle	2	$12	$24
Solenoid Lock	1	$12	$12
Power Source 1A @5v	2	$10	$20

Table 4.6: Bill of materials (Gesture detection)

The approximate cost of materials is $171.

Use case: Face detection

Image classification is used to detect faces while preserving privacy. The model identifies patterns consisting of facial contours and generic features such as eyes, mouth, nose, and hair. Detecting the identity of a specific person (face recognition), however, requires a completely different model and is outside the scope of this chapter.

People detector

Problem definition: A hotel front desk in NYC helps guests check in, book transfers to the airport, purchase theater tickets, and recommend tours, among other things. To improve their service, they need a way to detect anybody standing in front of the desk instantly. This will help the staff interrupt whatever they are doing around the lobby and address the guests immediately. This will guarantee the best service possible. As part of the solution, the client has suggested that the staff could be paged silently using a haptic bracelet.

Solution: As part of the solution, a camera that will be positioned to capture people getting close to the desk without detecting people passing by in the background. The camera will send every frame it captures to a processing Block to determine if there is a face in the image. If there is a face detected, a message will be sent to the Haptic pins.

The following figure shows the most relevant components and the flow of information: The faces, the camera, the wireless communication and the haptic pin actuator:

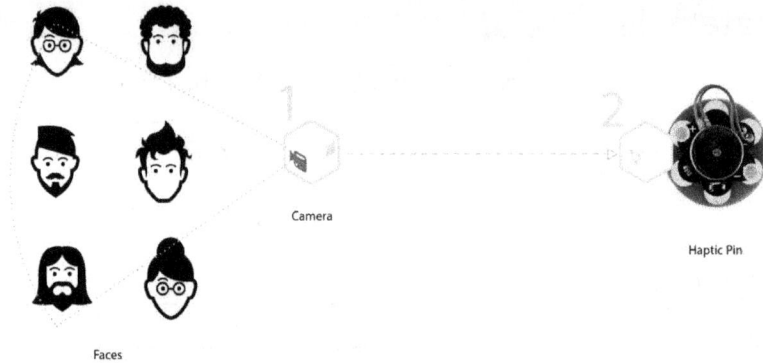

Figure 4.9: Concept diagram (People detector)

The haptic pins are battery-operated devices that front desk staff carry in their pockets or pin to their jackets. This is similar to a sound-based alarm except that it is silent and only perceptible by staff wearing the pin. The haptic pin has a microcontroller capable of subscribing to Mesh Network messages and a small battery that will power the haptic motor controlled by the microcontroller. The pin's battery should last at least 8 hours.

Data acquisition

For this use case, we used the existing dataset called *The Images of Groups Dataset* created by *A. Gallagher, T. Chen* for the IEEE Conference on *Computer Vision and Pattern Recognition, 2009*. We manually labeled faces using the Edge Impulse Labeling queue.

Using a single label to train the model is called Unary Classification or Class-Modeling, and it is very common. The goal is to identify objects of a specific class among others by learning from a dataset that exclusively includes objects of that class. It is more difficult than training multi-class models as there is no point of comparison between different classes. 400 face images have been used to train the model. Refer to the following figure:

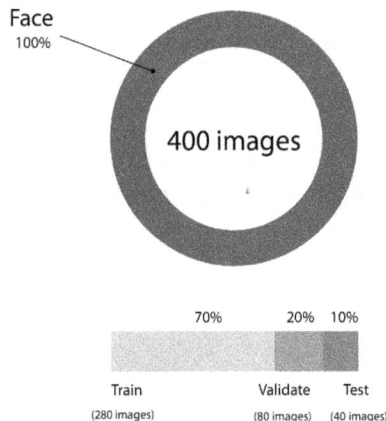

Figure 4.10: Training dataset (People detector)

Processing

As part of the processing process, we crop the image to a square ratio and resize it to 96x96 pixels. While we originally turned the face images to grayscale, we discovered that leaving them in color (RGB) improved the model's accuracy. It is possible that the different skin tones help the model differentiate faces from the background. The number of features per image is 96x96x3 = 27,648. Notice in the diagram how the samples representing a single class show together in a cluster. The model will create a limit around the cluster and classify everything inside it as a face. This is very similar to how **anomaly detection** works. You will see more about it in the following chapters.

The cluster diagram for **Unary Classification** in the following figure is still a useful way to verify that all samples are relatively close to each other forming a cluster:

A: FACE

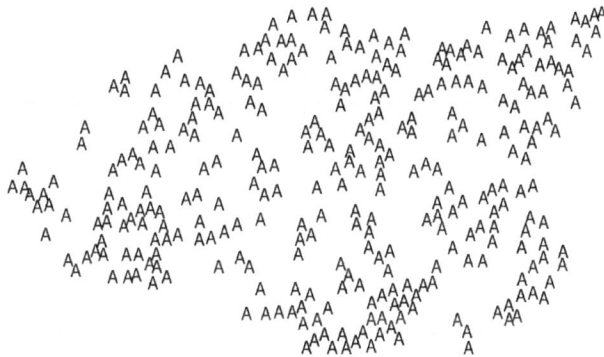

Figure 4.11: *Cluster diagram (People detector)*

Model

The model used is MobileNetV2. The input layer takes 27,648 features in its input layer. This model is trained with 90 epochs at a learning rate of 0.001 and batch size of 32. The original dataset to train this model contained samples with multiple faces. The way the model scores success is to compare the number of faces found vs the number of faces labeled in the sample. If, for example, the model finds 3 out of 6 faces it is considered 50% accurate for that sample in specific. However, because the goal of the project is to detect people in front of the desk and not to infer the exact amount of people in the group accurately, our accuracy, in reality, is 100% as people were successfully detected. To avoid this issue, we modified the dataset to train and validate single faces. By doing so, we achieve something unexpected: Because the model is looking for a single face close enough to the camera, it ignores people passing by in the background. The camera no longer needs to be positioned at a closed angle. The inference time using an Arduino Nicla Vision is 52ms, providing 20 frames per second, allowing us to create a voting algorithm at the model's output. If the person stays in front of the camera for more than 1 second (for more than 20 frames in a row), the program will declare the person is in front of the desk and start communicating the event to the service desk personnel. Refer to the following figure:

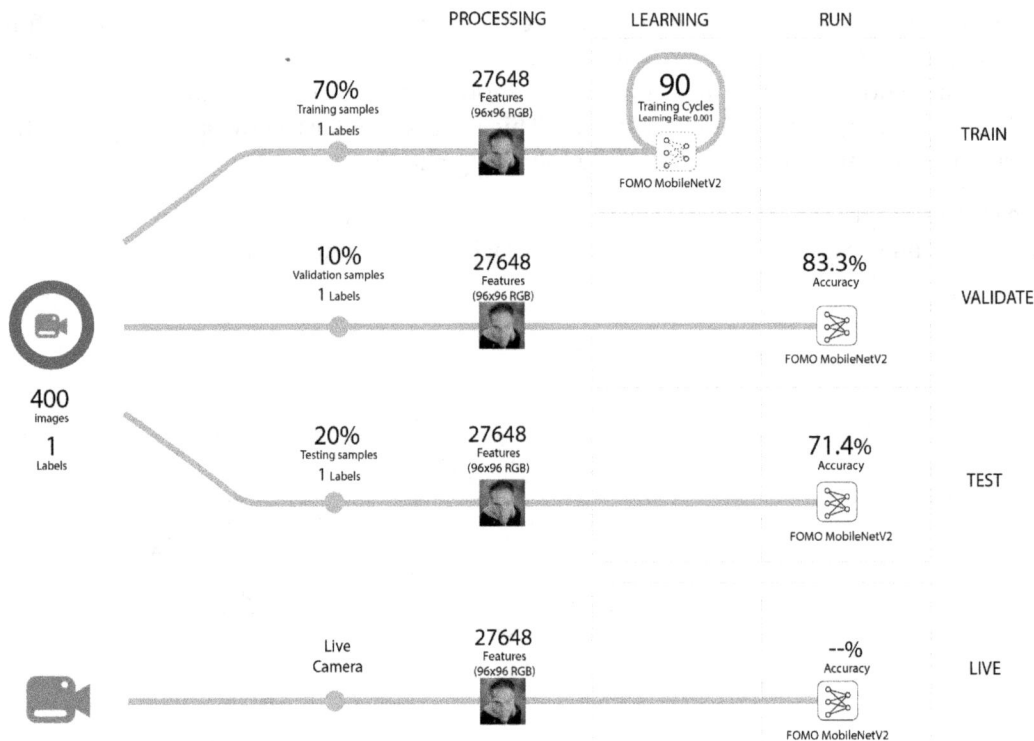

Figure 4.12: *Training, validation, testing and production model metrics (People detector)*

System implementation

The application is designed to have two main components. The first one, called Block 1, is responsible for capturing and processing images. The second one, called Block 2, is designed to receive notifications when a person stands in front of the camera. Once the person is detected, a haptic motor is activated to notify the user. There are multiple Block 2 components in the system, with at least one per person that needs to be notified. Refer to the following figure:

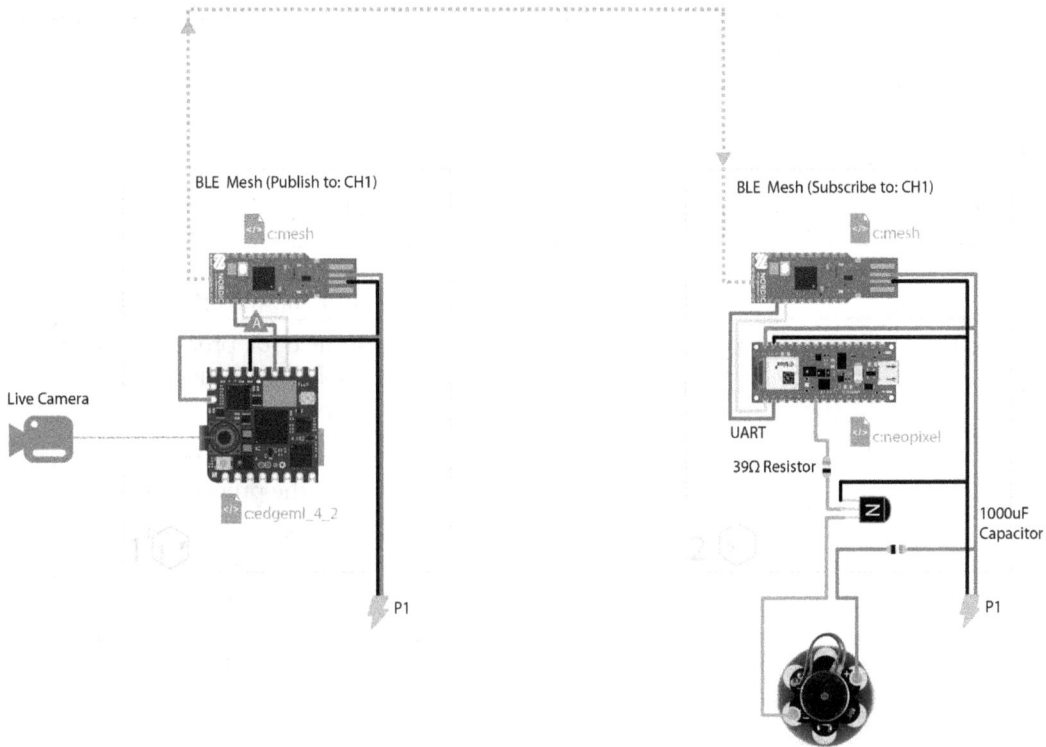

Figure 4.13: Connection diagram (People detector)

To ensure that the communication between Block 1 and Block 2 is seamless, the BLE Mesh Network is utilized. Block 1 publishes the message once to a dedicated channel, and every Block 2 component subscribed to that channel will receive the message. This approach ensures that the notification is delivered to the intended recipient without any delays or issues.

Block 1 uses two microcontroller boards; the first one, an **Arduino Nicla Vision**, captures the image, processes it, and runs it through the **Face Classification EdgeML** model that has been downloaded to its memory. The output of the model is sent to the postprocessing functions that use a voting mechanism that wait for more than 20 consecutive positive face identifications before sending out a command to the second microcontroller board. The second board is an NRF52840 Dongle in charge of network communication. The command it receives from the Nicla Vision is wrapped in a Mesh Network message and published to a predefined channel that all the instances of Block 2 are subscribed.

Block 2 uses two microcontroller boards; the first one is an NRF52840 Dongle in charge of connecting to the BLE Mesh Network and subscribing to the channel that Block 1 uses to send out commands. When a person is detected by Block 1, a message with a payload is received by Block 2, and the payload contains the command that needs to be executed. The NRF52840 Dongle does not process the command, but it sends it to the second board, an Arduino Nano 33. The Arduino outputs a signal that opens the transistor gate and lets current pass to the Haptic Motor, making it vibrate, notifying the user wearing it to be alerted without making any sound.

Source code

The logic in Block 1 is presented conceptually in the following table:

c:edgeml_4_2	Code location: Arduino Nano 33 BLE @ Block 1
	Capturing the data, processing, and running the EdgeML model. Pseudocode 1. Camera captures frames and sends them to the processing Block. 2. In the Processing Block, the frame is reshaped and resized. Features are sent to the EdgeML model. 3. The EdgeML model runs the inference with the provided data and returns an array of two results (face or background). 4. The Post Processing function waits for a series of positive face detections before notifying the main script. 5. The main script prepares the command for Block 2 to activate haptic motors and delegates it to the network microcontroller to publish it.

Table 4.7: Block 1 logic (People detector)

Network

The Camera (Block 1) publishes to a channel that every haptic pin (Block 2) is listening to. This is a simple example of the benefits of using a network that allows one publisher and multiple subscribers.

Block(s)	Action	Channel
1	Publishes to	CH1
2	Subscribes to	CH1

Table 4.8: Network configuration (People detector)

Power requirements

The power requirements per Block are as follows:

Block 1:

Power source	Device	Latent consumption	Active consumption	Notes
P1	Arduino Nicla Vision	0.032A @5V	< 1A @5V	
P1	NRF52 Dongle	0.04mA @5v	3mA @5v	Active when publishing messages as a client.

Table 4.9: Block 1 power requirements (People detector)

If running on battery, a 200 mAh Li-Po battery is recommended for reliable operation.

Block 2:

Power source	Device	Latent consumption	Active consumption	Notes
P2	NRF52 Dongle	0.04mA @5v	0.3mA @5v	Active when receiving messages as a server.
P2	Arduino Nano 33 BLE	0.034mA @5V	< 1A @5V	Activates Haptic Motor

Table 4.10: Block 2 power requirements (People detector)

We need a 1A power source for Block 2. Given the power requirements of the Solenoid, this Block must connect to a permanent source of power (wall outlet).

Bill of materials

The bill of materials offers an approximation of the cost of the project.

Description	QTY	Unit cost	Total
Arduino Nicla Vision	1	$85	$85
Arduino Nano 33 BLE	1	$30	$30
NRF52840 Dongle	2	$12	$24
LilyPad Wave Board	1	$9	$9
NPN Transistor 800mA	1	$0.5	$0.5
39Ohm Resistor	1	$0.5	$0.5
Power Source 1A @5v	2	$10	$20

Table 4.11: Bill of materials (People detector)

Approximate cost of materials (One Camera, One Haptic Kit): $169

Use case: Object recognition

Object recognition in computer vision refers to the ability of an AI system to identify and classify objects within images or video frames. It involves detecting the presence, location, and category of one or more objects by analyzing visual features such as shape, color, texture, and spatial relationships.

Component sorting

Problem definition: A company that sells DIY kits buys surplus electronic components at discount from component factories. The problem is that the surplus components come mixed up in boxes. You have been commissioned to create a system that sorts components. Assume components are already placed in a conveyor belt. The solution needs to recognize the component and move a lever to direct the component to the bucket to which it belongs.

Solution: The application consists of two stages. The first one captures an image of the conveyor belt with the components to be classified, then it runs an inference to determine the class of the component, and finally, determines the position the lever needs to be moved to, based on the classification. The second stage is the actuator. It receives the command that specifies the position, which is then translated into a signal sent to a servo motor. The servomotor moves the lever, which actuates the arm that sends the component to its bucket. The flow of information is shown in the following figure:

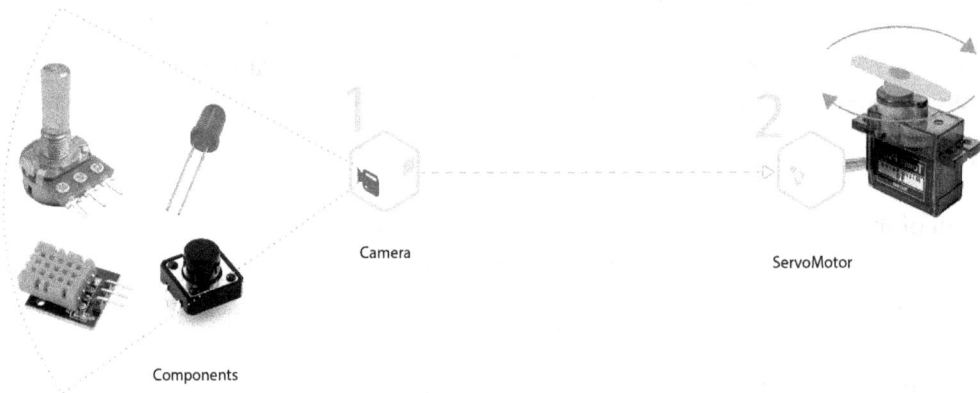

Camera

ServoMotor

Components

Figure 4.14: Concept diagram (Component sorting)

While the first prototype has only one camera and one actuator. Having multiple cameras in future versions will help the system see the components from different angles. One of the cameras could be listening to the classification results, and based on a voting algorithm, it could make the final decision on what command to send to the actuator. On the actuator part, the application could use more than one servo motor to create more complex movements that allow a more diverse set of parts to be classified. For this reason, it is convenient to use a wireless Mesh Network that helps cameras and actuators communicate with a simple Publish/Subscribe paradigm that allows one-to-many and many-to-one communication.

Data acquisition

A set was built to resemble the light conditions and background textures of the conveyor belt that will be used in the real environment. There are five different classes of components. However, this number is expected to increase as the real number of different components is much higher. Every class in the training dataset contains 50 samples with images taken from different angles, distances, and shadows. The samples have been labeled manually. There is only one piece per sample since we do not require the model to identify groups of components. Refer to the following figure:

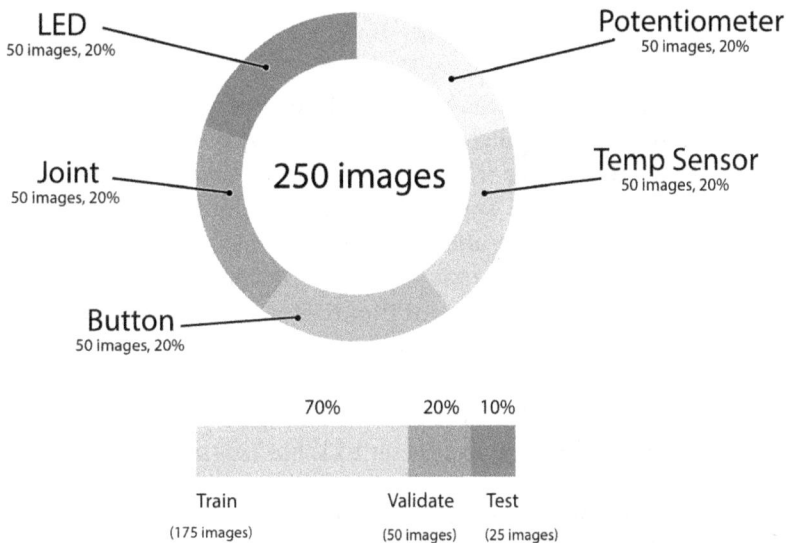

Figure 4.15: Training dataset (Component sorting)

Processing

Every sample is trimmed to a 1:1 (square) ratio and resized to 96x96 pixels. Because we will rely on the component colors to differentiate from different models, we leave the image in color (RGB). The number of features per sample is 96 x 96 x 3 = 27,648. An Arduino Nicla Vision (Cortex M7 at 480MHz) can execute the processing in less than 1 millisecond. Notice in the diagram below (cluster diagram) how the LED and the Joint clusters are clearly separated while the potentiometer, temp sensor, and button are much closer as they have many shapes in common. Nevertheless, the clusters are clearly defined. Refer to the following figure:

A: BUTTON
B: JOINT
C: LED
D: POTENTIOMETER
E: TEMP SENSOR

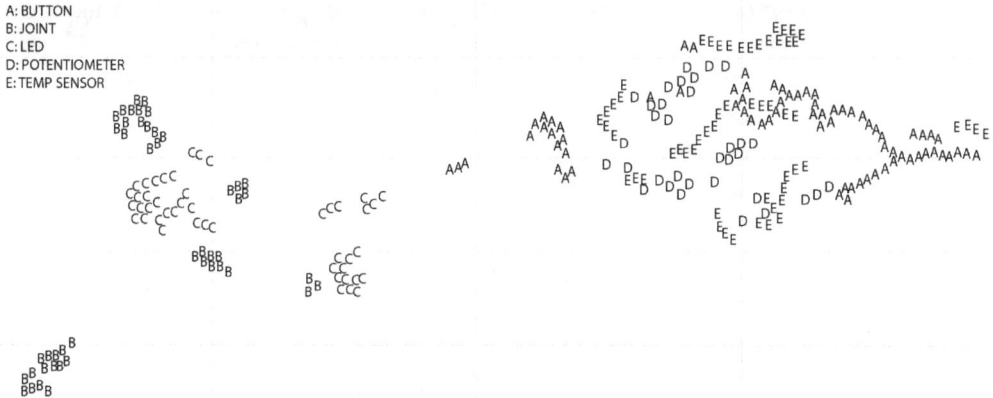

Figure 4.16: *Cluster diagram (Component sorting)*

Model

The model used to classify the components is MobileNetV2, with an alpha of 0.35. Alpha is also known as the width multiplier, and it is used to control the number of channels or channel depth. If you remember from the explanation on MobileNet at the beginning of this chapter, the convolution is separated into two parts: a Depthwise convolution and a pointwise convolution. Alpha affects the former. Alpha is by default equal to 1. By changing it to 0.35, you are indicating that you want the depth to be about ⅓, which means your convolution will be shallower and, for that reason, filter less effectively. This is only needed if you are trying to optimize for memory and convolutional power, which is what we are trying to do here. Only if you are not getting the results that you want and you have tried other things like increasing the amount of training cycles and making the Learning Rate smaller, then feel free to bring alpha closer to 1. For this model, we tried many things, but it became stable at around 60 cycles. We tried to make the Learning Rate larger to shorten the training time, but we only got the error to be all over the place. This model performs an inference in 86ms (Cortex M7 at 480MHz), which allows us to get about ten inferences per second. The conveyor will be moving at 0.1m/s; the camera covers an area of about 0.25cm, and the model will only have two frames to make a correct classification. For future versions of the model, it might be convenient to upgrade to a Cortex M55 at 400MHz, which would run the inference in 1ms (two orders of magnitude faster), giving the application 200 frames to correctly classify the component. The following figure shows the training, validation and test metrics:

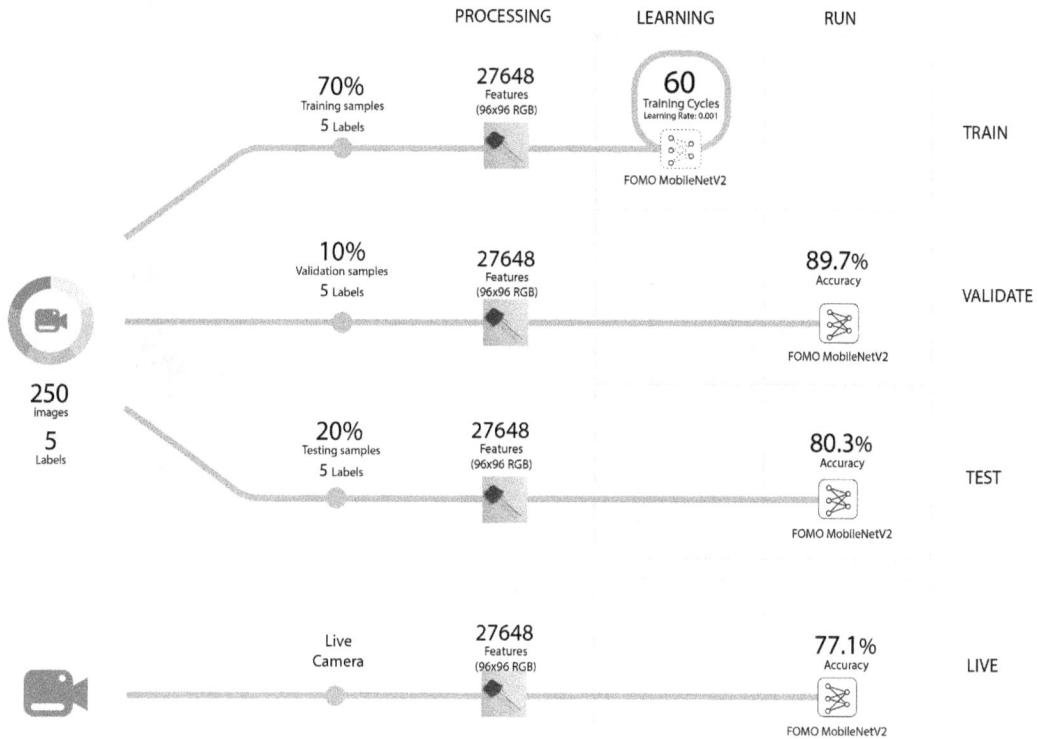

Figure 4.17: *Training, validation, testing and production model metrics (Component sorting)*

System implementation

The application consists of two Blocks: the following figure capture and classification on one side and the servo motor on the other:

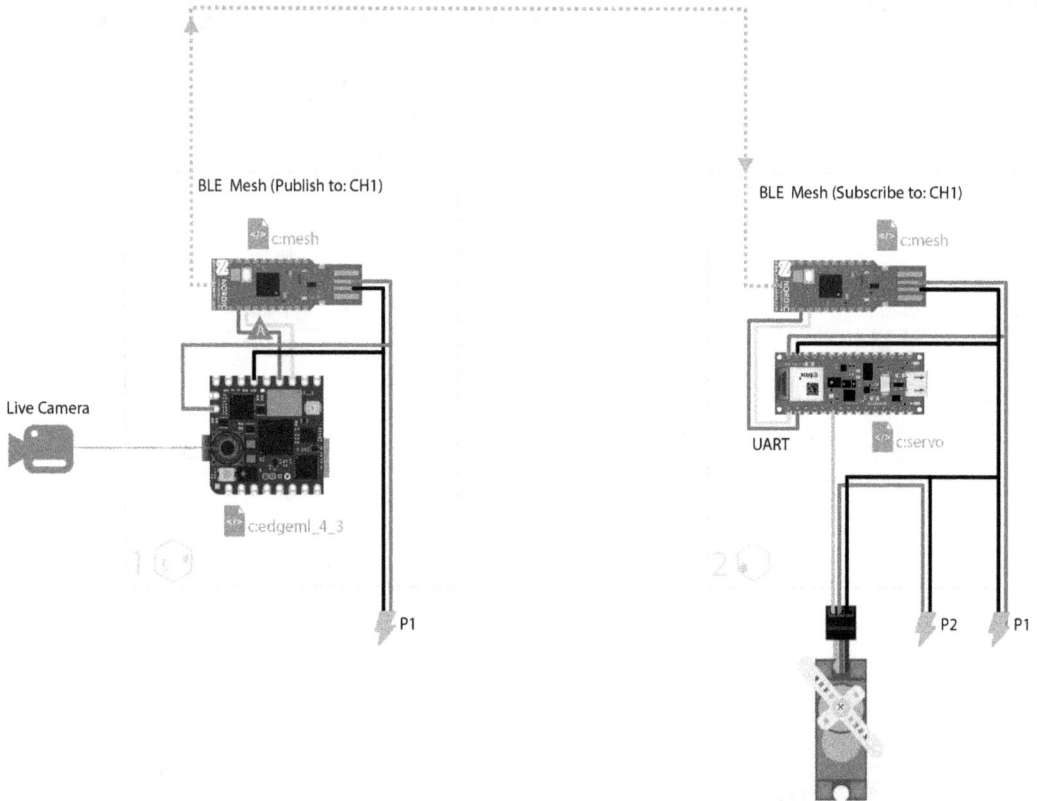

Figure 4.18: *Connection diagram (Component sorting)*

Block 1 uses two microcontroller boards, the Arduino Nicla Vision to capture the image in real-time, extract the features, run the model, and perform validation of results to declare a positive event that is communicated to the microcontroller board (NRF52840Dongle) in charge of preparing the message and to publish it to the BLE Mesh Network.

Block 2 uses two microcontroller boards as well, the first one in charge of all things Mesh Network and the second in charge of controlling the servo motor. The angle of the servo motor is controlled via a PWM signal output from the Arduino Nano 33. The servo motor has its own power source to avoid current peaks that could reset the two microcontrollers.

Source code

The logic in Block 1 is presented conceptually in the following table:

c: edgeml_4_2	Code location: **Arduino Nano 33 BLE @ Block 1**
	Capturing frame, detecting components, sending command out to control servo motor. Pseudocode 1. A camera captures frames to be processed. 2. The Processing Block reshapes and resizes the image and prepares the features to be sent to the model. 3. Image features are run through the model to infer what component in specific is being detected. 4. The post-processing functions use a voting algorithm to declare a positive classification of a component in specific. If that is the case, they communicate to the main script for further action. 5. The main script prepares the command to be sent to the servomotor controller. It sends the payload to the microcontroller in charge of network communication.

Table 4.12: Block 1 logic (Component sorting)

Network

The camera node classifies the image and publishes the class to channel 1. The actuator receives the message in almost real time as it is subscribed to the same channel.

Block(s)	Action	Channel
1	Publishes to	CH1
2	Subscribes to	CH1

Table 4.13: Network configuration (Component sorting)

Power requirements

The power requirements per Block are as follows:

Block 1:

Power source	Device	Latent consumption	Active consumption	Notes
P1	Arduino Nicla Vision	0.032A @5V	< 1A @5V	
P1	NRF52 Dongle	0.04mA @5v	3mA @5v	Active when publishing messages as a *client*.

Table 4.14: Power requirements, Block 1 (Component sorting)

If running on battery, a 200 mAh Li-Po battery is recommended for reliable operation.

Block 2:

Power source	Device	Latent consumption	Active consumption	Notes
P2	NRF52 Dongle	0.04mA @5v	0.3mA @5v	Active when receiving messages as a *server*.
P2	Arduino Nano 33 BLE	0.034mA @5V	< 1A @5V	Activates Servo Motor

Table 4.15: Power requirements, Block 2 (Component sorting)

We need a 1A power source for Block 2. Given the power requirements of the Servo Motor, this Block must connect to a permanent source of power (wall outlet).

Bill of materials

The bill of materials offers an approximation of the cost of the project:

Description	QTY	Unit cost	Total
Arduino Nicla Vision	1	$85	$85
Arduino Nano 33 BLE	1	$30	$30
NRF52840 Dongle	2	$12	$24
Servo Motor	1	$15	$15
NPN Transistor 800mA	1	$0.5	$0.5

Description	QTY	Unit cost	Total
39Ohm Resistor	1	$0.5	$0.5
Power Source 1A @5v	2	$10	$20

Table 4.16: *Bill of materials (Component sorting)*

Approximate cost of materials (One Camera, One Haptic Kit): $175

Conclusion

In this chapter, we explored the elements that make image classification work, including preparing the images, extracting their features, feeding them into a convolutional network, and converting the results into a statistical distribution that identifies the most probable class, referred to as the classification result.

Running image classification on a microcontroller introduces a new range of solutions where the detected event is not a physical phenomenon (like temperature) but the presence of a shape or movement. Moreover, on-site image classification eliminates the need to send images to a central server for processing, enabling solutions that prioritize privacy, data tenancy, and cybersecurity. The simplicity of a locally running solution also reduces infrastructure requirements, significantly lowering costs.

In the next chapter, we will discuss the principles of tracking and learn how to apply them.

References

- **https://techzeero.com/arduino-tutorials/vibration-motor-with-arduino/**

- **https://towardsdatascience.com/review-mobilenetv1-depthwise-separable-convolution-light-weight-model-a382df364b69**

- **https://paperswithcode.com/method/mobilenetv2**

- **https://www.sparkfun.com/products/11008**

- **http://chenlab.ece.cornell.edu/people/Andy/ImagesOfGroups.html**

- Image classification use case 1: **https://studio.edgeimpulse.com/public/321804/live**

- Image classification use case 2: **https://studio.edgeimpulse.com/public/323408/live**

- Image classification use case 3: **https://studio.edgeimpulse.com/public/322173/live**

Join our book's Discord space

Join the book's Discord Workspace for Latest updates, Offers, Tech happenings around the world, New Release and Sessions with the Authors:

https://discord.bpbonline.com

CHAPTER 5
Object Tracking

Introduction

Object tracking is the process of identifying and following the movement of one or more objects across a sequence of frames in a video feed. Unlike image classification, which focuses on identifying objects in a single frame, object tracking ensures that detected objects are consistently identified and their trajectories are maintained over time across multiple frames. This is essential in scenarios where understanding the behavior, interactions, or movement patterns of objects is critical, such as in surveillance, autonomous vehicles, sports analytics, or robotics. Object tracking bridges the gap between static image analysis and dynamic real-world applications, enabling systems to make decisions based on continuous observations rather than isolated snapshots.

Structure

This chapter covers the following topics:

- Tracking a single object
- Tracking multiple things at once
- Use case: Object counting
- Use case: People counting
- Use case: Event detection

Objectives

This chapter is a natural progression from image classification, now applied to video feeds. The principles remain the same, as each video frame is processed independently. What is new is the tracking algorithm, which maintains object positions across frames. The goal of this chapter is for the reader to understand the principles of tracking and learn how to apply them in real-life applications.

Tracking a single object

Tracking consists of identifying the same object in a sequence of video frames. The path the object takes is known as a track. To identify the object, we use an **object detection model** (as discussed in the previous chapter); to track the object across frames, we use a **tracking model**.

Figure 5.1 demonstrates the principle of tracking by visually representing the object's path. This path allows the model to predict the object's next position based on previous readings. When a new frame is captured, the model searches for the object within the predicted area. For example, if the path is straight, the model expects the object to continue in a straight line. If the path curves, the model anticipates the object will follow the curve.

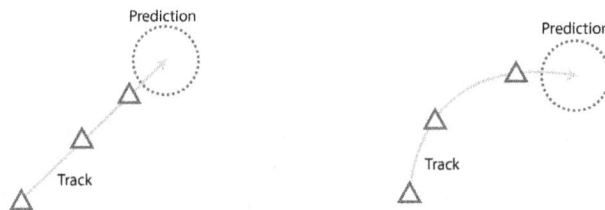

Figure 5.1: Prediction of the next position

The way tracking works is straightforward. It first guesses where the object will be in the future, using a set of rules or a model. Then, it looks at the next frame and adjusts its initial guess to be more in line with what is happening.

Things to consider

Following things is hard because we might not have direct access to what we are tracking. We must rely on radar or cameras instead of built-in sensors like GPS. The goal is to get the best possible picture of where the object is by combining different types of sensor information.

One of the biggest challenges in tracking is ensuring we are following the right object and not getting fooled by something else nearby (false positives) or failing to detect an object (false negatives). The accuracy of the TinyML object detection model plays a vital role in this aspect.

Predicting where an object will go next is especially tough when we cannot control it. We must consider all sorts of things, like how fast it is moving, any changes in direction, and even unexpected factors like the wind. Our tracking tools use a mix of math, educated guesses, and smart corrections when things do not go as expected.

Tracking multiple things at once

When tracking multiple objects, we need to assign each object to a different track, create new tracks for newly detected objects, and delete tracks when an object leaves the frame.

Assignment

We must ensure to match the right sensor data to the correct object, especially when they are close together or it is hard to tell them apart.

This puzzle of figuring out which piece of data belongs to which object is known as the **data association problem** crucial for ensuring accurate tracking in complex scenarios. And to keep things interesting, the number of objects we are tracking can change. New ones might appear, or old ones might vanish, requiring us to adjust our tracking setup constantly.

The assignment is based on the prediction from the tracking model of where the object should be. The model computes the probability of every object belonging to every track and assigns them based on the most likely option.

Shown in *Figure 5.2* is a visual example of the assignment challenge where two objects are being tracked (circles), the new reading, represented by a triangle belongs to track B because it is located within the predicted space B:

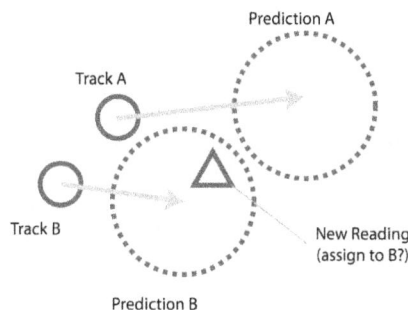

Figure 5.2: Track assignment

Track maintenance

Track maintenance involves observing, matching observations to objects, and maintaining an up-to-date list of what we are tracking. It keeps tracks in a healthy state. If a track has not gotten any object associated with it in a couple of frames, it might be time to eliminate it.

Observe how the track has a series of missing matches in the following figure:

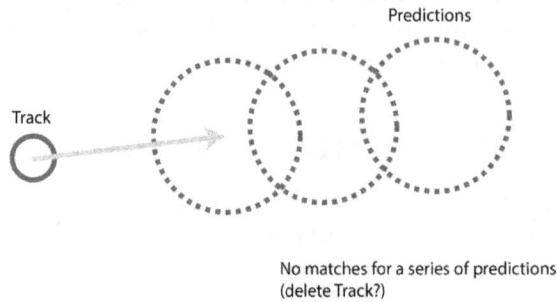

Figure 5.3: Track maintenance

If there is a new object that cannot be associated with an existing track, it might be time to create a new track. This is shown in the following figure:

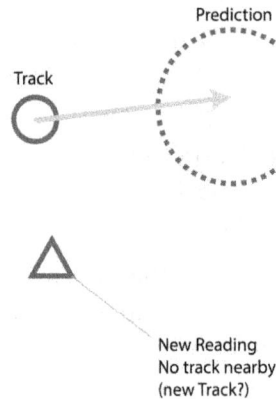

Figure 5.4: Track creation

However, we cannot just eliminate and create tracks freely; sometimes, the track does not receive associations because the model has failed to identify the object in a couple of frames. In other instances, an obstacle temporarily occludes the object (Blocked visually). On the other hand, if the model identifies something incorrectly, the best option is to wait for a couple of identifications before creating a track.

Gating

The strategy to optimize track maintenance, i.e., to save memory and computational power, is called **gating**. It is like setting up a fence around each object we are tracking. Only the data within the fence gets considered, helping us focus on what is close and ignore the rest.

Take a look at the following figure, there is a rectangle around an area of interest. Objects will only be tracked within that area:

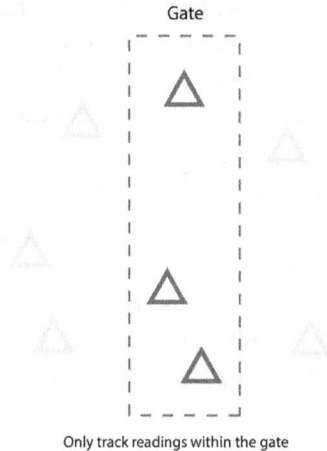

Figure 5.5: *Gating*

Applications

Once our system can identify objects and create reliable tracks with them, there are many applications we can enable with it. Few of them are listed as follows:

- **Counting**: We can count objects by detecting the intersection between the track and a predetermined area or limit. For example, we can count how many objects are transported on a conveyor belt.

- **Detecting events**: We can detect when an object enters an area or crosses a limit by following its track. For example, we can detect when a player crosses the field's boundary.

- **Timing**: We can count how much time an object has spent in a frame. For example, we could track how much time a car has spent in a parking lot.

Use case: Object counting

An incredibly useful application of image tracking is counting moving objects. This requires a specialized classification model that is both highly accurate and fast at detecting the objects being counted. The model provides the locations of objects in the frame, which the tracking algorithm uses to assign tracks to each moving object. Conditions can then be set to trigger a count (e.g., when an object crosses a boundary), allowing the tracking system to output a real-time count.

Conveyor belt counting

Problem definition: A factory in *Long Island City* produces a series of baked products. While their production manager has a process to count the number of items produced based on the number of boxes at the end of the line, it has been detected that items get lost, fall aside, or are removed by employees along the production line. The production manager would like to count the number of items at different stages of the production line to understand the wastage and develop solutions to reduce it.

Solution: To address the problem, the production manager is considering implementing a new strategy: To count the number of items at various points along the production line. This approach will provide quantitative metrics and detailed insights into the production flow, enabling the identification of stages exhibiting higher loss rates. This plan involves the installation of cameras at key intervals along the production line. These cameras are tasked with counting the number of items as they pass through each production stage. The following figure shows the concept diagram of the solution:

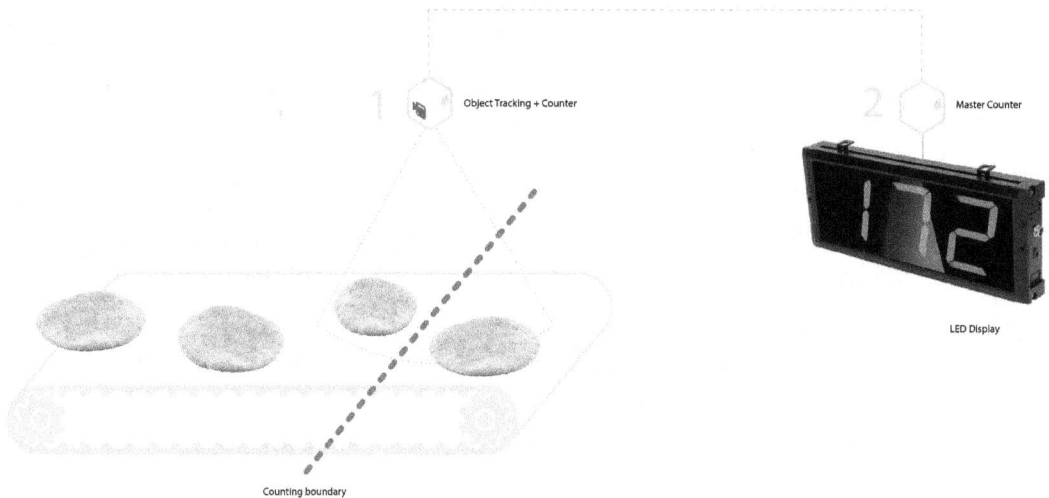

Figure 5.6: *Concept diagram (Conveyor belt counting)*

Because this solution will be installed in a food facility, the device will be encased in a transparent, airtight container. This is an ideal use case for a wireless and battery-operated sensor network. The device consists of a digital camera sending frames to a microcontroller. The microcontroller will extract the frame features and feed them to an object recognition model paired with a tracking algorithm that follows the objects and increases the count when they cross a predetermined limit in the conveyor belt. The count of that specific device is passed to a secondary microcontroller in charge of wireless communication. The secondary MCU packages and publishes the count to a channel that sends counts from that device. The count of all the devices placed at different positions in the production line is received wirelessly by a central MCU that shows all the counts in a display for the operator and line manager to make decisions based on the available data.

Data acquisition

Under ideal conditions, a production line operates in a controlled environment where illumination remains consistent, objects move at a predictable speed, and their shapes are uniform. However, real-world scenarios often differ. A well-prepared training set for counting objects on a conveyor belt should account for normal states as well as corner cases, such as overlapping objects or objects in different orientations. It is essential to capture the training dataset from a location and angle similar to the final position of the cameras.

A regular camera will acquire data at about 25 frames per second. Including all frames in the training set may be unnecessary, as moving objects look the same as they move through the band. A better approach is to create a collection of objects in different positions, orientations, light conditions, and groupings. The model will thus learn how to recognize the object from diverse scenarios. Regardless of where the model is used along the production line, it is essential to train it with the same objects against varying backgrounds. This training will help the model learn to recognize the objects independently from the background. If, in the future, the texture or color of the band (the background) changes for a reason, the model will still work. Since we use transfer learning, we do not need to train the model from scratch. However, we still need around 500 images of the same class to create a stable model. In the following figure, we show that we have created a data set with a balanced number of regular and corner cases:

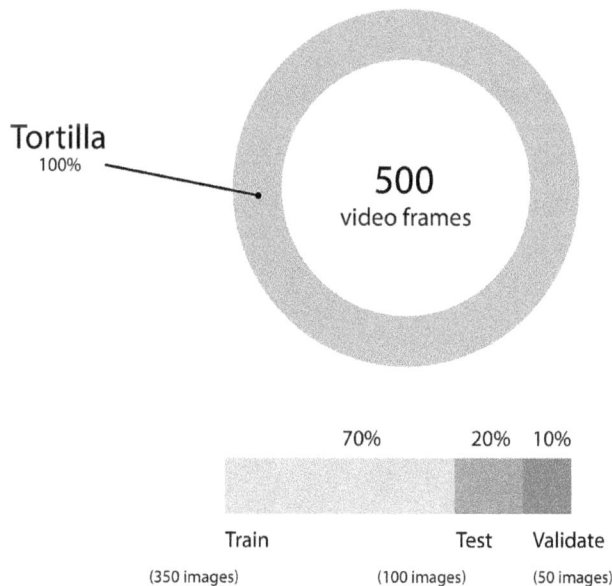

Figure 5.7: Training set (Conveyor belt counting)

Processing

Preparing images for a production line counting system begins with adjusting the image to a square ratio. This initial step ensures that the square encompasses the entire width of the conveyor belt, which is crucial for accurate counting. It is also essential to eliminate potential noise sources within the image, such as individuals passing by or moving fans, as these can affect the system's accuracy.

Following the initial adjustment, the image's dimensions are reduced to a more manageable size, typically around 96 pixels on each side. This reduction is vital for processing efficiency. However, if the results from the trained model are unsatisfactory, it may be necessary to consider larger dimensions, such as 160x160 or 320x320 pixels, to improve accuracy.

The final consideration in this setup is whether to use color images. While color images can provide additional detail, they also increase the computational load due to the three-color channels they contain. Converting images to grayscale is advantageous for most applications as it reduces the features to a third, requiring less computational power. This simplification is particularly effective unless the products counted on the conveyor belt have distinct color characteristics crucial for differentiation. In scenarios where specific color attributes are essential for distinguishing products or when multiple counters are tracking different objects, maintaining the color information becomes necessary. The following cluster diagram shows the grouping of different samples in the data set:

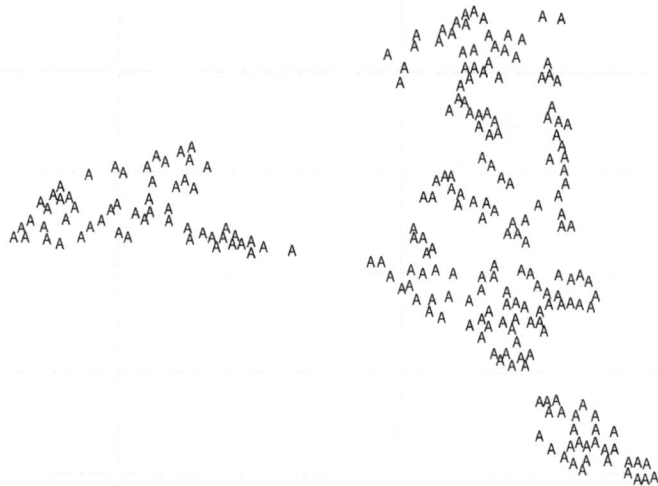

Figure 5.8: Cluster diagram (Conveyor belt counting)

Model

Multiple counting devices are being deployed throughout the entire line to achieve the highest level of accuracy in the production line counting system and minimize the issues associated with confusing waste for missed counts. This setup allows for a comparison of counts to ensure accuracy. However, a significant challenge in this process is ensuring that the model can process all frames quickly enough to keep up with the production line's pace.

Several strategies are being implemented to address these challenges effectively. Let us look at them in detail:

- The model is trained using high-quality data encompassing various real-life conditions, lighting situations, and product orientations. This comprehensive training approach enhances the model's ability to accurately recognize and count objects under diverse conditions.

- A quantized 8-bit version of the model is utilized to optimize processing speed without significantly compromising accuracy. This version reduces the computational load, enabling faster processing times.

- The model is designed to use the minimum necessary number of features by utilizing the smallest possible frame size and number of channels. This approach is carefully balanced to ensure that while inference times are improved, the model's accuracy remains high during the validation phases.

- The base of the counting system model is built on the MobileNetV2 architecture, known for its efficiency and effectiveness in mobile and embedded vision applications.

- Furthermore, the system employs the **faster objects, more objects (FOMO)** algorithm to accurately generate coordinates for the identified objects.

This combination of strategies and technologies ensures that the counting system can operate swiftly and accurately, addressing the need for speed in processing frames and the imperative for high accuracy in counts.

The *Figure 5.9* shows the metrics obtained during the training, validation, testing and deployment of the conveyor belt counting tracking model. Notice the 70/10/20 split of the sample set. Also, pay attention to the number of features (27,648), the amount of training cycles (60) and the difference between the F1 score (97.5%) and the accuracy (98.86%) in the validation and testing stage. The high F1 score accuracy might reflect overfitting however the test showing also a high score shows consistency without bias. Please be aware that only a real deployment will show the real accuracy of the model.

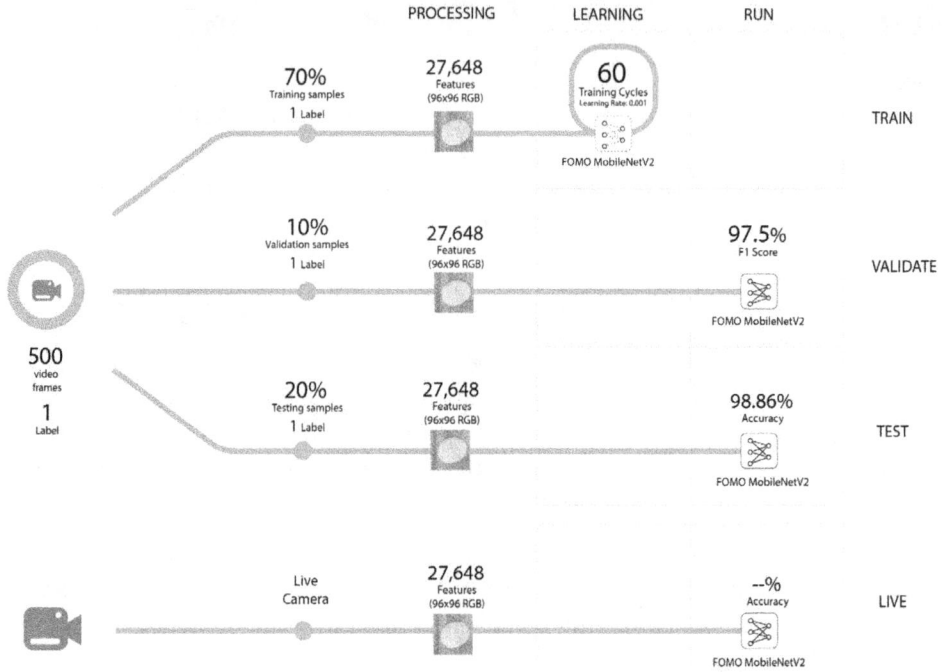

Figure 5.9: *Training, validation and testing metrics (Conveyor belt counting)*

System implementation

The production line counter system is designed with a two-Block architecture to ensure efficient and accurate counting of objects on a conveyor belt, culminating in showing results on a prominent LED display as shown in the following figure:

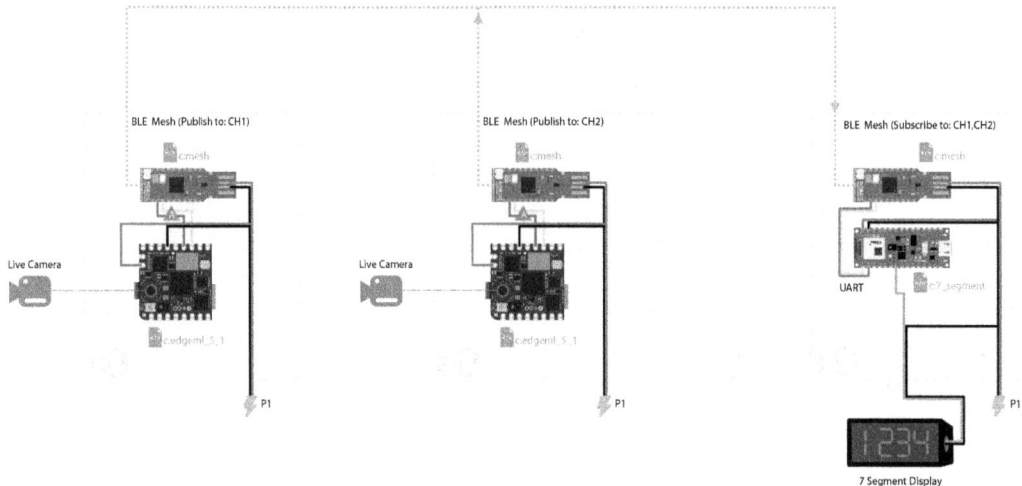

Figure 5.10: *Connection diagram (Conveyor belt counting)*

The first Block of this system focuses on video capture and processing. It utilizes an Arduino Nicla Vision, a powerful device capable of capturing video from the conveyor belt and processing these video frames into features. These features are then used to train and run a **Convolutional Neural Network (CNN)** on the same device to generate object counts. In addition to video processing capabilities, this Block includes a secondary microcontroller that handles wireless network communications. Communication between the primary video processing unit and the secondary communication unit is facilitated through **Universal Asynchronous Receiver-Transmitter (UART)**. After processing, the secondary unit publishes the count to a **Bluetooth Low Energy (BLE)** Mesh Network, assigning each count to a specific channel corresponding to its counter. This setup allows for a scalable system where multiple counters transmit data simultaneously to the aggregator.

The second Block of the system is centered around data aggregation and display. It employs an Arduino Nano 33 BLE equipped with a secondary microcontroller (NRF52840) for receiving counts from the various counters across the production line. By subscribing to each counter unique channel, the Arduino can gather and compare counts from different sources to establish the master count. This finalized count is displayed on a 4-digit, 7-segment LED display, which updates with every new count. The connection to the display is made through **Inter-Integrated Circuit (I2C)**, a serial communication protocol that allows multiple devices to communicate with the Arduino.

Given the system's deployment in a factory setting, where power access is ubiquitous, both Blocks of the counter system are powered by a 5V power source connected to the electric grid. The power sources ensure the system remains operational without interruption, providing reliable and accurate counting results in a real-time manufacturing environment.

Source code

Table 5.1 presents the pseudocode for the program that handles object tracking and counting on the conveyor belt. The process is divided into four stages: capturing the image, extracting its features, running the classification, and executing the tracking algorithm.

c:tinyml_5_1	Code location: Arduino Nano 33 BLE @ Block 1
	Capturing video frames, classifying objects, tracking and counting. Pseudocode 1. A camera captures video frames from the conveyor belt. Frames are sent to the processing Block. 2. In the processing Block, the image is resized and reshaped. The resulting features are sent to the model 3. The TinyML model runs the inference with the provided data and returns an array of identified objects. The array is sent to the tracking algorithm. 4. The tracking algorithm checks whether each identified item is close enough to an identified object in the last step. If there is a match, the new item acquires the same ID as the old item. By doing this, the ID persists, and tracking takes place. 5. The counting algorithm checks whether a tracked object has crossed a predetermined line. If the check is positive, a counting event is declared. A count increase is sent to the secondary MCU for publishing events to the Mesh Network.

Table 5.1: Pseudocode (Conveyor belt counting)

Network

The two components in this use case are wirelessly connected via a pub/sub Mesh Network. Wireless communication is essential since the facility handles food. The counting component is enclosed in an insulated transparent box and communicates in real-time with the large number counter located in a different part of the facility. Both components operate on the same channel. In future implementations with additional sensors along the production line, each counting device would send updates through separate channels, all of which the main counter would be subscribed to. Refer to the following table:

Block(s)	Action	Channel
1	Publishes to	CH1
2	Subscribes to	CH1

Table 5.2: Network configuration (Conveyor belt counting)

Power analysis

Block 1 performs real-time image classification and tracking while also publishing high-frequency messages with the latest count. For these reasons, powering the component with a battery would be impractical, as it would require frequent recharging. Instead, a low-voltage power line is necessary to supply power to the sensor. Considering the industrial setting, it is reasonable to assume that providing power to this device will not be a significant challenge. Refer to the following table:

Power source	Device	Latent consumption	Active consumption	Notes
P1	Arduino Nicla Vision	0.032A @5V	< 1A @5V	
P1	NRF52 Dongle	0.04mA @5V	3mA @5V	Active when publishing messages as a *client*.

Table 5.3: Power profile for Block 1 (Conveyor belt counting)

Block 2 is in charge of driving a 7-segment display showing the count in real time. Given the fact that the display uses big bright numbers and that it will be permanently installed on a wall, it makes sense to also connect it to the electric grid. It is important to mention that the low energy consumption of LEDs could give you the option to make this Block battery operated as well. Refer to the following table:

Power source	Device	Latent consumption	Active consumption	Notes
P2	NRF52 Dongle	0.04mA @5V	0.3mA @5V	Active when receiving messages as a *server*.
P2	Arduino Nano 33 BLE	0.034mA @5V	< 1A @5V	Sends data to a big 7-segment display. The display is powered directly from a 5v power source.

Table 5.4: Power profile for Block 2 (Conveyor belt counting)

Bill of materials

This bill of materials show the approximate cost of a proof of concept that includes two Block 1 components and one 7 segment display:

Description	QTY	Unit cost	Total
Arduino Nicla Vision	2	$85	$170
Arduino Nano 33 BLE	1	$30	$30
NRF52840 Dongle	3	$12	$36
Big 7 segment Display	1	$90	$90
Power Source 1A @5v	2	$10	$20

Table 5.5: Bill of materials (Conveyor belt counting)

Approximate cost of materials is $346.

Use case: People counting

A highly useful application is the simultaneous tracking of multiple different objects. The complexity arises not only from predicting the object's next position based on its trajectory (as shown in the previous use case) but also from ensuring that the object remains the same throughout its trajectory. This is achieved using a multiclass model capable of generating a unique ID for each classified object, which the tracking algorithm uses to link its trajectory consistently.

People counting in supermarket

Problem definition: A prominent supermarket chain faces a challenge impacting customer satisfaction; prolonged waiting times at the checkout registers. This issue has been identified as a critical factor contributing to a decline in the overall quality of service provided to shoppers. The supermarket's management team is exploring a new approach to optimize the checkout process to address this.

The proposed solution involves closely monitoring the flow of customers entering and leaving the store. The management can gain valuable insights into customer traffic patterns by accurately counting the number of individuals coming into the store and those leaving. This data is crucial for estimating the total number of customers in the store at any given time.

Understanding the approximate customer count inside the store is instrumental in determining the required number of open registers. The goal is to have a proportional relationship between the number of customers and the number of active checkout lanes. By achieving this balance, the supermarket aims to significantly reduce waiting times at the registers, thereby enhancing the shopping experience for its customers and improving overall service quality. Implementing this customer counting system will enable the supermarket to adjust its checkout operations based on real-time customer traffic, leading to a more efficient and satisfactory service.

Solution: The solution consists of a set of cameras mounted on the frame of every entrance and exit door. The cameras are installed on the highest part of the frame, pointing down to the floor, covering an area of a couple of square meters. The cameras use a wide-angle lens to cover a greater distance at a short focal point. The camera sends video frames to the microcontroller. The MCU processes the frames and runs a person classification model. The embedded tracking algorithm uses its results to count the number of people crossing the door. The result is sent to a secondary microcontroller wirelessly, sending the count to a central microcontroller, which receives the counts of all the supermarket cameras. The main job of the central MCU is to make sense of all the data and come up with the official count of people in the supermarket. Based on that information, the real-time people count will be displayed for the floor manager to decide whether to open more registers. Refer to the following figure:

Figure 5.11: Concept diagram (People counting)

Data acquisition

When acquiring data to train a person recognition model, you should consider the specific conditions the model will find when it is used in a real scenario. In the case of a camera installed on the frame of an entrance door, the objects that need to be recognized (the humans) will be observed from a top-down perspective. Training a model with pictures from a different perspective, e.g., a full-body view, might deliver unexpected results. We captured the training set from a camera installed on the door frame for this use case. Additionally, the model should be trained to recognize people dressed for different seasons. A person wearing a simple shirt might look different from someone wearing a hat, a coat, or a scarf. If you use a shot that shows people of different sizes because of perspective, provide enough samples in your training data set to teach the model how to recognize them. An example is having a camera pointing to the street; the frames will contain people walking on the closest sidewalk and from the sidewalk across the street.

The process of data acquisition also needs to cater to the tracking algorithm. For this use case, the camera is positioned at an angle that prevents people from Blocking each other, given that the camera is high up on the doorframe.

Most importantly, the acquired frames must be aligned to the door frame itself as the counting algorithm will use an imaginary line parallel to the door frame to create the boundary that will be used to count objects (humans) once they cross it.

The training set for this use case has been acquired in a commercial space in New York City. The office has a unique entrance that employees and clients use to enter and exit the business. The door is located at street level. To avoid capturing people passing by, the camera is pointing into the inside of the space. The camera is at an angle of approximately 30° from the door. This covers an area of about 2x2 meters. We captured 5 video segments of 15 minutes each at different times of the day. Then, we transferred the video to Final Cut Pro, where we trimmed and resized the frames. The result was five sequences at 25FPS. That is 112,500 frames. Not all the video frames were helpful in training, as many contained no persons walking by. After eliminating those, we kept a subset of the video frames that showed people walking by. We focused on having a diverse set of people rather than the same person walking in different positions. The dataset has 600 frames with hundreds of combinations of people walking alone or in groups. The following figure demonstrates this division of people:

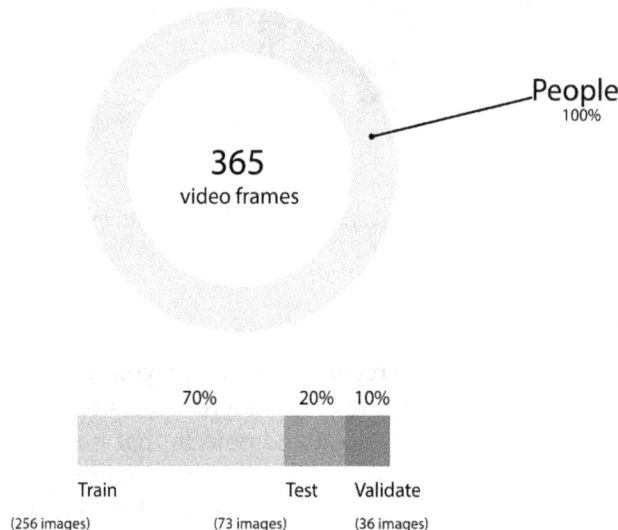

Figure 5.12: Training dataset (People counting)

Processing

Extracting the features from the frames is straightforward. First, the processing functions trim the image to a square format and resize it to 90x90 pixels. As indicated in the last section, this was done with the Final Cut Pro when the video was prepared to obtain the training data set. You do not need to use a specialized video software to do that. Instead, you can take snapshots of the frames you consider worthy of the dataset and have a Python script or Edge Impulse resize and trim them for you. We trained the model with both color images and grayscale. There was no significant difference. We selected the grayscale as it requires three times less memory and processing power. To augment the data, we created new samples by flipping them (horizontally and vertically) and mirroring them.

The process will generate 8,100 features, one per pixel. Features will be fed to the fully connected input layer of the Convolutional Neural Network we will train.

Figure 5.13 shows only one cluster in the clustering graph, which is okay as we have only one class (person). It would be interesting to extend the model in the future for specialized classes like **children** or **wheelchairs**.

A: PEOPLE

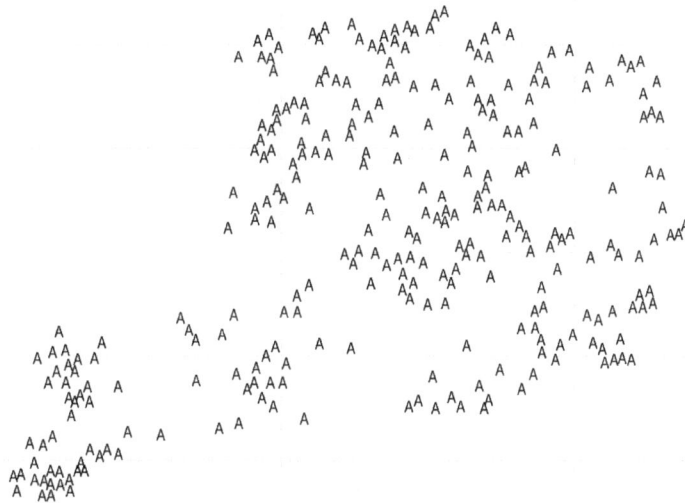

Figure 5.13: *Cluster diagram (People counting)*

Model

The model used in this case is based on MobileNet V2, a prevalent object recognition model used in devices with minimal memory and a CPU. To reuse MobileNet V2 in our specific case, we rely on a technique called **transfer learning,** where we remove the specialized layers in charge of recognizing particular objects and replace them with a layer that will recognize and classify our use case. To do this, we will re-train the model with our training dataset so that it can adjust the weights for the new specialized layers. Additionally, the FOMO algorithm is used to indicate the position of the detected objects by their centroid, which saves a lot of memory and makes the model go much faster as it does not need to infer the area covered by the object, but just its location in the frame.

Figure 5.14 presents key metrics for this use case. The sample set is divided into three parts: 70% for training, 10% for validation, and 20% for testing. The 95.6% F1 score during validation suggests that the model performs very well on the validation dataset. However, the 86.67% accuracy during testing is significantly lower than the validation F1 score, which may indicate that the model does not generalize well to new data. This discrepancy could be due to overfitting or data imbalance. If the validation dataset is too similar to the training set, the model may appear to perform well during validation but struggle with truly unseen data. To mitigate this, we could increase the dataset size and improve its diversity.

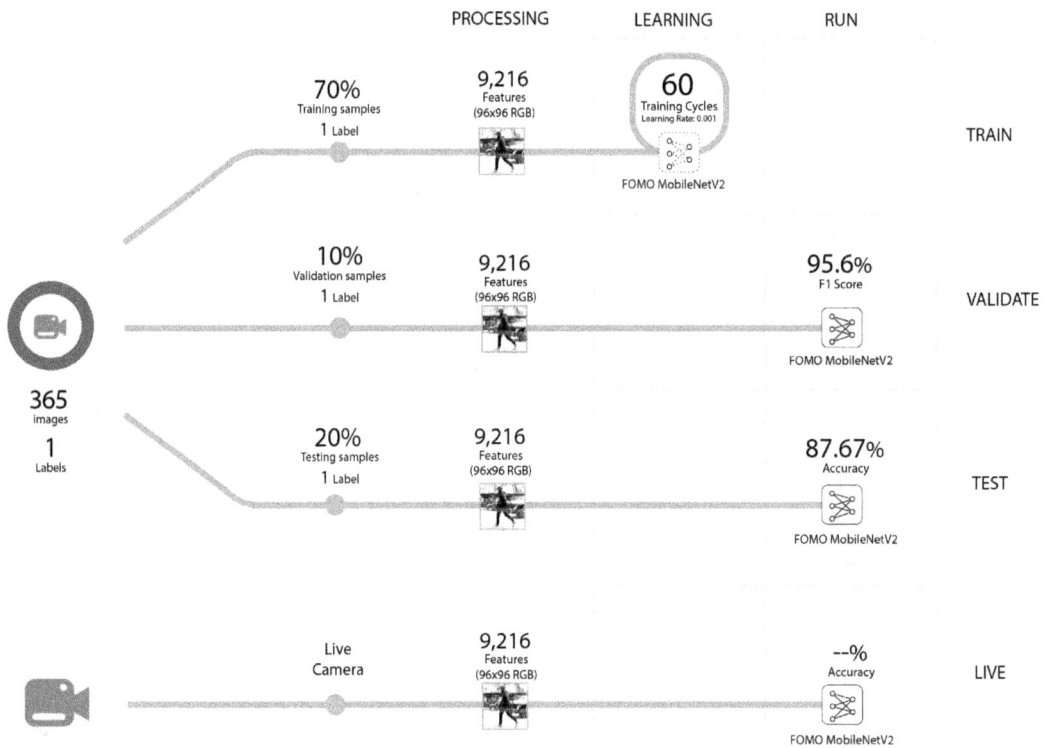

Figure 5.14: *Training, validation and testing metrics (People counting)*

System implementation

The solution is implemented in two Blocks: the first one counts objects, and the second one displays the count. The Blocks are connected wirelessly and powered independently as shown in the following implementation diagram:

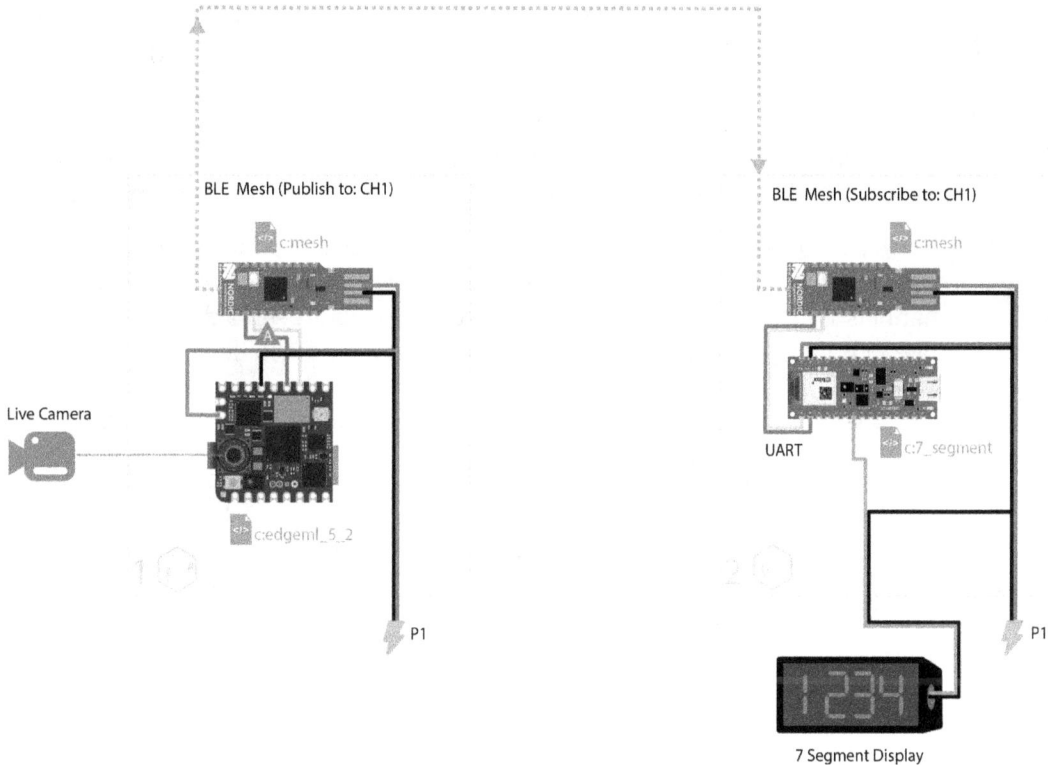

Figure 5.15: Connection diagram (People counting)

There are two types of Blocks, given as follows:

- The first is a data capture Block that contains the camera, the microcontroller running the people counting algorithm, and a secondary microcontroller in charge of communicating the count increments to other devices in a wireless local network.

- The second Block contains a microcontroller in charge of receiving the people count increments from every door in the supermarket and passing them to the main microcontroller that calculates the total number of people in the space. The second Block communicates the count to the supermarket manager via a small OLED display.

We use the Arduino Nicla a low energy and compact device known for its ability to capture high-quality video, run local machine learning models, and perform custom functions such as object tracking for people counting.

The model is obtained from Edge Impulse, where training and testing occur. The tracking and counting algorithm is written in MicroPython using the OpenMV IDE. Once a count event has occurred, the Arduino Nicla sends the count increment to the secondary microcontroller (NRF52840 dongle) to publish to a BLE Mesh Network. The Mesh Network has been configured to have as many channels as doors with a people counter installed. The device publishes the count to the channel assigned to its door. The door counters do not keep track of their total count of the day; instead, they only report how many people have entered and left the place in the last 10 seconds. We refer to it as **count increment**.

We use an NRF52840 dongle for the second Block to obtain all incoming counts. The dongle is subscribed to all the channels doors use to send count increments. While having multiple channels is not strictly needed, as all the doors could send their counts in the same channel without a problem, having a channel dedicated to each door allows for easier troubleshooting and identification of the origin of the counts. Once a count increment has been received, the dongle sends it to the main microcontroller (an Arduino BLE 33). The Arduino keeps track of all the door counts in an array in its memory and stores it in a non-volatile SD card connected via I2C. If the Arduino must reset, the initialization functions will pull the latest count from the SD card. The OLED display used to communicate the total count is connected to the Arduino using an I2C interface. It is refreshed every 10 seconds, displaying the total sum of all doors.

Source code

The pseudocode in *Table 5.6* shows the 5 stages of the data transformation. The first one is the raw image capture, the second is the extraction of its features, the third is the classification run, the fourth one consists of assigning a track to the identified objects, and the last one checks whether the conditions have been met to consider a tracking event a count.

c:tinyml_5_2	Code location: Arduino Nano 33 BLE @ Block 1
Image Classification Model Process-ing · Track-ing · Detec-tion ① → ② → ③ → ④ → ⑤ → A	Capturing video frames, identifying objects, tracking and counting. Pseudocode 1. A camera captures video frames from the camera mounted on the door. Frames are sent to the processing Block. 2. In the processing Block, the image is resized and reshaped. The resulting features are sent to the model. 3. The TinyML model runs the inference with the provided data and returns an array of identified objects. The array is sent to the tracking algorithm. 4. The tracking algorithm checks whether each identified item is close enough to an identified object in the last step. If there is a match, the new item acquires the same ID as the old item. By doing this, the ID persists, and tracking takes place. 5. The counting algorithm checks whether a tracked object has crossed a predetermined line. If the check is positive, a counting event is declared. A count increase is sent to the secondary MCU for publishing events to the Mesh Network.

Table 5.6: Pseudocode for Block 1 (People counting)

Network

People-counting devices must be installed in strategic locations that provide an optimal angle for the counting model. In many cases, this location is on the ceiling. Running a wired connection is often impractical, making wireless communication essential. For privacy reasons, these devices must process images locally and output only a numerical count rather than transmitting raw images. Given the low bandwidth requirements, a wireless Mesh Network capable of handling just a few kilobytes per second is sufficient, enough to transmit count data but not images. The counting device, represented by Block 1, publishes messages to a shared channel that the data consumer is subscribed to. Refer to the following table:

Block(s)	Action	Channel
1	Publishes to	CH1
2	Subscribes to	CH1

Table 5.7: Network configuration (People counting)

Power analysis

The same space and location constraints described in the network section also apply to power supplies. Accessing hard-to-reach devices for battery replacement is impractical. However, a viable solution is to extend a low-voltage line from an electrical register used for lighting, providing a permanent power source for the device. Refer to the following table:

Power source	Device	Latent consumption	Active consumption	Notes
P1	Arduino Nicla Vision	0.032A @5V	< 1A @5V	
P1	NRF52 Dongle	0.04mA @5V	3mA @5V	Active when publishing messages as a **client**.

Table 5.8: Power profile for Block 1 (People counting)

Block 2 and the 7-segment display acquire power from a power source connected to the electric grid:

Power source	Device	Latent consumption	Active consumption	Notes
P2	NRF52 Dongle	0.04mA @5V	0.3mA @5V	Active when receiving messages as a *server*.
P2	Arduino Nano 33 BLE	0.034mA @5V	< 1A @5V	Sends data to a big 7-segment display. The display is powered directly from a 5v power source.

Table 5.9: Power profile for Block 2 (People counting)

Bill of materials

The following bill of materials accounts for the installation of a single people counter and a single 7-segment display, both communicating wirelessly and powered by the electric grid:

Description	QTY	Unit cost	Total
Arduino Nicla Vision	1	$85	$85
Arduino Nano 33 BLE	1	$30	$30
NRF52840 Dongle	2	$12	$24
Big 7 segment Display	1	$90	$90
Power Source 1A @5v	2	$10	$20

Table 5.10: Bill of materials (People counting)

Approximate cost of materials is $249.

Use case: Event detection

An advanced application of image tracking is to flag events that can only be detected across a series of frames. The key is to detect the states before and after the event occurs and then issue a classification event. This can be thought of as classification across time, which differs from classifying a single image, as discussed in *Chapter 4, Image Classification*.

Car tracking

Problem definition: The police department is trying to detect drivers who cross a double line, violating the transit code. They have identified a highway exit where this behavior has been the cause of many accidents. The solution should track the trajectory of the car where the car crosses the double line from an outer lane into the exit lane. When the event occurs, the solution should send a signal to a traffic camera. The camera will take a picture that will serve as evidence for the transit violation ticket issued to the driver.

To effectively address this issue, a monitoring solution is being proposed. The core of this system revolves around tracking the movement of vehicles, specifically focusing on instances where a car veers across a double line from an outer lane into the exit lane. This maneuver is dangerous and illegal, making it a critical intervention point. The following figure illustrates the violation:

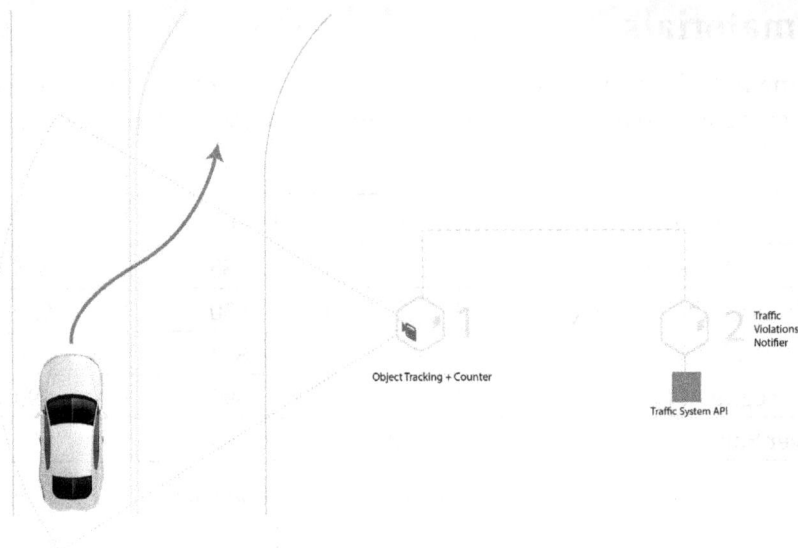

Figure 5.16: *Concept diagram (Car tracking)*

The proposed solution involves a mechanism that triggers a response when such an event is detected. Upon recognizing a vehicle crossing the double line, the system automatically sends a signal to a strategically placed traffic camera. Upon receiving the signal, this camera will photograph the offending vehicle.

The photograph taken by the camera serves a crucial role in the enforcement process. It will be used as concrete evidence of the traffic violation, aiding in issuing a transit violation ticket to the driver. This approach not only aids in penalizing those breaking the law but also serves as a deterrent to prevent future incidents. By implementing this solution, the police aim to reduce accidents at the identified highway exit and promote safer driving practices.

Solution: The solution consists of one or more auxiliary cameras detecting when a car crosses a double line and a central microcontroller in charge of sending a digital signal to the police department traffic camera that will take the photograph included in the traffic violation. Implementing the traffic camera is out of the scope of this use case. Instead, we focus on the auxiliary cameras that work together to signal when the violation event occurs. In a way, the system we are creating can be abstracted as a sensor that detects violations. The separation is essential as we could modify the internal workings of the system to improve its accuracy (e.g., adding a sonar to corroborate the event) without having to reimplement the interface with the traffic camera.

Data acquisition

The data we acquire for this dataset must help us achieve three different goals. 1. To recognize cars, 2. To track cars, 3. To follow trajectories.

To achieve the first goal, the model needs to recognize the changes in the car shape as it moves through the video frame. If the shot is looking at the street from a perspective where the car is becoming larger as it gets closer, the dataset must have a balanced mix of vehicles of many sizes from that perspective. On the other hand, if the video frame shows a side shot where the car moves from one side to the other without modifying its apparent size, the dataset needs to consider the effects of a moving object on any given instant. Is the car going to look blurry? Or is your model fast enough to capture the event at all? For example, if the vehicle moves across the frame in less than one second and your model can only process 7 frames per second, you only have a little room for error. The module would need to be accurate enough to avoid missing three classifications in a row to be able to at least detect the car before, during, and after it crosses the boundary.

A common error during data acquisition for model training on a tracking implementation is to capture and train the model with objects moving at a rate that does not take into consideration the actual performance of the microcontroller. The model's training and verification results will look great when running on a regular computer. Still, when deployed in the device in tandem with the tracking algorithm, the results might not work.

Cameras that detect traffic events are generally outdoors. The device must likely be installed in a pole or under the bridge to protect it from tampering. The remote access to the camera installation place makes capturing training data difficult. This hurdle makes an excellent opportunity to consider generating a synthetic training dataset. Synthetic datasets are computer-generated variations of a specific phenomenon. To create such a dataset, you need to use a photo editor to cut images of cars that match the camera's perspective and paste them on top of a picture of an empty street. Generate as many variations as possible and train the model with the synthetic dataset. The dataset should have a good variety of types of cars to increase accuracy and reduce overfitting. If done correctly, a synthetic dataset should not be easily noticeable from one generated in an actual situation.

For this use case, we generated 290 images, which was enough to reach an F1 score of 95.2%. Refer to the following figure:

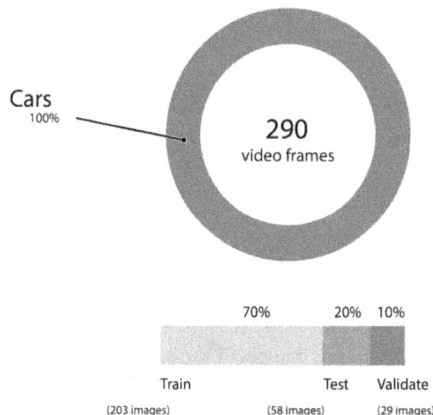

Figure 5.17: Training dataset (Car tracking)

The camera angle affects the tracking directly, so avoid perspectives where other cars can Block cars. A car's trajectory should be visible 100% from entering the frame, crossing the double line, and leaving it.

We labeled each car independently under a single class. In future implementations, we might create different classes for buses, motorcycles, and vans.

Processing

Processing a synthetic dataset is not different from any other. Everything starts with a reshape to a square format and a subsequent resize. After a couple of attempts, we discovered that a size of 96x96 pixels was enough for the model to recognize the cars consistently. The additional dataset augmentation has been automatically implemented via Edge Impulse.

Each video frame is converted to 27,648 features. That is 9,216 features per channel (RGB). The following cluster diagram groups similar images based on their features. Each sample represents a different car. The fact that they are clustered closely together is a positive sign, as it indicates that the model can effectively distinguish cars from other objects. Refer to the following figure:

Figure 5.18: *Clustering diagram (Car tracking)*

Model

The model for this use case is based on the MobileNetV2 model proposed by Google Research, which, as of the writing of this book, is the golden standard for object detection in resource-constrained devices. The strategy is similar to the other use cases in this book: To strip the specialized layers from MobileNetV2 and replace them with a customized layer that is trained with the training set of this use case. The technique used is called Transfer Learning. To give a sense of perspective, training an object recognition from scratch would require a dataset with millions of images and hundreds of computation hours.

The FOMO MobileNetV2 model demonstrates strong performance in validation (95.2% F1 score) but exhibits lower accuracy during testing (88.52%), indicating a possibility of overfitting and suggesting the need for further evaluation of the model's generalization capabilities. Since this is a single-class model, the high validation score indicates that the model has learned to classify cars well on seen data, but its generalization to new, unseen images is weaker. The relatively small dataset (290 images) compared to the high feature count (27,648) might contribute to this, as the model could be memorizing patterns instead of learning robust generalizable features. To improve generalization, we could consider increasing dataset size, applying data augmentation, or adding regularization techniques like dropout or weight decay. Additionally, reviewing the test set for data distribution differences from training could help identify biases affecting performance. Refer to the following figure:

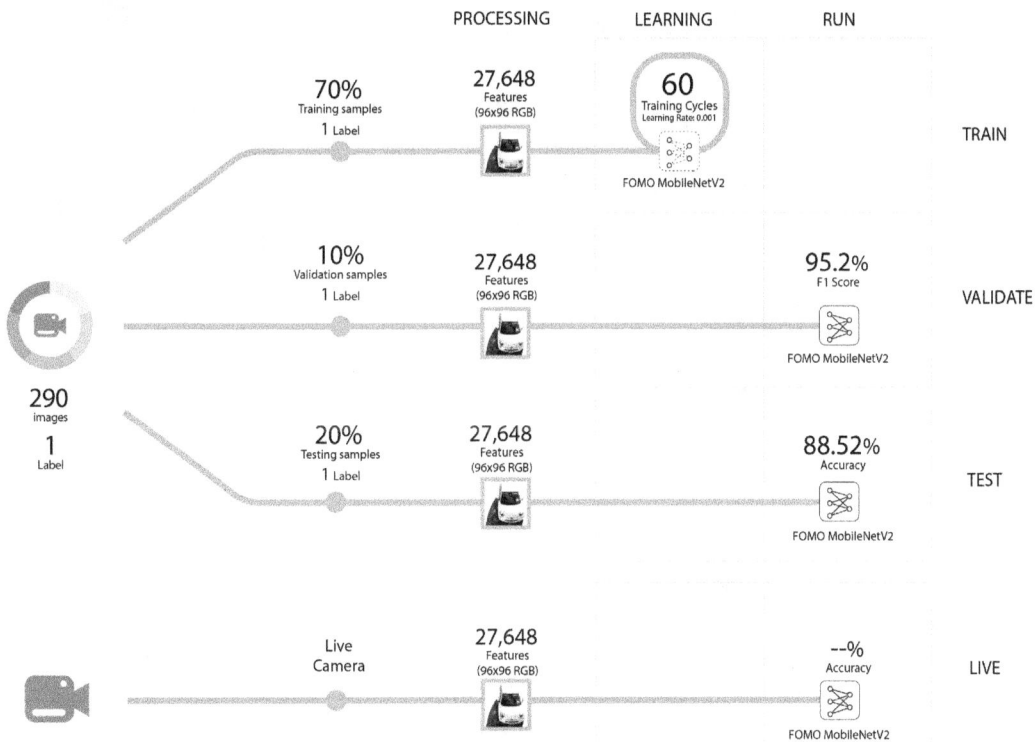

Figure 5.19: Training, validation and testing metrics (Car tracking)

Leveraging an existing model to require just a couple hundred images and a dozen computation minutes is truly an incredible feat. Because we do not need to know the exact area the object occupies, we optimize the response time further using the FOMO algorithm, which determines the object's centroid. With this optimization, we only get one coordinate per recognized object, making the math to determine whether the centroid has crossed the boundary much easier.

System implementation

The system consists of two different Blocks. The first one contains the camera that captures the video frames, the model that classifies the cars, and the algorithm that tracks and counts the number of times a vehicle crosses a double line. The second Block subscribes to the notifications from the first Block and sends a signal to the traffic system when a traffic violation occurs. The following figure shows the connection between both Blocks, the peripherals and their power sources:

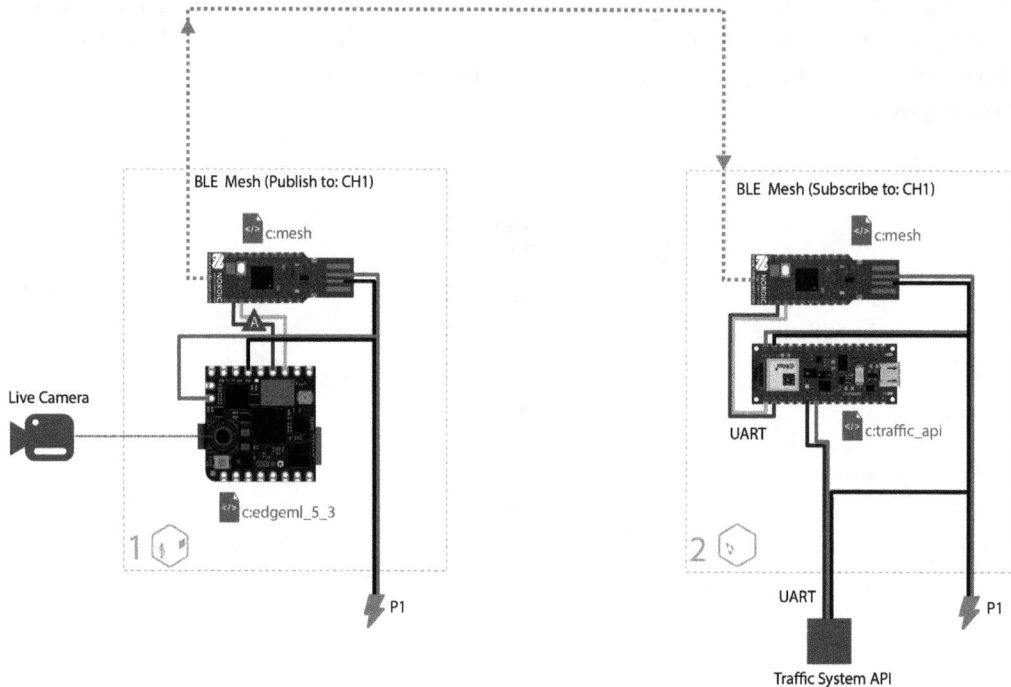

Figure 5.20: Connection diagram (Car tracking)

The first Block (the data acquisition Block) is implemented with an Arduino Nicla Vision capable of performing the video frame capture and inference and running the tracking algorithm. A secondary microcontroller mounted on an NRF52840 dongle receives the notification from the Arduino Nicla via UART that a traffic violation event has occurred. The dongle prepares the payload with the notification contents and publishes the message to the Mesh Network.

The second Block (the proxy Block) receives messages from the Mesh Network via an NRF52840 Dongle subscribed to the same channel used by the data acquisition Block to send the violation notifications. The dongle is a full-featured microcontroller that can be re-programmed to send a signal to the traffic controller. For this reason, this use case does not require a primary microcontroller like the other use cases. The dongle is capable of communicating via UART, I2C, or SPI. It can also output a custom signal if it is required.

If the interface requires a different higher voltage (like 5 volts), a buck and MOSFET gate can provide reasonable output in real time. The dongle also features a multicolor LED that will be used to show the communication status for troubleshooting purposes. It will show **green** if connected to the Mesh Network, **blue** if a message is received, and **red** if there is a problem.

Source code

The pseudocode for the Block 1 shows the sequence to infer whether there has been a violation. It starts with the video frame acquisition, followed by the feature extraction, the image classification run and the feed of its results to the tracking model that keeps track of all the cars in the frame detecting if a violation has been incurred. If that is the case, a signal is sent out.

c:tinyml_5_3	Code location: Arduino Nano 33 BLE @ Block 1
	Capturing video frames, identifying objects, tracking and detecting traffic violations. Pseudocode 1. A camera captures frames from the street video feed. Frames are sent to the processing Block. 2. In the processing Block, the image is resized and reshaped. The resulting features are sent to the model. 3. The TinyML model runs the inference with the provided data and returns an array of identified cars. The array is sent to the tracking algorithm. 4. The tracking algorithm checks whether each identified car is close enough to a previously identified car from the last step. If there is a match, the vehicle acquires the same ID as the previous one. By doing this, the ID persists, and car tracking takes place. 5. The counting algorithm checks whether a tracked car has crossed a double line. The double line is hard coded to the software as two coordinates. The check is performed geometrically by calculating the distance between the line and the object. If there is a cross, a traffic Violation has been detected, and a message is sent to the network MCU to publish a notification message.

Table 5.11: Pseudocode (Car tracking)

Network

A component mounted at the top of a pole is an excellent example of an ideal use case for a wireless network. Since the device does not need to capture images, relying instead on a specialized camera for that function, a low-bandwidth network, such as a low-power Mesh Network, is sufficient. The component will transmit messages to a receiver device installed next to the traffic camera. Refer to the following table:

Block(s)	Action	Channel
1	Publishes to	CH1
2	Subscribes to	CH1

Table 5.12: *Mesh network configuration (Car tracking)*

Power analysis

The component mounted at the top of the pole is also an ideal candidate for a solar-powered device. However, given the critical nature of the operation (ensuring that all violations are penalized without exception), a permanent power source is recommended. If the device is installed on a traffic pole, power is likely included in the original specifications, making it reasonable to assume that extending a low-voltage line to the device would be feasible. Refer to the following table:

Power source	Device	Latent consumption	Active consumption	Notes
P1	Arduino Nicla Vision	0.032A @5V	< 1A @5V	
P1	NRF52 Dongle	0.04mA @5v	3mA @5v	Active when publishing messages as a *client*.

Table 5.13: *Power profile, Block 1 (Car tracking)*

For the receiver Block, given the fact that it will be installed in close proximity to the traffic camera, we can also assume that power will be available to it:

Power source	Device	Latent consumption	Active consumption	Notes
P2	NRF52 Dongle	0.04mA @5v	0.3mA @5v	Active when receiving messages as a *server*.
P2	Arduino Nano 33 BLE	0.034mA @5V	< 1A @5V	Sends data to a proprietary Traffic system **application programmable interface (API)**

Table 5.14: *Power profile, Block 2 (Car tracking)*

Block 2 acquires power from a power source connected to the electric grid.

Bill of materials

The following bill of materials considers a minimal implementation of one violation detecting device and a receiver. Both of them powered directly from the electric grid.

Description	QTY	Unit cost	Total
Arduino Nicla Vision	1	$85	$85
Arduino Nano 33 BLE	1	$30	$30
NRF52840 Dongle	2	$12	$24
Power Source 1A @5v	2	$10	$20

Table 5.15: Bill of materials (Car tracking)

Approximate cost of materials is $159.

Conclusion

In this chapter, we explored how running image classification multiple times per second while tracking detected objects and their locations enables a new set of solutions for detecting events over time. These solutions include counting objects from a video feed, tracking people, and detecting traffic violations. In the following chapters, we build upon this knowledge to detect anomalies.

References

- Tracking use case 1: **https://studio.edgeimpulse.com/public/339554/live**

- Tracking use case 2: **https://studio.edgeimpulse.com/public/344166/live**

- Tracking use case 3: **https://studio.edgeimpulse.com/public/340135/live**

- FOMO: Object detection for constrained devices https://docs.edgeimpulse.com/docs/edge-impulse-studio/learning-blocks/object-detection/fomo-object-detection-for-constrained-devices

Join our book's Discord space

Join the book's Discord Workspace for Latest updates, Offers, Tech happenings around the world, New Release and Sessions with the Authors:

https://discord.bpbonline.com

CHAPTER 6

Sensor Fusion

Introduction

Sensor fusion combines data from multiple sensors to create a more accurate or informative set of information than each sensor could provide individually. This definition can be extended to include creating derived data that would be unattainable using individual sensors alone.

With the advent of advanced machine learning technologies and models trained on a vast array of data sources, it could be argued that employing a Neural Network to synthesize new data is a form of sensor fusion. However, we will focus on explicit sensor fusion, where data is fused before it is sent to the Neural Network. Once we have generated new data with sensor fusion, we can use it to train a model and infer data from it.

Two main challenges arise in sensor fusion: dependability and time synchronization. Dependability refers to the system's ability to provide a reliable data stream consistently. It is crucial to consider and plan for scenarios where one or more sensors might fail or produce inaccurate data. We must establish strategies for detecting and correcting such issues while keeping sensor fusion reliable. Time synchronization is equally critical, as the data from various sources must be correlated in time. Without proper synchronization, there is a risk of generating misleading information, as asynchronous data might not truly reflect the interactions or the sequence of events among various readings.

Structure

The chapter covers the following topics:

- Types of sensor fusion
- Sensor fusion algorithm
- Kalman filters
- Use case: Scoring
- Use case: Profiling
- Use case: Correction

Objectives

The main objectives of this chapter are to identify opportunities for implementing sensor fusion by understanding the various approaches used in combining data from multiple sensors. Learn the steps involved in the sensor fusion algorithm to enhance accuracy and reliability in applications. Additionally, explore the concept of a Kalman filter and its significance in sensor fusion, as it plays a crucial role in estimating and refining sensor data for improved performance.

Types of sensor fusion

Sensor fusion is a departure from the methodologies discussed in previous chapters, where data is typically captured from a single sensor, processed to extract features and input into a Neural Network for inference and insight derivation. Sensor fusion introduces an additional complexity: it involves the integration of readings from multiple sensors to create a unified representation of a specific environmental characteristic.

A standard categorization of sensor fusion identifies three distinct configurations: complementary, competitive, and cooperative. In a complementary configuration, sensors collaborate rather than compete, each contributing unique data to form a more comprehensive view of the environment. This approach does not just add data; it enriches the overall context. *Use case 1* shows this configuration by providing readings of temperature and relative humidity present in living and working spaces that help define the **comfort index** of an indoor space.

The competitive configuration is designed for reliability and redundancy. Multiple sensors can measure the same property or provide similar information in this setup. This redundancy ensures that if one sensor fails or provides inaccurate data, the system can still function correctly by relying on data from the remaining sensors. *Use case 2* shows this configuration by capturing temperature with multiple sensors to generate the thermal profile of an indoor space.

The following figure illustrates the three different approaches to sensor fusion and highlights their distinctions:

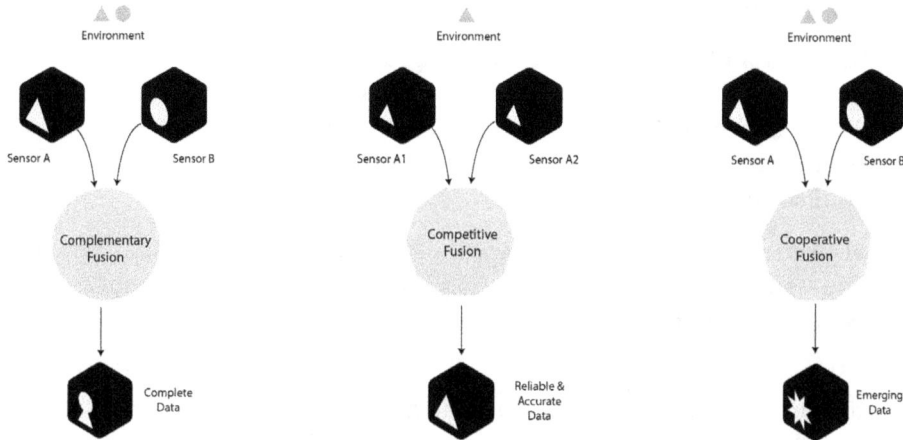

Figure 6.1: *Sensor fusion types*

Lastly, the cooperative configuration involves different sensors contributing varied data that, when combined, can deduce information that would be impossible to measure directly. This collaborative approach leverages the strengths of diverse sensors to create a detailed and multifaceted understanding of the environment. Each configuration offers unique advantages and is suited to different tasks and objectives within the broader scope of sensor fusion. The Correction use case in this chapter shows this approach by leveraging the unique qualities of a gyroscope and an accelerometer data to calculate the roll and pitch angle of an object that is more accurate than that acquired independently by each sensor.

Sensor fusion algorithm

Sensor fusion algorithms integrate data from multiple sensors to produce more accurate, reliable, and comprehensive information than what is available from any single sensor. The steps involved in a sensor fusion algorithm typically include the following:

1. **Data collection**: Gathering raw data from various sensors, each of which may measure different aspects of the environment or object of interest (e.g., temperature, motion, distance).

2. **Pre-processing**: Cleaning and preparing the data for fusion. This step may involve filtering noise, scaling, and converting data into compatible formats or units. It is crucial for ensuring the quality and consistency of the input data.

3. **Data alignment**: Aligning data in time and space. Since data may come from sensors with different sampling rates or at different positions, aligning data is essential for accurate fusion. This may involve interpolation, timestamp matching, and spatial transformations.

4. **Data association**: Determining which data points across sensors correspond to the same phenomenon or object. This step is crucial in environments with multiple entities or when sensors measure overlapping areas.

5. **Estimation and integration**: Combining data from multiple sources to estimate the state of the environment or object. sensor fusion can be done through various mathematical models and algorithms, such as Kalman filters, Bayesian networks, or Neural Networks. The goal is to leverage the strengths of each sensor to improve overall accuracy and reliability.

6. **Post-processing**: Further refining the fused data, if necessary, this step might include smoothing the results, applying thresholds, or extracting higher-level information from the raw fused data.

7. **Feedback loop:** In some sensor fusion systems, there is a feedback loop where the outcome of the fusion process is used to adjust the parameters of the sensors or the fusion algorithm itself, enhancing future data collection and processing.

It is important to note that using multiple sensors in a TinyML application does not automatically qualify it as a sensor fusion system. For a system to be considered as employing sensor fusion, the integrated data from multiple sensors must culminate in a new, unified representation of the information. This distinction is crucial in understanding and categorizing different multi-sensor applications.

The following figure illustrates how sensor fusion produces information that differs from the simple aggregation of two sensors:

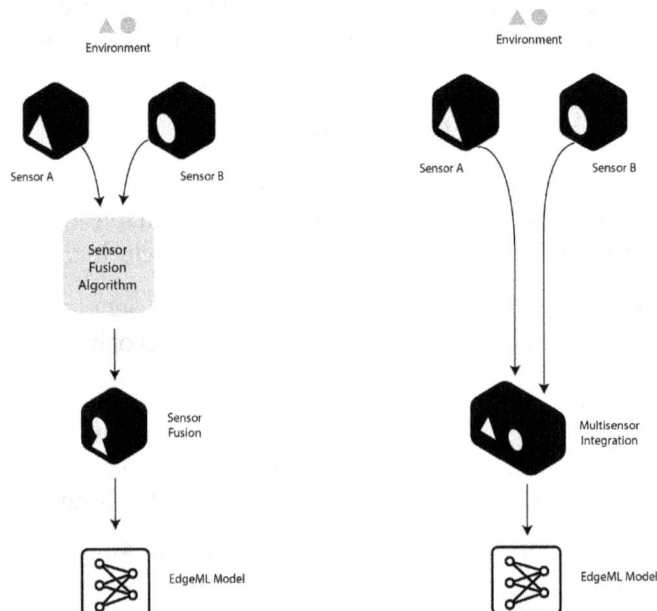

Figure 6.2: Sensor fusion versus multiple sensors aggregation

Kalman filters

Kalman filters are great to smooth and correct curves, but their real value is in estimating system parameters such as position, velocity, or sensor bias, which cannot be measured or observed directly or with a high level of accuracy. Sensors are typically unpredictable, noisy, and slow to detect changes. Therefore, you cannot assume that a sensor's readings reflect a system's real state. A Kalman filter can turn a few raw readings and knowledge about the system into a more accurate value you can trust.

A real-life application of Kalman filters is in NASA's Mars Rovers, such as *Perseverance* and *Curiosity*, which rely on them for accurate navigation, sensor fusion, and motion tracking in the harsh and unpredictable Martian environment. Since GPS is not available on Mars, the rovers must estimate their position, velocity, and orientation using onboard sensors while accounting for sensor noise, delays, and uncertainties.

The Kalman filter is like an intelligent assistant that helps you make the best guess about the current state of something you are interested in tracking, such as the location of a moving car or the temperature in a room, even when your measurements have some errors or noise.

A Kalman filter combines measurement data with prior knowledge to produce an accurate estimate of a system's state. The process begins by capturing one or more measurements, which are assumed to contain inaccuracies due to the limitations of the components. In the prediction step, the current state and uncertainty are estimated using a mathematical model of the system and prior knowledge, such as physics-based principles or statistical data. In the update step, this prediction is refined by incorporating new measurements while accounting for uncertainties in both the prediction and the data. By continuously comparing new readings against prior knowledge and previous estimates, the filter maintains an optimal balance between the predicted and measured states. This dynamic process ensures an improved and continuously evolving output estimate. The sequence of the prediction and update steps is illustrated in the following figure:

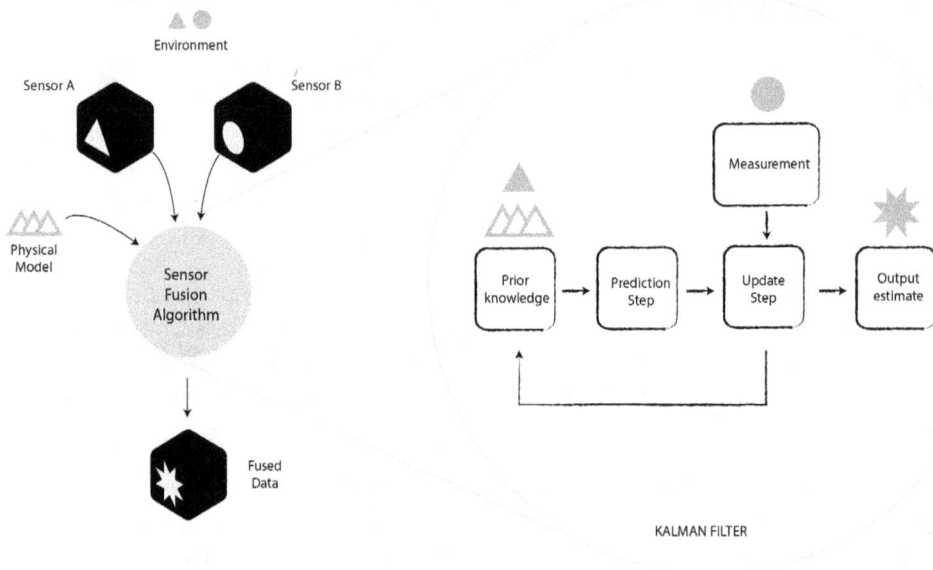

Figure 6.3: Sensor fusion algorithm

As an example, imagine you are trying to guess the speed of a bicycle as it moves past you while you have a slightly blurry vision. Each time you see the bike, you guess how fast it is going, but because of your blurry vision, you are not entirely sure if your guess is accurate. Here is where the Kalman filter steps in to help you make a better guess.

As mentioned before, the Kalman filter works in two main steps: Prediction and update:

1. **Prediction**: Based on what you already know about the bicycle's behavior (like its previous speed and direction), you predict its current speed and position. This is like saying, based on how fast it was going a moment ago, I think it should be here now.

2. **Update**: Then, you take a new observation or measurement of the bicycle's position. Because of your blurry vision, this measurement is not perfect. The Kalman filter combines your prediction with this new, noisy measurement to make a new and improved guess about the bicycle's speed and position. It does this by weighing its confidence in the prediction and the measurement. If your prediction is usually reliable, it will trust it more; if the measurements are generally accurate, it will lean more on them.

The beauty of the Kalman filter is in how it balances these two things (the predictions and the measurements) to adjust its guesses. Over time, as it gets more information, it becomes better at predicting the state of whatever it is tracking. It is like gradually adjusting your glasses to see the bicycle more clearly, helping you make more accurate guesses about its speed, even if each measurement is not perfect.

Use case: Scoring

Sensor fusion is often employed in situations where directly measuring a metric is not possible. In this use case, there are multiple levels of sensor fusion: the first level combines the readings from individual sensors, while the second level integrates the indices from multiple areas into a single aggregated score.

Degree of comfort score for shelters

Problem definition: A shelter located in New York City is taking proactive steps to enhance the living conditions of its guests by focusing on the degree of comfort monitoring within its premises. The primary objective is to ensure that guests enjoy a comfortable experience throughout their stay. The shelter has decided to implement a system that measures comfort based on a combination of humidity and temperature **(Humidex Index)**. This system is designed to communicate the comfort conditions clearly and concisely to various stakeholders, including the guests and staff.

The **Humidex Score** is a comprehensive metric that provides a singular numerical value representing the overall degree of comfort within the shelter. This index is calculated based on humidity and temperature levels present in a room. These factors play a significant role in determining the shelter's health, comfort, and safety conditions, making their monitoring crucial.

To ensure a thorough assessment of the degree of comfort, Humidex must be calculated in each room and common area within the shelter. The Humidex scores should be provided to the operations staff in near real time, allowing for targeted actions to improve comfort in a timely fashion where necessary. A general comfort-building score has also been requested to offer a location-based performance scorecard. The building-level score will be published publicly to stakeholders for transparency and accountability.

Solution: The solution consists of a network of standalone clusters of sensors. Each set contains all the sensors necessary to capture the data and perform sensor fusion to generate the Humidex index for each space in the shelter. Refer to the following figure:

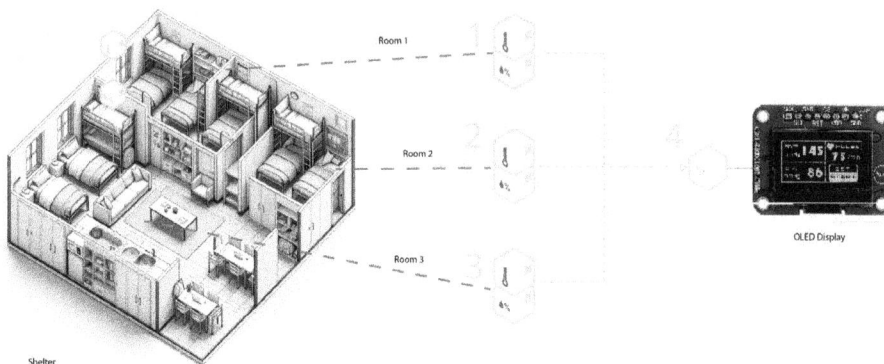

Figure 6.4: Concept diagram (Degree of comfort)

Each cluster will transmit sensor fusion output to a centralized device that will aggregate them using a weighted average to generate the building-level comfort score, effectively executing sensor fusion at that level.

Data acquisition

Each room (to be monitored) will have a device capable of capturing humidity and temperature readings. The device is a microcontroller that communicates with each one of the sensors by polling every 20 seconds. Each sensor reading is filtered after acquisition using a simple Kalman filter corrected by the comfort index generated in the last reading. The microcontroller keeps two buffers in parallel (one per metric). Each buffer holds the last two readings of each metric. The buffers allow the metrics from the different sensors to arrive at slightly different times. In the case of a faulty sensor, if fresh data does not make it to its buffer for more than two readings, it will be flushed to avoid misleading results. In the event of a missing sensor, we could be misleading the user into believing the comfort index is okay if we do not emphasize that data is missing. Therefore, the node will output an error value if at least one sensor is missing instead of trying to compensate for the missing ones. Please notice that while technically speaking, we could try to infer the missing sensor with the rest of the readings (check *Chapter 7, Deep Learning Regression* to learn how to do it) because this is an application that could affect the health of a person, it is preferable to return an error.

The training set includes an equal number of space temperature and relative humidity readings, as shown in *Figure 6.5*:

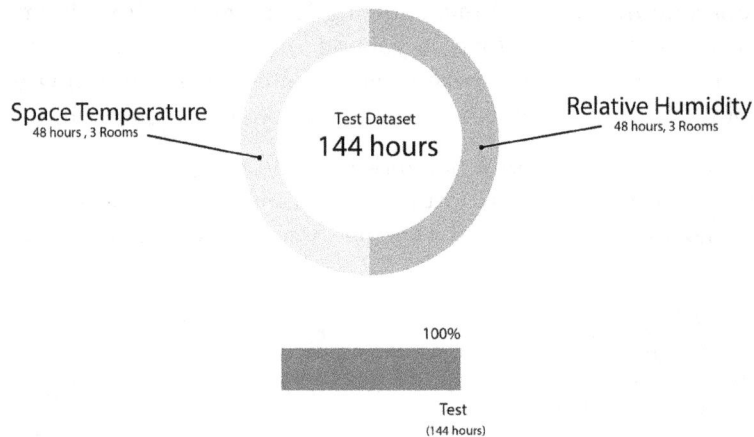

Figure 6.5: *Training data set (Degree of comfort)*

Processing

Once the metrics have been captured and available in the buffers, we calculate the comfort index. The frequency at which this calculation is run is extremely low (1/60 Hz) if you compare it to the frequencies we used for sound or movement analysis (*Chapter 2, Sound Classification and Chapter 3, Movement Classification*). The reason is that we are only interested in events that span more than a few minutes. The humidity % could drop and rise instantaneously because of specific events like somebody momentarily opening a window. However, the goal of the project is to provide insight to the operations team in charge of improving the living conditions of the shelter on situations they can address. Such teams are so busy that they will not be able to attend and troubleshoot transient events. Instead, if they see a trend where the comfort index starts getting worse in a room, they will compare it against neighboring spaces and be able to isolate the root of the problem. For that reason, capturing data every 30 seconds and running calculations every minute or so is sufficient for the goals of this application.

The standard Humidex ranges and their corresponding degree of comfort are listed in the following figure:

HUMIDEX RANGE	DEGREE OF COMFORT
16-29	Comfort
30-39	No Comfort
40-45	Some Discomfort
46-54	Great Discomfort
55-60	Dangerous
61-65	Heat Stroke

Figure 6.6: Humidex range and degree of comfort

Humidex is a measurement of how hot humans feel. It is intended to express how the combined effects of warm temperature and humidity are perceived. It is an equivalent of the *Wind Chill Factor* but for warm environments.

The formula to calculate it requires only two inputs, relative humidity and temperature, as shown in the following equation:

$$h = T + \frac{5}{9} \times \left(6.112 \times 10^{7.5 \times \frac{T}{237.7+T}} \times \frac{RH}{100} - 10\right)$$

Calculating a new piece of information from a function that does not change in time is the most straightforward way of doing sensor fusion. Simple, however, does not mean it is easy; data from multiple sources must be available simultaneously and not be corrupt.

Once we obtain the comfort index from each one of the rooms, it is time to generate the building level comfort score. We could feel tempted to average the **Indoor Air Quality Index (IAQI)** from all rooms and output that. However, we need to consider the goals of the building level score, which are to communicate to stakeholders how comfortable the shelter is in real time. Comfort is based on human perception. Let us assume that the score is equivalent to the results from a poll performed by asking all the guests to rate their comfort level from 0 to 5. We must give more weight to larger groups' rooms to reflect this in the equation. The same goes for common areas that everybody shares. Comfortable common areas also affect the perception of the entire population. We will add a factor that will be multiplied by the humidex index of every room. The following equation will calculate the factor:

$$Fn = G / R$$

Where G is the number of guests living in that room, and R is the average room size for that shelter.

For example, a room for six people in a shelter where the average room size is four and weighs $6/4 = 1.5$. A space for four people in the same shelter weighs $4/4 = 1$. A room for two people in the same shelter weighs $2/4 = 0.5$.

The comfort index for those three bedrooms, assuming the first room has a score of 15, the second a score of 23, and the third a score of 40, would be.

$((1.5 \times 15) + (1 \times 23) + (0.5 \times 40))/3 = 21.8$

This raw **Degree of Comfort** score calculation is performed in the device that receives the comfort indices from the sensor devices scattered around the shelter. To obtain the final output, we pass the building score through a Kalman filter which will consider past readings. The output is a corrected version of the Degree of Comfort score for the building.

System implementation

The system is composed of two primary components. The initial component (Block 1) is dedicated to data acquisition. In contrast, the second (Block 2) is the aggregation component, tasked with collating data from each room to compute an overall score for the entire building as shown in the following figure:

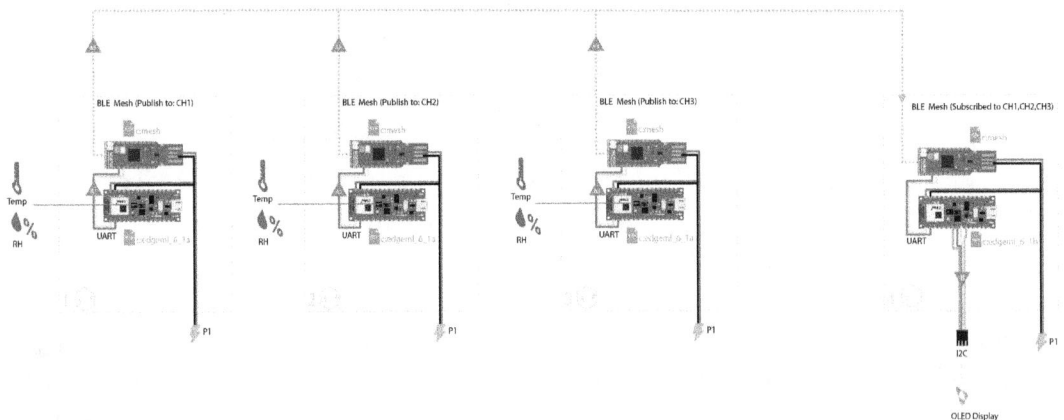

Figure 6.7: Connection diagram (Degree of comfort)

The data acquisition components are powered by an Arduino Nano 33 BLE Sense, equipped with a **Relative Humidity** (**RH**) sensor and a temperature sensor. This setup allows for direct data collection without the need for external devices. Each room to be monitored will have its instance of this data acquisition unit. Each calculates the humidex index independently and sends the score to the central aggregation component.

The aggregation component utilizes an Arduino Nano 33 BLE and gathers data from each room. It does this by tuning into the specific channels on which the rooms broadcast their data within a BLE Mesh Network, allowing for a direct stream of information from every monitored room. Each room is assigned a unique channel, facilitating the aggregation unit's ability to discern the source of data not by the content of the messages but through the channels they are received on. To manage memory efficiently, the aggregation unit keeps only the recent two scores from each data acquisition unit.

For simplicity, the overall score calculated for the building is displayed on an OLED screen connected to the aggregation component.

Source code

Presenting the pseudocode of an algorithm helps you understand the fundamental principles of the software without being tied to the specifics of any programming language. Once the pseudocode is clear, it can be implemented on different platforms or used as a basis to generate code with the help of AI. A highly effective way to present pseudocode is by using columns to represent specific components and arrows to indicate the flow of information between them. In the following tables, the main components are the data buffer, which captures and holds the data, and the sensor fusion component, which executes the Kalman filter:

c:tinyml_6_1a	Code location: Arduino Nano 33 BLE @ Block 1-3
	Capturing RH and temperature and calculating the comfort index. Pseudocode 1. The microcontroller polls the relative humidity and temperature sensors. Readings are received and stored in a buffer. 2. The sensor fusion function pulls the readings from the buffer and calculates the humidex index. 3. The index is sent to the networking microcontroller for the message to be sent to the aggregator.

Table 6.1: Pseudocode (Degree of comfort)

c:tinyml_6_1b	Code location: **Arduino Nano 33 BLE @ Block 4**
	Receiving data from every room, calculating the building wide comfort score. Pseudocode 1. The device subscribes to the channels of every room, receives synchronous messages, and organizes inputs in an array. 2. The general comfort score is calculated using a weighted average. 3. Data is sent to the driver in charge of the OLED display. The score is displayed.

Table 6.2: Source code (Degree of comfort)

Network

The Blocks communicate asynchronously using a subscription-publication paradigm. Blocks 1-3 are data producers while Block 4 is a data consumer. This can be implemented in various types of low energy mesh networks like BLE Mesh. Refer to the following table:

Block(s)	Action	Channel
1-3	Publish to	CH1-CH3
4	Subscribes to	CH1-CH3

Table 6.3: Asyncrhronous communication between Blocks (Degree of comfort)

Power analysis

For Block 1:

Power source	Device	Latent consumption	Active consumption	Notes
P1	Arduino Nano 33 BLE Sense	0.032A @5V	< 1A @5V	
P1	NRF52 Dongle	0.04mA @5v	3mA @5v	Active when publishing messages as a *client*.

Table 6.4: Power requirements for Block 1 (Degree of comfort)

Block 1 can be powered by a battery if the refresh rate is kept low enough (e.g., capturing and calculating the index only once an hour). However, the battery would eventually deplete and require replacement, creating an operational burden for the facility team. An alternative is to power the sensor directly using a 5V power source from the electrical installation. While this provides a permanent solution, it requires the involvement of an electrician, which could increase the capital expenses of the installation.

For Block 2:

Power source	Device	Latent consumption	Active consumption	Notes
P2	NRF52 Dongle	0.04mA @5v	0.3mA @5v	Active when receiving messages as a *server*.
P2	Arduino Nano 33 BLE	0.034mA @5V	< 1A @5V	Executes sensor fusion for the general score

Table 6.5: *Power requirements for Block 2 (Degree of comfort)*

A permanent 1A power source is required for Block 2, as it needs to actively listen for messages from the various data capture components (Block 1) distributed throughout the building.

Bill of materials

The following table provides an approximate reference for the quantity and cost of elements needed to create a proof of concept that calculates the **Comfort** score from a sample of 10 rooms:

Description	QTY	Unit cost	Total
Arduino Nano 33 BLE Sense	10	$45 (n=10 for pilot program)	$450
Arduino Nano 33 BLE	1	$30	$30
NRF52840 Dongle	10+1	$12	$132
OLED Display	1	$5	$5
Power Source 1A @5v	10+1	$30	$330

Table 6.6: *Bill of materials (Degree of comfort)*

Approximate cost of materials is $947.

Use case: Profiling

A great use case for sensor fusion is augmenting existing readings with inferred readings. This may be necessary when it is physically impossible to place a sensor in a specific location (e.g., measuring the temperature inside a rocket engine) or when installing too many sensors is economically unfeasible.

Temperature profiling in a commercial building

Problem definition: The owner of a recently renovated commercial building wants to create a temperature profile of each floor before commissioning a new **heating, ventilation, and air conditioning (HVAC)** implementation. They require a detailed understanding of the temperature distribution across each building floor to achieve this. The HVAC designer working on this project has enlisted your expertise to install a temporary network of wireless sensors. These sensors should help capture a comprehensive temperature profile that shows the temperature distribution on the floor plan and its rate of change in time across the day.

Given that this is a temporary setup, it is essential to maintain cost-effectiveness while deploying the sensor network. The primary challenge is creating a representative temperature profile for each floor without installing an excessive number of sensors. The number of sensors and their placement within the floor plan must be carefully considered. On one hand, we don't need a sensor in every corner and crevice, as sensor fusion allows us to infer data for unmeasured areas. On the other hand, sensor fusion cannot generate data where no input exists, so at least one or two sensors must capture temperature variations in every space being profiled.

The following figure illustrates the concept being developed in this use case: multiple sensors placed in different areas of the location and a sensor fusion Block that generates the inferred readings:

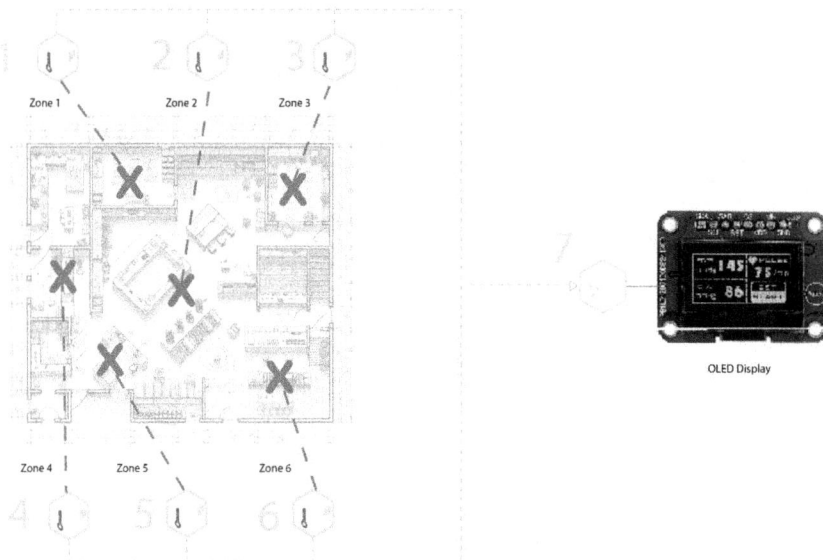

Figure 6.8: Concept diagram (Temperature profiling)

Solution: The solution involves installing a wireless sensor network that captures temperature data across every floor. There are two advantages to creating independent setups per floor. The first one is that the sensor fusion algorithm will be more straightforward as it will not have to handle grouping and managing data from different floors. Typically, air handling units control every floor independently, so having a temperature profile per floor makes sense. The second reason is that low-powered sensor networks struggle to cross thick concrete floors. Having standalone setups per floor eliminates this problem, avoiding the need for complex network architectures. Once we have a setup for one floor, we can replicate it on as many floors as needed.

Each temperature sensor will be placed strategically, representing a particular temperature zone of the floorplan. For example, one of the sensors would be placed by the windows, another in the kitchen, and another by the entrance.

The sensor fusion solution's analytical part uses a Kalman filter to estimate the actual floor temperature by combining multiple readings and estimating the temperature rate of change for every zone. This is useful for designers to understand what parts of the floor loose or gain temperature faster than the others.

Data acquisition

Acquiring multiple readings of the same floor brings up the interesting challenge of simultaneously keeping all the devices synchronized to output the same timestamp. Microcontrollers do not have dedicated **real-time clocks** (**RTCs**) for accurate long-term timekeeping; instead, they have timers. These timers count the number of machine cycles from the microcontroller and infer the length of a second from it. If you have a point of reference in time, you can add seconds using the MCU timers. The problem is that this is, at best, an approximation; the time will often drift away because the microcontroller is using its cores for other tasks. A dedicated clock called RTC is added as a peripheral to each microcontroller to address this issue. A real time clock uses a dedicated crystal to measure the passing of time with high accuracy and usually has an integrated battery that allows it to keep track of time even if the microcontroller is reset or turned off. Once you have the RTCs in place, you need to ensure that all the RTCs have the same time and date. To do that, one of the sensors broadcasts its timestamp every minute. The rest of the sensors will update their RTC based on that timestamp.

Each sensor stores its raw readings and timestamps on an SD card for analysis after the temperature profiling has been completed. The training set consists of 1,008 hours of readings from six different areas on a commercial building floor. Refer to the following figure:

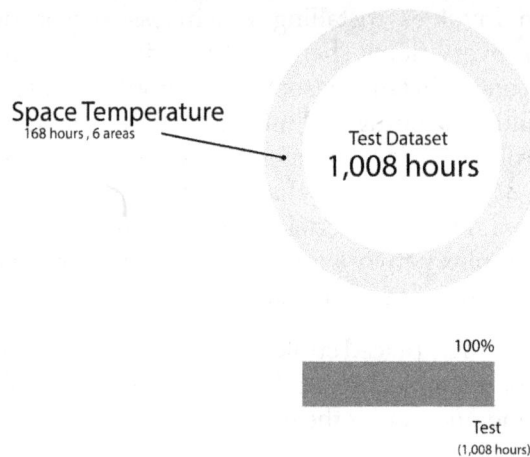

Figure 6.9: *Training set (Temperature profiling)*

Processing

In this use case, we will use the Kalman filter to calculate the true temperature (remember that sensors are noisy) and the rate of temperature change in the measured zone. A zone with a high-temperature change rate cannot hold temperature easily. On the contrary, an area with a low rate of temperature change indicates a space where temperature does not swing so easily. The analysis does not try to explain why this is the case; it just shows it is happening. A more thorough thermodynamic analysis, which is outside the scope of this book, might reveal the root cause of the temperature swings that the nearby windows, insulation, floor materials, or geometry of the space could be causing. Notice how the Kalman filter is helping us calculate states that cannot be measured directly.

Temperature and rates of change states will be calculated independently for every zone. The location of a sensor represents a zone.

The sensor fusion algorithm works as follows:

1. We combine each sensor reading with its immediate neighbors using a multiple-input Kalman filter. This works by making one prediction per reading and as many corrections as sensors participating in the aggregation. This way, every sensor contributes independently to calculate the true temperature state. *Figure 6.10* shows the raw readings. The output is a single timeseries that represents the corrected temperature for a given space. We will input that timeseries to the next step. Refer to the following figure:

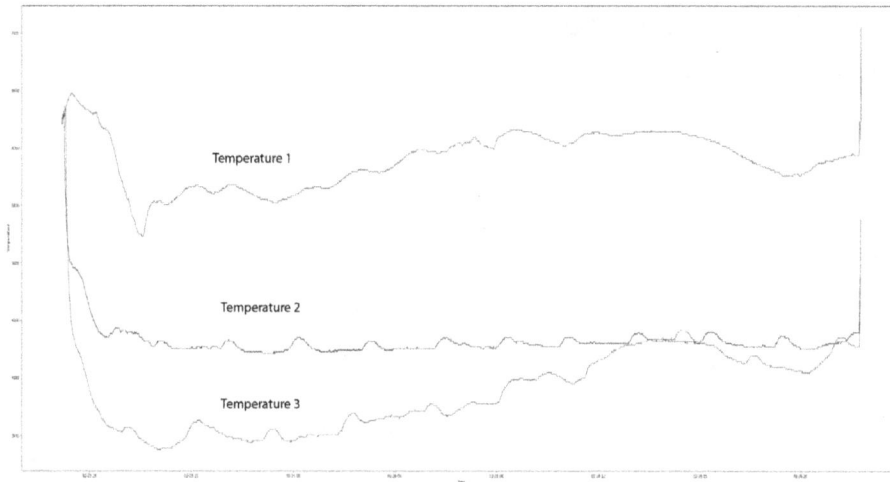

Figure 6.10: *Multiple sensor input (Temperature profiling)*

2. Using the output from the previous step, we calculate the rate of temperature change by determining the derivative of temperature over time. This is achieved by calculating the difference between the current and predicted temperatures and dividing it by the time interval between the two states. A Kalman filter is used for this process, where the **State Transition Matrix** incorporates the differential equation that translates the rate of change predictions into the current state, which is then corrected using the latest measurements. *Figure 6.11* illustrates the output of the first stage of fusion (Fusion 1) and its derivative (Fusion 2). The physical interpretation of the derivative is the room's ability to retain temperature. Engineers use this information to design HVAC equipment and make architectural improvements.

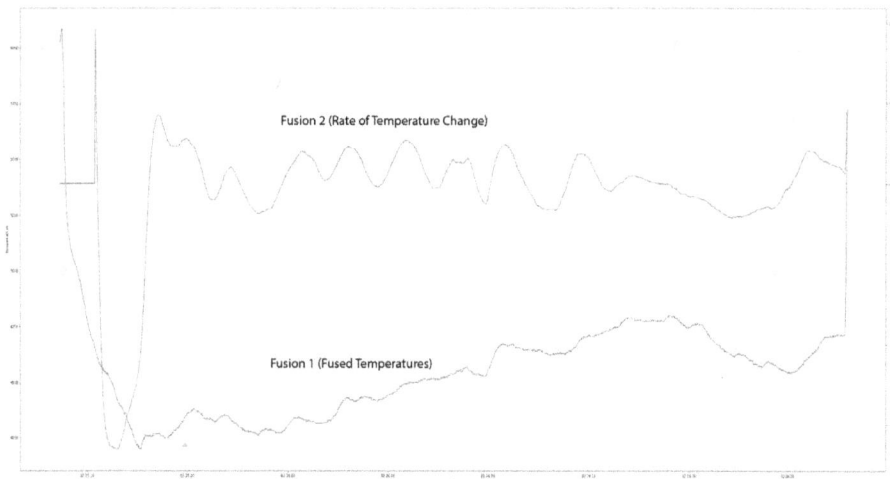

Figure 6.11: *Fused temperature and rate of change (Temperature profiling)*

System implementation

Refer to the following figure:

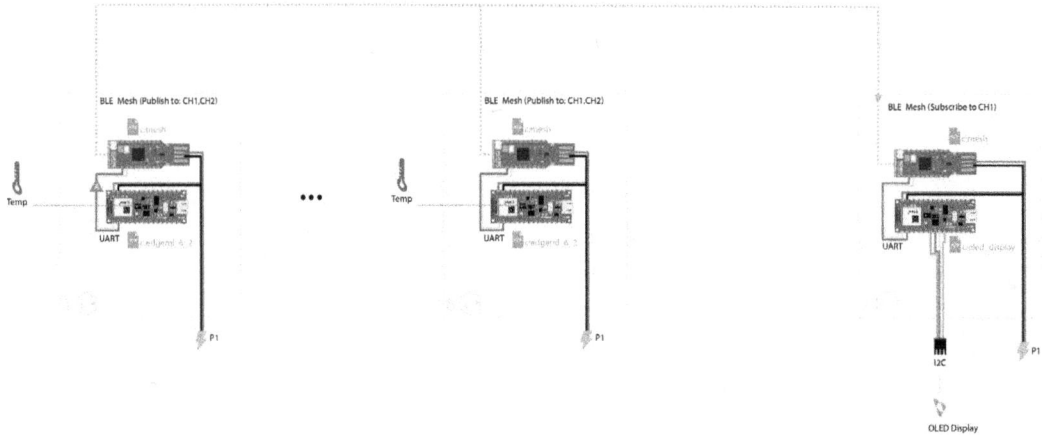

Figure 6.12: Connection diagram (Temperature profiling)

This use case is implemented using several data acquisition units that communicate with each other to exchange temperature readings. This collaboration enables local sensor fusion with the aggregated data saved to an SD card.

Each unit has a temperature sensor and an SD card module for data logging connected to the main microcontroller board via the I2C protocol. A timer in the main script triggers the scheduled temperature readings from the sensor. Additionally, a secondary microcontroller, the NRF52840, is integrated via **Universal Asynchronous Receiver-Transmitter (UART)** to handle the publication of the raw temperature data as soon as it is collected.

Furthermore, this secondary microcontroller is set up to receive updates from adjacent sensors, forwarding any new data to the primary microcontroller. This incoming data is then stored in a circular buffer, which the sensor fusion algorithm utilizes to calculate the most current temperature and its rate of change.

Source code

In the following table, the main components are the data processing component, which captures and holds the data, and the sensor fusion component, which executes the multi-sensor Kalman filter:

c:tinyml_6_2	Code location: **Arduino Nano 33 BLE @ Block 1**
	Capturing local temperature, capturing neighboring temperature, and performing sensor fusion, storing results in SD Card. Pseudocode 1. The microcontroller receives data from neighbor sensors and stores it in a buffer. 2. Sensor fusion algorithm fuses local temperature readings with neighbor sensor data. 3. Sensor fusion algorithm estimates the rate of temperature change. 4. Results are stored on an SD card.

Table 6.7: Pseudocode (Temperature profiling)

Network

The wireless network is particularly important for this use case, as it is a temporary network. This enables a proof of concept to be installed and begin generating insights on the same day. Block 1 consists of sensors that capture readings from other sibling Block 1 sensors.

Block(s)	Action	Channel
1	Publishes to	<Own assigned Channel>
1	Subscribes to	<Neighbor Channels>

Table 6.8: Network configuration (Temperature profiling)

Power analysis

Due to the temporary nature of the profiling network, the Block 1 must operate on batteries. Polling data at 1Hz, storing it on an SD card, and publishing messages to a mesh network are all power-intensive operations. However, certain optimizations can be implemented to extend battery life, such as using a larger battery, reducing the frequency or putting the node to sleep between readings.

Power source	Device	Latent consumption	Active consumption	Notes
P1	Arduino Nano 33 BLE Sense	0.032A @5V	< 1A @5V	Arduino will be polling temperature sensors and storing data on an SD Card continuously (1Hz) continuously (1Hz)
P1	NRF52 Dongle	0.04mA @5v	3mA @5v	The dongle will publish and receive messages from subscriptions at about 1Hz.

Table 6.9: Power profile (Temperature profiling)

Bill of materials

Assuming a temperature profiling network consisting of 9 sensors and a data aggregator, the following table provides an approximate bill of materials, including microcontrollers, sensors, power sources, and SD loggers.

Description	QTY	Unit cost	Total
Arduino Nano 33 BLE	10	$30	$300
NRF52840 Dongle	10	$12	$120
Temperature Sensor	10	$6	$60
SD Card Logger	10	$19	$190
128 Mb SD Card	10	$5	$50

Table 6.10: Bill of materials (Temperature profiling)

Approximate cost of materials is $720.

Use case: Correction

A common application of sensor fusion is using a complementary sensor to correct errors and drift in a calculation. This is achieved by calculating the same metric two different ways (one for each sensor type) and then giving more weight to one or the other based on the uncertainties associated with each. These uncertainties are represented as covariances in the filter's mathematical model.

Accelerometer and gyroscope for drones

Problem definition: A consumer electronics company is developing a new product: a compact flying drone equipped with a camera. This innovative drone incorporates an advanced **Inertial Measurement Unit (IMU)**, essential for its operation. The IMU provides precise readings of the drone's motion, including acceleration and gyroscope data across three axes (X, Y, and Z). These measurements are crucial for understanding and controlling the drone's movements in real time.

The sensor fusion component in this use case is self-contained in the drone informing its navigation systems. The following concept diagram shows no communication or links to an external device:

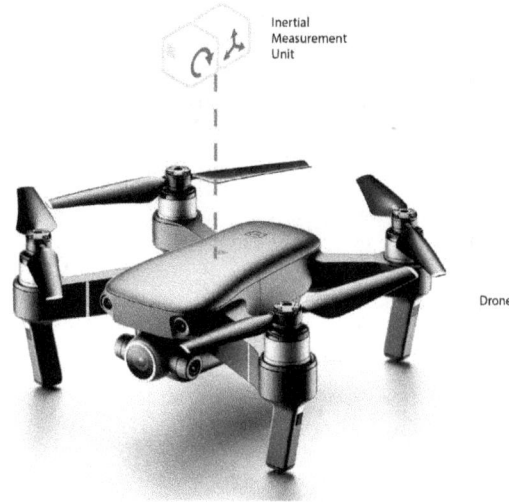

Figure 6.13: *Concept diagram (Gyroscope correction)*

One of the primary uses of the gyroscope readings is to determine the drone's attitude, which refers to its orientation in space at any given moment. Accurate attitude information is vital for stable flight and effective maneuvering. However, the design team encountered a significant challenge during the testing phase. They observed that the angle readings from the gyroscope began to drift over time during the flight. As the flight progressed, the drift became more severe, eventually making the readings unreliable and the drone unusable.

Solution: The team is exploring a sensor fusion solution to address this angle drift issue. sensor fusion is a method that combines data from multiple sensors to improve the accuracy of the overall system. In this case, the proposed solution involves using the accelerometer readings to correct the drift experienced in the gyroscope data. By integrating the accelerometer data with the gyroscope readings, the team aims to achieve a more stable and accurate measurement of the drone's pitch and roll angles. This correction is essential to ensure the drone's reliable performance and operational stability.

The readings on an inertial measurement unit will be sent to a microcontroller running a Kalman filter that will correct the gyroscope readings with real-time data from a set of accelerometers. The output will be a corrected signal indicating the actual **Roll and Pitch** angles. The signal will be sent to the drone's central controller.

Data acquisition

There are six data points of interest coming from the IMU: The X, Y, and Z gyroscope readings and the X, Y, and Z readings of the accelerometers. The frequency of acquisition is 62,5Hz (one reading every 16ms) as shown in the *Figure 6.14*. We are using the Arduino Nano 33 BLE Sense LSM9DS1 IMU and performing the real-time calculations. Sensor fusion allows us to disregard the raw data and only save the last state of the Kalman filter.

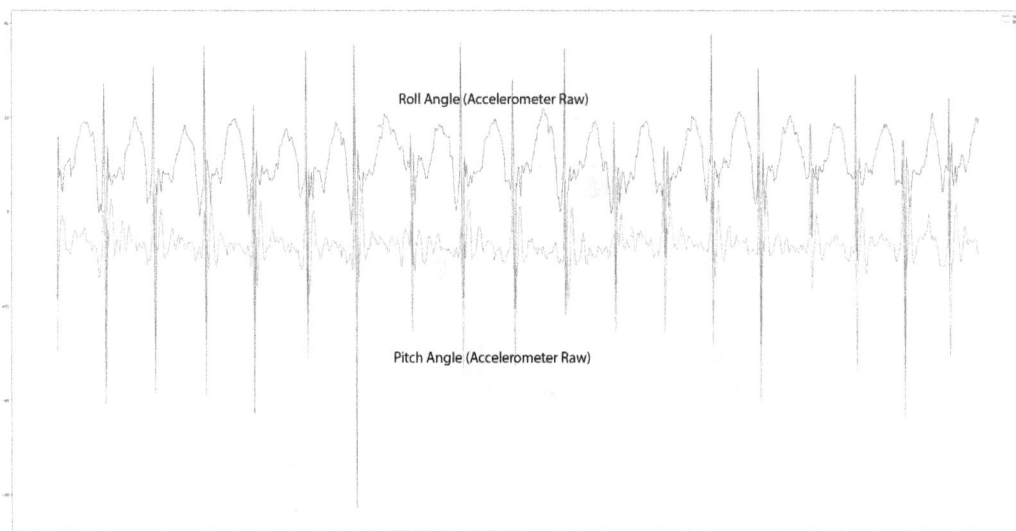

Figure 6.14: *High frequency roll and pitch readings*

The test dataset is conformed from 6 data points: X, Y and Z accelerometers and X, Y and Z gyroscopes as shown in the following figure:

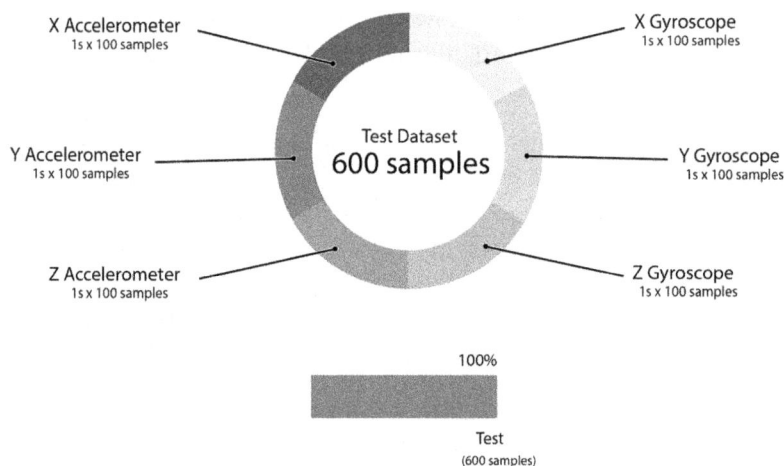

Figure 6.15: *Training dataset (Gyroscope correction)*

Processing

A notable limitation of gyroscopes is their lack of a stable reference point, leading to a measurement drift over time. While precise in detecting any form of acceleration, accelerometers can produce misleading rotation angles due to their sensitivity to all movements. However, accelerometers benefit from a reliable reference point: the constant gravitational pull of the Earth.

We will employ sensor fusion techniques to counteract each sensor type's shortcomings. This approach will generate a refined set of roll and pitch angles by harnessing the gyroscope's accuracy and accelerometer's stable reference point, effectively mitigating drift and enhancing the overall precision.

Before we can use the gyroscope and the accelerometer's readings in the Kalman filter, we must perform several transformations.

First, we must translate the gyroscope's raw data to physical units by dividing the readings by 131. The digital signal from the gyroscope returns a signed 16-bit integer with values between -32768 and +32767. According to the IMU spec, that range represents -250 to 250 degrees/second values. In other words, if we divide 32767/250, we get 131.072, the value of 1 degree/second. Notice that the gyroscope does not return an angle but an angular speed. Later, we will transform that speed to an angle the filter can use.

The next step is to calculate the roll and pitch angles from the accelerometer readings that we will use to correct the gyroscope angles. We could calculate the total acceleration vector (using the Pythagorean theorem with its components) and then calculate the angle from the component to the X and Z axis. A more straightforward way to do it is to use the **arcTan( )** function, where we can input the component values directly. The result will be in radians. Multiply the result by 180/Pi to convert it to degrees.

The first step of the Kalman filter consists of estimating the pitch and roll angles from the gyroscope input. It converts the angular speed to an angle. Assuming that the body is not accelerating during the small period between readings, it multiplies the rate by the time between this reading and the next to obtain the traveled angle. The roll angle corresponds to the angle traveled around the X-axis, and the pitch angle corresponds to the angle traveled around the Z-axis. To understand this better, let us look at the following figure:

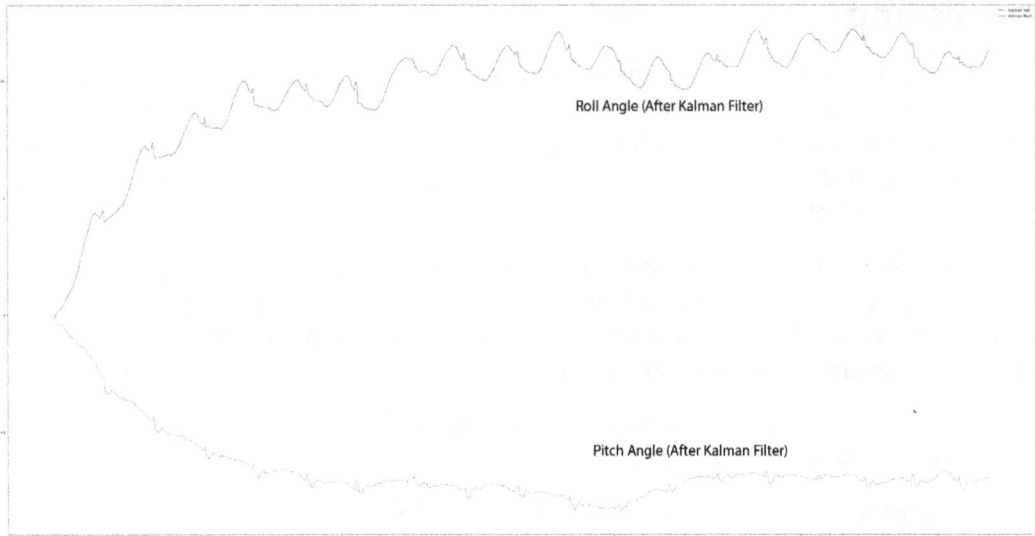

Figure 6.16: Roll and pitch angles after Kalman filter

The Kalman filter then estimates the measurement error covariance and the estimation error covariance matrices. In other words, it figures out who it should trust more: the estimations obtained from the gyroscope data or the readings obtained from the accelerometer. It outputs its decision in the form of a factor called **Kalman Gain**. The Kalman Gain will give more weight to one or the other but still consider both sets of angles. The output is the true roll and pitch angles of the drone obtained from fusing the gyroscope and accelerometer as shown in the following figure:

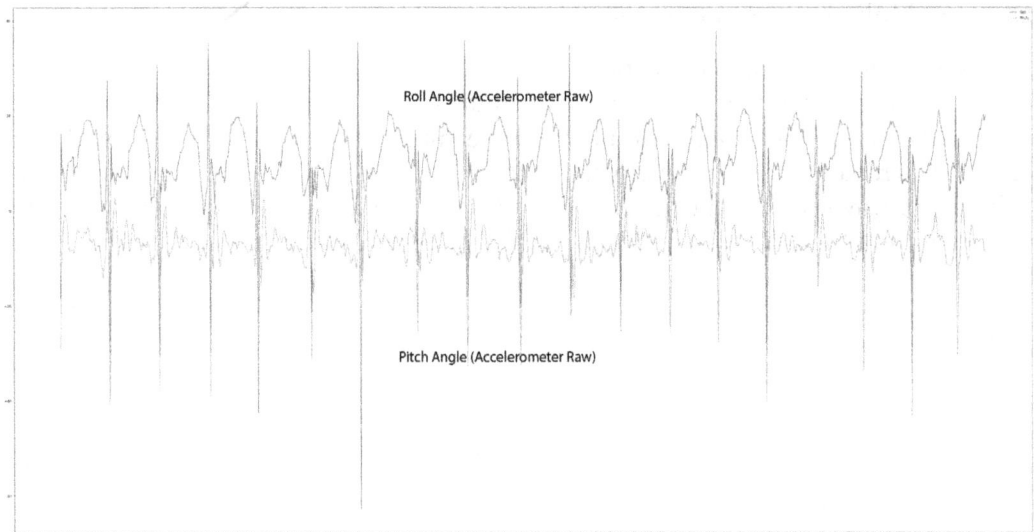

Figure 6.17: True pitch and roll angles

System implementation

The implementation consists of a single Block containing an Arduino Nano 33 BLE receiving its IMU's accelerometer and gyroscope readings. Refer to the following figure:

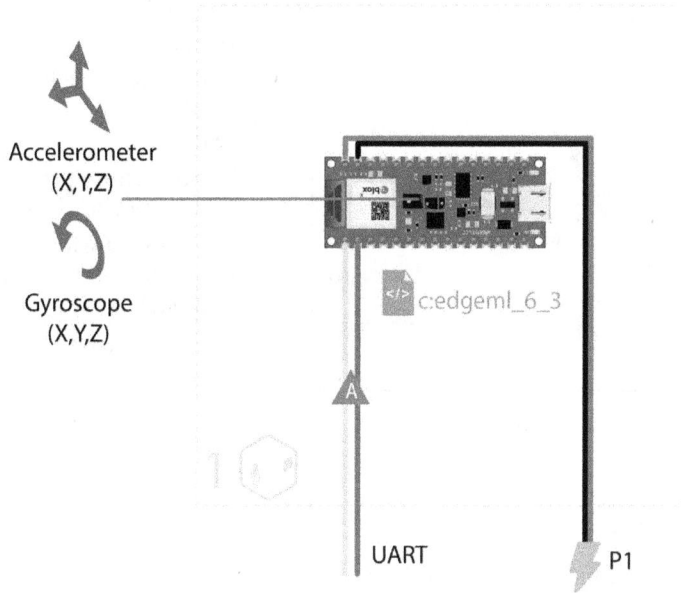

Figure 6.18: Connection diagram (Gyroscope correction)

The sensor fusion algorithm runs in the Arduino microcontroller (NRF52840), and its outputs are sent to the drone using a UART interface. This setup is simple because we need to make it as light as possible, as it adds to the overall weight of the drone.

Source code

The pseudocode highlights three main components. The first is the data buffer, which in this case captures readings at a high frequency, unlike the previous use cases. The preprocessing component operates at the same frequency to capture input but does not necessarily output features at the same frequency. In some cases, it may return an averaged window to reduce the output frequency. This is critical because not all sensors generate data at the same frequency. The sensor fusion component requires normalized data (e.g., both accelerometer and gyroscope readings must have the same order of magnitude and frequency to avoid bias). Once the sensor fusion component processes the data, it calculates and returns the true roll and pitch in the output. Refer to the following table:

c:tinyml_6_3	Code location: Arduino Nano 33 BLE @ Block 1
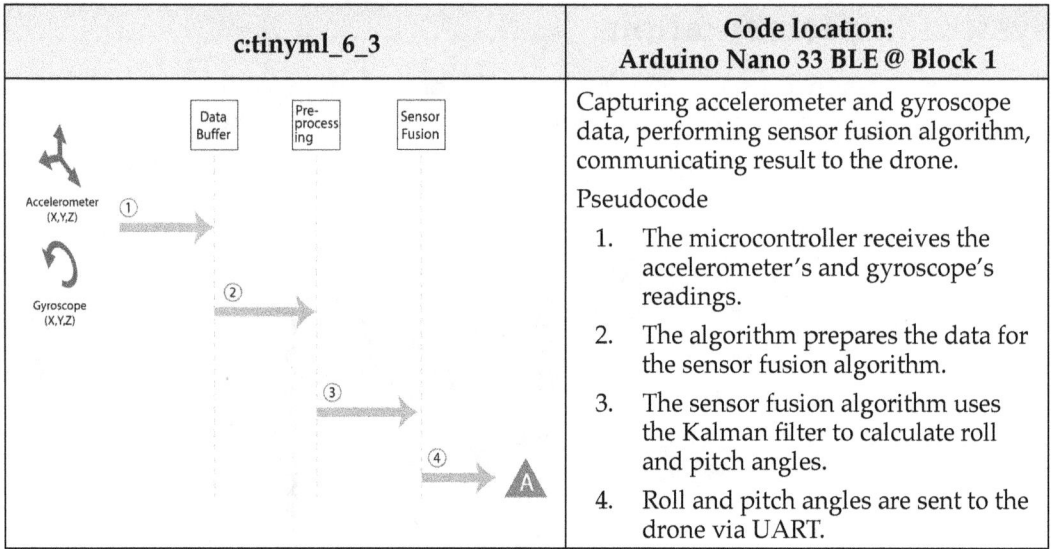	Capturing accelerometer and gyroscope data, performing sensor fusion algorithm, communicating result to the drone. Pseudocode 1. The microcontroller receives the accelerometer's and gyroscope's readings. 2. The algorithm prepares the data for the sensor fusion algorithm. 3. The sensor fusion algorithm uses the Kalman filter to calculate roll and pitch angles. 4. Roll and pitch angles are sent to the drone via UART.

Table 6.11: Pseudocode (Gyroscope correction)

Power analysis

For Block 1: Because this is a self-contained component, it will depend on the drone battery to operate. Navigation systems require real time angle calculations, this would not allow for certain power optimizations like sleep modes or low frequencies. Refer to the following table:

Power source	Device	Latent consumption	Active consumption	Notes
P1	Arduino Nano 33 BLE	0.034mA @5V	< 1A @5V	IMU is active 100% of the time UART sends data in real time.

Table 6.12: Power analysis (Gyroscope correction)

Bill of materials

Components like the Arduino Nano 33 BLE come with embedded gyroscopes and accelerometers.

Description	QTY	Unit cost	Total
Arduino Nano 33 BLE	1	$30	$30

Table 6.13: Bill of materials (Gyroscope correction)

Approximate cost of materials is 30.

Conclusion

This chapter introduced the concept of sensor fusion by explaining the inner workings of the Kalman filter. However, there are many other specialized filters that may be better suited for specific cases. The use cases demonstrate the diversity of real-life sensor fusion applications, including the chaining of sensor fusion, the augmentation of readings, and the ability to correct metrics in real time.

In the next chapter, we will discuss Deep Learning regression, which, similar to sensor fusion, is able to use one or multiple inputs to generate one or more numeric values.

References

- O. Univ.-Prof. Dr. Hermann Kopetz Institut fur Technische Informatik 182 **https://mobile.aau.at/~welmenre/papers/elmenreich_Dissertation_ sensorFusionInTimeTriggeredSystems.pdf**

- H. F. Durrant-Whyte. Toward a Fully Decentralized Architecture for Multi-Sensor Data Fusion. In IEEE International Conference on Robotics and Automation, volume 2, pages 1331–1336, Cincinnati, OH, USA, 1990.

- Humidex, **https://www.ccohs.ca/oshanswers/phys_agents/humidex.html**

- Kalman filter, Alex Becker, **https://www.kalmanfilter.net/kalman1d.html**

- **Sensor fusion use case 1:** https://studio.edgeimpulse.com/public/350891/live

- **Sensor fusion use case 2: https://studio.edgeimpulse.com/public/350888/live**

- **Sensor fusion use case 3: https://studio.edgeimpulse.com/public/350887/live**

Join our book's Discord space

Join the book's Discord Workspace for Latest updates, Offers, Tech happenings around the world, New Release and Sessions with the Authors:

https://discord.bpbonline.com

CHAPTER 7

Deep Learning Regression

Introduction

Deep learning regression is a machine learning technique that uses deep Neural Networks to predict continuous values. In this approach, the algorithm learns to map input data to a continuous output (e.g., real numbers) rather than classifying data into categories.

This technique is named after its similarity to traditional regression methods, such as linear regression or polynomial regression. These methods establish a mathematical equation to transform an independent variable (X) into a dependent variable (Y) using a set of data samples.

Figure 7.1 illustrates the three steps involved in performing regression. First, we acquire a training dataset that represents the behavior we want to model. Next, we generate a model that captures and codifies that behavior. Finally, we use the trained model to infer new data points.

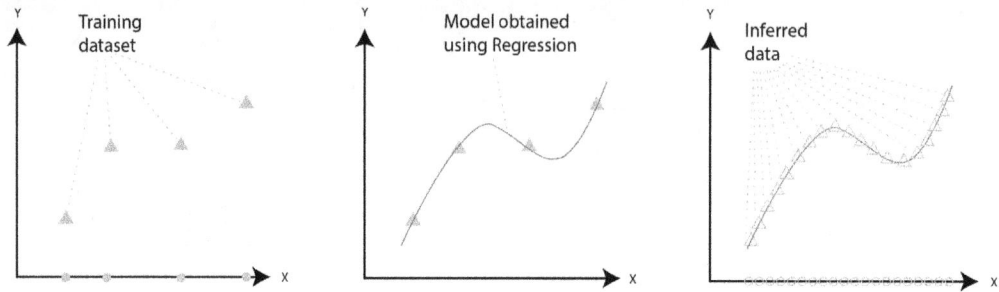

Figure 7.1: Regression

Structure

The chapter covers the following topics:

- Non linearity
- Preparing data for regression
- Training the regression model
- Use case: Controlling
- Use case: Forecasting
- Use case: Estimating

Objectives

The main objective of this chapter is to help you understand how deep learning regression can be used to create systems capable of learning non-linear relationships directly from data. This serves as a fundamental building Block for teaching a system almost anything from a set of examples. We will demonstrate this concept by teaching a greenhouse controller to manage its environment, implementing a thermostat that can predict future conditions, and determining the weight of an object using an image.

Non linearity

In deep learning regression, each neuron in the dense layers represents a linear equation defined by a weight (the slope) and a bias (the Y-axis intercept). These linear equations form the foundation of the network, computing a weighted sum of inputs. However, to capture more complex relationships and patterns in the data, the output of this weighted sum is passed through an activation function, typically a **Rectified Linear Unit (ReLU)**. While the weighted sum itself is a linear equation, the activation function introduces non-linearity, enabling the model to learn intricate patterns beyond simple linear relationships. A helpful metaphor for understanding this concept is a metal chain: while each link is straight, the entire chain can assume almost any shape (as shown in *Figure 7.2*). Similarly, while individual neurons perform simple linear computations, the collective network can model complex, non-linear functions with the help of their activation functions.

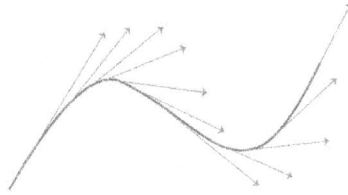

Figure 7.2: *Non-linear functions*

The training process involves passing all the data samples through the network multiple times. With each pass, the weights and biases of the neurons are adjusted to reduce the difference between the predicted and actual values (as shown in *Figure 7.3*). This iterative process is akin to refining a complex mathematical equation. The result is a trained Neural Network, a sophisticated model capable of predicting a wide range of values based on inputs. This network represents not just a single equation but a compilation of many, working in concert to effectively map inputs to outputs.

Figure 7.3: *Training process*

Inputs and outputs

Deep learning models are not limited to a single output. They can be designed to produce multiple outputs simultaneously, which is particularly beneficial for control scenarios requiring various actions based on environmental inputs. For instance, a deep learning regression model in a greenhouse can simultaneously adjust lights, fans, and water supply by analyzing factors like temperature, humidity, and light conditions. This multi-output capability enables a more integrated and responsive approach to managing and controlling complex systems.

Let us look at the following table to illustrate each type of regression based on inputs and outputs:

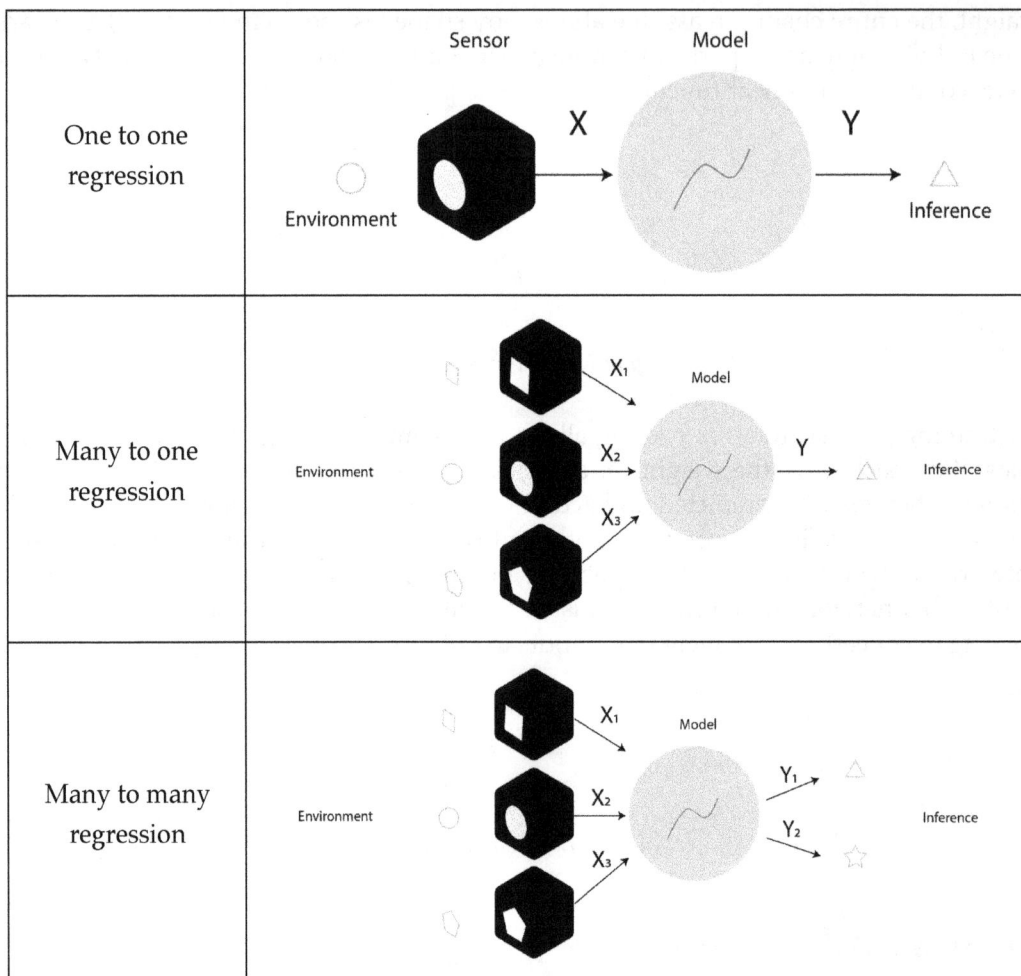

Table 7.1: Types of regression based on inputs and outputs

Preparing data for regression

Deep learning regression models can process diverse data types, including time series, shapes, images, and sound waves. However, before these varied inputs can be used, they must be converted into a numerical format compatible with **Dense Neural Networks**. If the resulting features come in different orders of magnitude, you should scale them. Scaling in machine learning refers to adjusting the range or distribution of variable values. This step is crucial because it ensures that features contribute equally to the analysis, preventing features with larger magnitudes from dominating the model's decision-making process. Scaling can enhance the model's stability and increase overall algorithm performance.

In the following figure, the left column shows readings before scaling, while the right column shows readings after scaling:

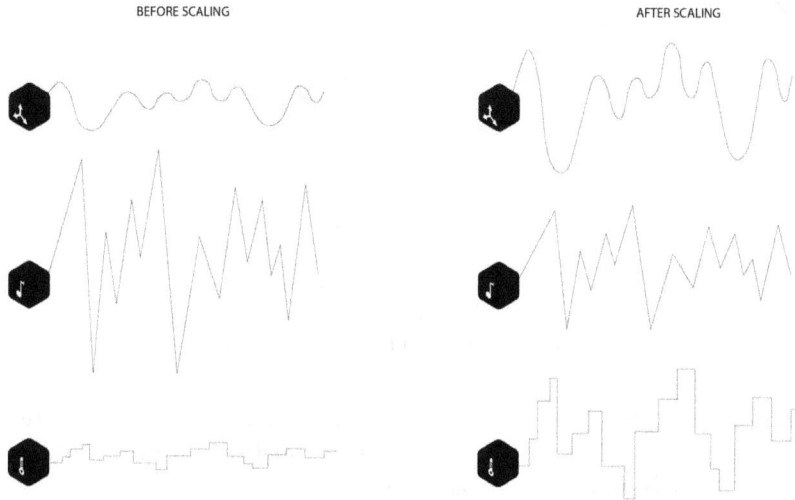

Figure 7.4: Scaling

Once the data has been scaled there are two main approaches to represent these features. A) as a single value: Each number is treated as a value, such as an integer or a normalized floating-point number. This approach is simpler, reduces dimensionality, and works well. B) As a bit-level representation. In this approach, each number is broken down into individual binary features (0s and 1s). This approach preserves the fine-grained details of the data and allows the model to capture relationships at the bit level, which may be critical for certain applications, such as cryptographic or hash-based data. Regardless of the chosen representation, it is essential to normalize or scale the features to a similar range (e.g., 0 to 1 or -1 to 1) to ensure the model performs efficiently and avoids numerical instability. Preparing the data requires converting all the input variables to a matrix that contains all the inputs in a row. Each row becomes one training sample. Then you would tag each row with the solution. The solution can be a single number (for **one to one** or **many to one** regressions) or a vector (for **one to many** or **many to many** regressions).

Training the regression model

A deep learning regression model differs significantly from a classification-oriented model. The key distinction is that, instead of producing categorical probabilities, the output is a continuous numeric value. As a result, no additional transformation is applied after the output layer to normalize values. The model directly generates numerical predictions that align with the scale of the label values used during training.

It is typical to use the **mean square error** to determine the regression error during training. In a deep learning regression, the most critical layers of the network are the dense layers. As part of the optimization process, you can include more hidden layers or make them wider. Refer to the following figure:

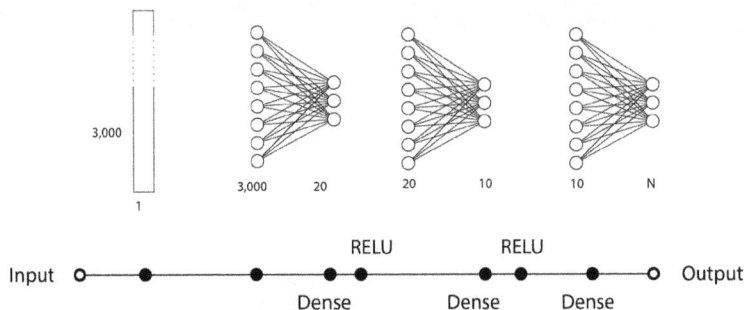

Figure 7.5: Regression Deep Neural Network

In traditional regression models, managing multiple inputs and outputs often presents a significant challenge due to the complexity of the relationships between variables. However, this complexity is much more manageable in a deep-learning regression approach. One needs to increase the number of neurons in the network's input layer to accommodate multiple inputs. Each additional neuron can process an extra feature. Similarly, the number of neurons in the output layer is expanded to handle multiple outputs. Each of these neurons is responsible for generating one of the desired outputs. This straightforward scalability is one of the critical advantages of deep learning regression, making it a flexible and powerful tool for handling complex, multi-dimensional data.

Use case: Controlling

A novel approach to control is to use deep learning regression to determine control metrics based on a set of inputs. The model is trained in advance with examples that demonstrate how outputs should behave given specific inputs, similar to teaching by example. In traditional control systems, this knowledge is encoded as explicit rules (e.g., 'if this, then that'). However, these systems struggle to handle corner cases or unforeseen scenarios without predefined rules. In contrast, deep learning regression generalizes from its training data, allowing it to infer patterns and make predictions for new inputs, including some corner cases. While this approach reduces reliance on manual rule creation, its effectiveness depends on the quality and diversity of the training data.

Greenhouse control

Problem definition: The team operating a hydroponic farm is embarking on an ambitious project to enhance their farming practices. Their objective is to implement automation across various aspects of the farm, including irrigation, lighting, fresh air intake, and room temperature control. The farm is already equipped with multiple light, temperature, and humidity sensors.

In pursuit of this automation, the team is exploring an innovative approach that minimizes the need for extensive coding and mathematical modeling. They want to develop a system that can learn to manage these environmental factors by observing manual operations. The challenge lies in the vast number of possible settings' combinations for these environmental factors, making it impractical to teach the system every possible scenario manually.

The ideal solution is a system that can learn and adapt based on limited examples. The system could extrapolate and make informed decisions in similar situations by learning from these examples. Despite this automated decision-making capability, the team emphasizes the importance of maintaining control. They intend to establish predefined limits to prevent the system from making adjustments that could potentially jeopardize the farm's production.

Additionally, the team desires real-time notifications regarding the actions planned by the system. This feature would allow them to monitor the system's decisions and intervene, if necessary, especially when they believe a different approach might be more beneficial. Integrating these features would automate farm operations and ensure the team retains oversight, balancing efficiency with precision and care.

Solution: The system consists of sensor groups that capture ambient conditions for each one of the areas of interest in the hydroponic farm where plants are grown. Each sensor group reads temperature, **Relative humidity (RH)**, and ambient light situation. Additionally, the system can capture the actuators' position and status that affect the zones' readings, namely, whether windows are open or closed, whether fans are running or not, whether lights are on or off, and whether the irrigation system is operating (see *Figure 7.6*):

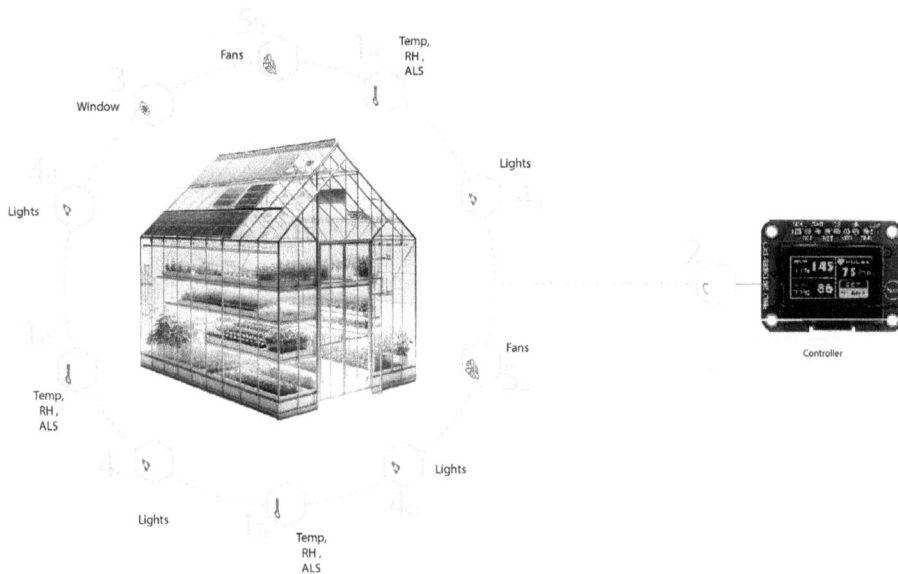

Figure 7.6: *Concept diagram (Greenhouse control)*

It is important to stress that the actuators do not have a 1:1 relationship with the area metrics measured by each one of the sensor groups. Instead, you can think of this problem as a black box where the actuators are the inputs, and the area metrics are the outputs. The model will perform a deep learning regression that will be able to output the area metrics based on the inputs.

Conversely, the model will perform a deep learning regression that can output the actuator settings to obtain a set of desired metric readings. Since a greenhouse is a dynamic system (it changes with time), we do not rely on absolute measurements but rates of change. In other words, the regression will output the rates of change (how fast the metrics are changing) when actuators are set in a specific configuration.

A secondary function that uses a control function will help the system establish the path to a desired state based on the regression's outputs.

Data acquisition

For this use case, we need to capture cause-and-effect relationships within the environment to generate sufficient data for creating a regression model. Sensors and encoders capture the state of the actuators responsible for controlling air and light from outside, as well as illumination from interior lights. Meanwhile, a group of environmental sensors measures metrics such as temperature, RH, and ambient light levels for each area of interest in the hydroponic farm.

The goal is to capture 3,300 examples of cause-and-effect relationships during a well-run day (this becomes the **positive sample**). Each example will include six variables: **Temperature, Window Status, Relative Humidity, Fan Status, Ambient Light Conditions**, and **Light Status**. Ideally, we should have samples of good days and bad days for the system to have a diverse set of examples to learn from. In order to do this, you can cause problems intentionally, and have an expert operator fix the situation while you are capturing the input and output metrics. Refer to the following figure:

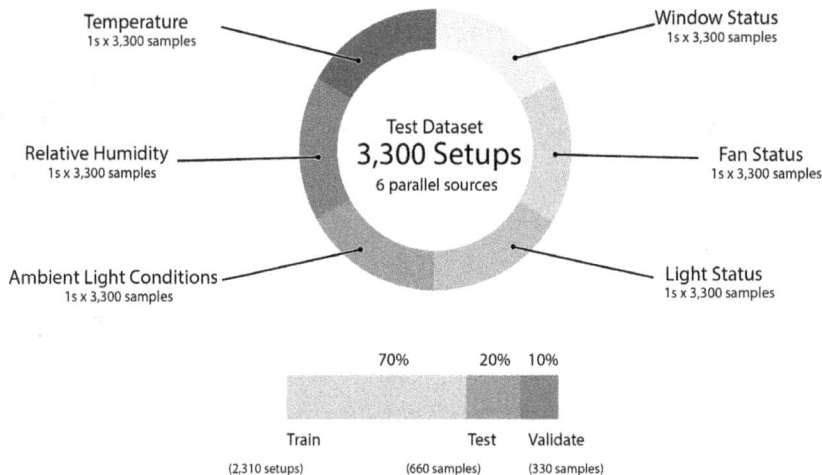

Figure 7.7: Training set (Greenhouse control)

The system is influenced by three types of actuators:

- **Ceiling window**: This actuator opens and closes to allow fresh air and sunlight into the interior space. The window's position affects multiple sensors, including temperature and RH (by introducing outside air) and ambient light (by letting sunlight in).

- **Fans**: A series of fans facilitates air circulation, with sensors detecting each fan's status through an intelligent switch. For simplicity, we assume the fan speed remains constant. The fans primarily impact temperature and RH readings.

- **Interior lights**: These LED lights are controlled by an intelligent switch that reports their on/off state. Unlike the other actuators, the lights do not influence temperature or RH readings.

The system operates at a low frequency, with one reading every 30 seconds being sufficient. Changes in temperature and light lasting less than a minute are inconsequential for this use case.

Each zone generates three time series: one for temperature, one for RH, and one for ambient light. Thus, the total number of time series to be aggregated is three times the number of zones.

On the actuator side, each device being tracked generates a time series of states. For instance, if a fan is on, the time series will show a value of 1 for every reading, and if the fan is off, it will show a 0.

All time-series data is sent to a central aggregator device, where the regression process takes place. To ensure data from all devices is synchronized, each device is equipped with a **real-time clock** (RTC). A main RTC periodically broadcasts synchronization messages to the other devices, typically once per minute. This synchronization ensures that all devices align their RTCs with the broadcasted timestamp. As a result, every recorded data point is timestamped consistently across all devices, maintaining precise synchronization throughout the system.

Processing

Once all the data has reached the aggregator device that will handle the regression, we need to process it slightly to simplify calculations. The steps are given as follows:

1. Ensure that all the time series are at the same frequency. If they are not, we can run a simple resampling step. Be careful to detect significant gaps in the data. If that is the case, you could also extrapolate or predict its values with a regression model, which is out of the scope of this use case.

2. Normalize the data. Deep learning networks work better when all the data exists in the same order of magnitude.

3. Eliminate outliers. You can use a Kalman filter (*Chapter 6, Sensor Fusion*) or establish maximum and minimums for the type of reading and replace any reading beyond the limits.

Figure 7.8 shows how the deep learning model organizes similar input samples based on their features. Data points close to each other indicate that the model perceives them as having similar feature characteristics, which may result in similar regression solutions.

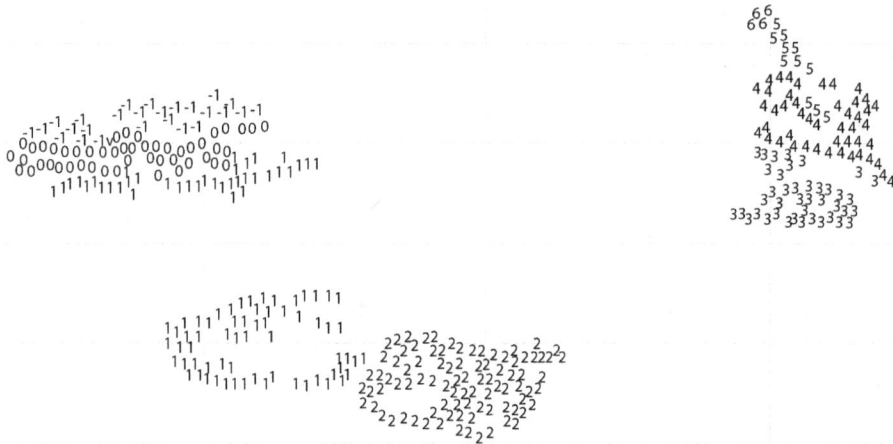

Figure 7.8: Cluster diagram (Greenhouse control)

Model

The question we want the regression model to answer is: given the current state of the system, if we modify the inputs (or leave them unchanged), what will the system's state be in the next step?

In this context, the system refers to a zone in the hydroponic farm. The system state represents that zone's temperature, RH, and light conditions. The inputs include anything that could influence the system's state in the near future, such as the status of windows, fans, lights, outdoor temperature, light conditions, and even the system's current state. The next step refers to a specific (but predictable) point in time when the system's readings will be taken again to determine its new state. Using regression, we aim to predict this future state.

Additionally, we could approach the problem from the opposite perspective: given the current state of the system, if we wanted the system to move closer to a desired state in the next step, what inputs would we need to adjust?

This regression model does not provide a complete path to the destination but helps move one step closer with each iteration. The process involves running the regression model to determine the next step, executing the recommended actions, and then rerunning the model based on the updated state. This step-by-step approach ensures the system remains responsive to disturbances or external factors, preventing divergence.

Understanding how to manipulate inputs to achieve a desired output is highly useful, it is akin to knowing how to operate a car. However, just as a car requires a map or GPS to guide turns, this model also needs a guiding framework. To achieve this, we pair the regression model with a traditional control algorithm, such as a **Proportional-Integral-Derivative (PID)** controller. In this setup, the PID function defines a goal (or setpoint) for each metric, calculates how far the current state is from the objective, and determines the corrections needed to minimize the error. The regression model translates these corrections into specific actions for the actuators, enabling the system to achieve its goals one step at a time.

To make accurate recommendations, it is essential to analyze the direction and speed at which the metrics change over time. This is done by calculating the rate of change, which involves subtracting the previous value of a metric from its current value and dividing the result by the time elapsed between measurements. This calculation provides the rate and direction of the metric's change over time.

This raises an important question: should the model be trained using a system's absolute values or its rates of change? The answer is both. Absolute values anchor the model to the initial conditions, while rates of change anchor it to the behavior from that point forward. The more diverse and richer the input data, the better the model's performance.

The input features for the fully connected layer of the deep Neural Network consist of time-series data, including readings from ambient sensors (temperature, RH, ambient light) and actuators (windows, fans, lights). These features also include their rates of change over time (derivatives). The data is labeled with respect to the target outputs. As a result, when the system's current conditions and the desired rate of change for the next step are provided as input, the model outputs a set of instructions specifying which actuators to adjust to achieve the desired outcome.

The deep learning regression model, using a 20-10 dense network, demonstrates a strong performance with a low validation loss of 0.07 and a high testing accuracy of 98.64%. The low loss indicates that the model is effectively minimizing the error between predicted and actual values on the validation dataset, while the high testing accuracy suggests the model generalizes well to unseen data. This balance between validation loss and testing accuracy indicates that the model is not overfitting and has learned the underlying patterns in the data effectively. The architecture appears well-suited for the problem, and the dataset likely provides sufficient coverage of the input-output relationships needed for accurate predictions. Refer to the following figure:

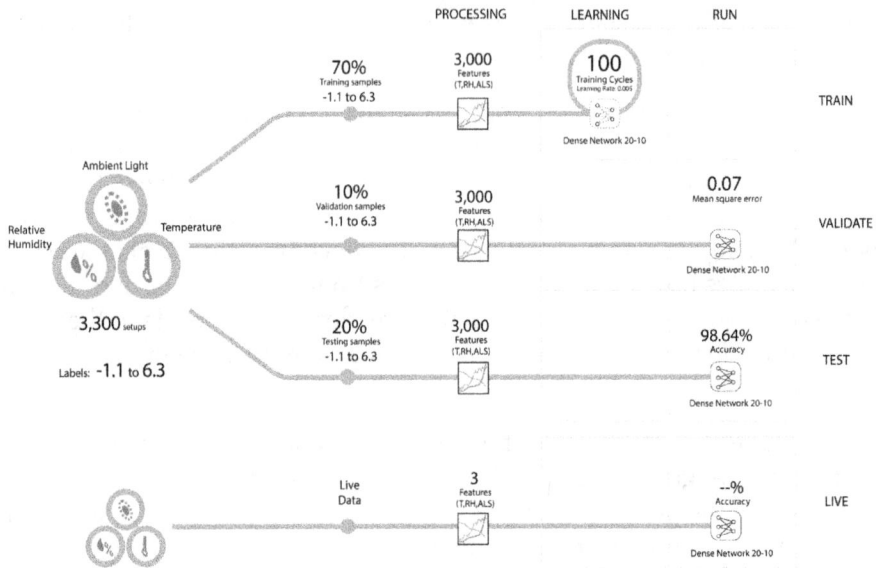

Figure 7.9: Training, validation and testing metrics (Greenhouse control)

System implementation

The implementation consists of two different types of building Blocks. The first is an acquisition Block that captures temperature, RH, and light intensity. There are as many acquisition Blocks as areas of interest in the hydroponic farm. The second one is the aggregator Block that receives data from all the acquisition Blocks and performs the deep learning regression and the PID control iterations. The rest of the Blocks are actuator Blocks that control lights, fans and window position. The full setup is shown in the following figure:

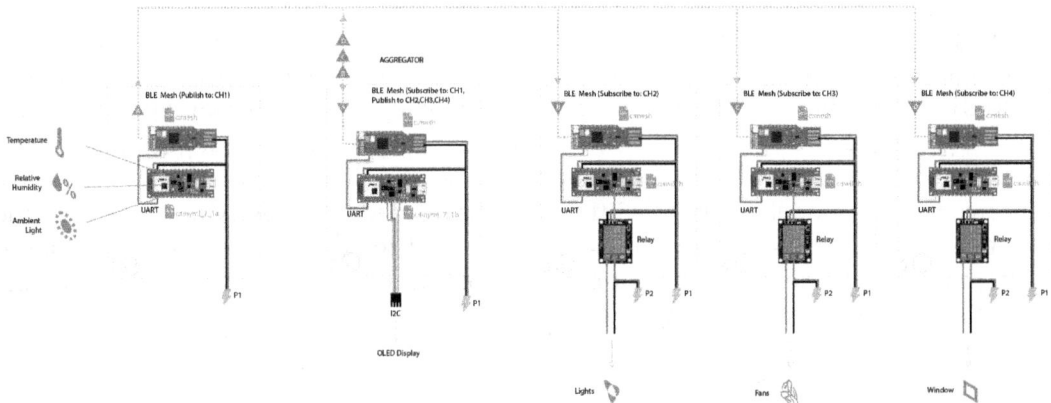

Figure 7.10: Connection diagram (Greenhouse control)

The acquisition Block is built with an Arduino Nano 33 BLE Sense, which has a temperature sensor, a RH sensor, and a light intensity sensor on the same board. This Block uses the NRF52840 Dongle as a secondary microcontroller board in charge of all network functions, sending the data to the aggregator and updating the RTC.

Source code

Block 1 serves two main functions: capturing data from three different sensors (Temperature, Relative Humidity, and Ambient Light Situation), and removing noise from the data before sending it to the aggregator. The pseudocodes are shown in the following tables:

c:tinyml_7_1a	Code location: Arduino Nano 33 BLE @ Block 1
	Capturing the data and sending it out to the aggregator. Pseudocode 1. The Block acquires temperature, RH and light intensity readings. 2. Noise is removed from data. 3. Data is sent to the central aggregator.

Table 7.2: Pseudocode for Block 1 (Greenhouse control)

Block 2 aggregates data from all greenhouse sensors, processes it, runs it through the regression model to determine actuator actions, refines those actions using a PID function, and sends out the resulting control commands.

c:tinyml_7_1b	Code location: Arduino Nano 33 BLE @ Block 2
	Receiving data from all sensors and actuators, running control function and performing regression. Pseudocode 1. Data from all sensors (ambient metrics and actuator status) is received. 2. Data is resampled, normalized and filtered. 3. Regression is run to translate inputs to actuator actions 4. PID function is executed to figure out the best path to run the actuator commands. 5. Control commands are sent to actuators.

Table 7.3: Pseudocode for Block 2 (Greenhouse control)

Network

The constantly changing conditions inside the greenhouse and the need to reposition equipment to optimize measurements and actuator effects make a strong case for using a wireless network to connect the sensors and actuators. A wireless network also simplifies the addition of new components for an easy integration. The data acquisition Blocks publish their data to a shared channel that the aggregator subscribes to, while control commands are published on a separate channel monitored by the actuators. Each message payload includes an identifier to specify the target actuator.

Block(s)	Action	Channel
1	Publishes to	CH1
2	Subscribes to	CH1
2	Publishes to	CH2
Actuators	Subscribe to	CH2

Table 7.4: Network configuration (Greenhouse control)

Power analysis

The data acquisition Blocks can be powered by batteries since readings are generated at a very low frequency (approximately once per minute). The Block remains in a sleep mode during the intervals between readings.

Power source	Device	Latent consumption	Active consumption	Notes
P1	Arduino Nano 33 BLE Sense	0.032A @5V	< 1A @5V	Arduino will be polling temperature, RH and light intensity sensors.
P1	NRF52 Dongle	0.04mA @5v	3mA @5v	Dongle is in charge of publishing and receiving messages from the network.

Table 7.5: Power profile for Block 1 (Greenhouse control)

The regression Block must remain always on, as it continuously listens to the acquisition channel. Once it receives data, it processes it and runs it through the regression model, which is a power-intensive operation. For these reasons, Block 2 must be powered directly from the electric grid.

Power source	Device	Latent consumption	Active consumption	Notes
P2	NRF52 Dongle	0.04mA @5v	3mA @5v	The Dongle is in charge of consuming the messages from all Data Acquisition Blocks.
P2	Arduino Nano 33 BLE Sense	0.032A @5V	< 1A @5V	Arduino will be aggregating data and running the Regression model.

Table 7.6: Power profile for Block 2 (Greenhouse control)

The actuator Blocks are responsible for receiving control commands from Block 2. They are powered by the same power source as the actuator they control.

Power source	Device	Latent consumption	Active consumption	Notes
A1	Light Switch	0.025A @5V		Actuator is in charge of turning lights in the hydroponic farm. There are as many as light groups.
A2	Fan Switch	0.025A @5V		Actuator is in charge of turning the fan on and off.
A3	Window Actuator	0.5A @5V		Actuator is in charge of opening and closing motor activated windows.

Table 7.7: Power profile for actuator Blocks (Greenhouse control)

Bill of materials

This bill of materials considers 3 data acquisition zones, 2 fans, 1 window and 4 lights:

Description	QTY	Unit cost	Total
Arduino Nano 33 BLE	10	$30	$300
NRF52840 Dongle	10	$12	$120
Window Actuator	1	$120	$120
Fan Switch	2	$20	$40
Light Switch (Relay)	4	$10	$40
Power Sources	10	10	$100

Table 7.8: Bill of materials (Greenhouse control)

Approximate cost of materials is $720.

Use case: Forecasting

The ability to forecast a variable is a transformative capability for control systems. Instead of relying on reactive strategies that involve correcting a system's state after the fact, often requiring significant effort to counteract inertia, forecasting enables early adjustments to guide the system toward the desired state. This proactive approach can lead to substantial energy savings and streamline the control process. However, the effectiveness of this approach depends on the accuracy of the forecasts and the system's specific dynamics.

Thermostat temperature prediction

Problem definition: An appliance company has asked you to design an innovative thermostat that aims to revolutionize indoor temperature regulation. Unlike traditional thermostats, which adjust the temperature based on current readings, this new model proactively manages the climate by predicting future temperature changes within a room.

Solution: The solution consists of a standalone device that captures temperature and RH and runs an inference model to predict the temperature and RH of the room in the next 20, 40, and 60 minutes. The device interacts with the HVAC like a regular thermostat, which uses three cables, two for power and a third for a switch. To show the room's current state and offer a way for the user to change the setpoint (the desired temperature), the device communicates wirelessly with a UI Block dedicated to interface with the user. The UI can also show the temperature of multiple thermostats at once. The following figure shows the conceptual connections between the Blocks:

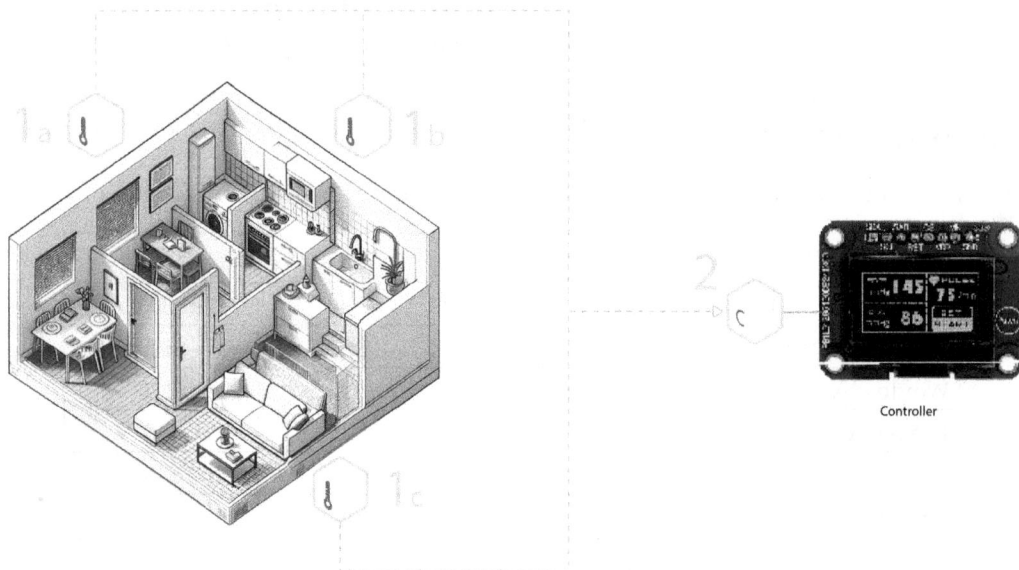

Controller

Figure 7.11: Concept diagram (Temperature prediction)

The thermostat must be capable of accurately forecasting the room's temperature for the upcoming hour. This capability hinges on the thermostat's ability to learn and adapt to the specific environment in which it is placed. As part of its initial setup, the thermostat is designed to gather temperature data from the room over a few days. This critical data collection phase allows the thermostat to understand the room's unique thermal characteristics and patterns.

Once the thermostat has accumulated sufficient data, it can make informed predictions about future temperature fluctuations. By proactively adjusting the heating or air conditioning systems in anticipation of these changes, the thermostat can maintain a comfortable indoor climate more efficiently.

The potential benefits of this predictive approach are substantial. This advanced thermostat could lead to energy savings of up to 20% in heating and cooling costs. Such savings not only reduce expenses for homeowners but also contribute to broader energy conservation efforts. This innovative thermostat represents a significant leap forward in climate control technology, combining convenience, efficiency, and environmental responsibility.

Data acquisition

The temperature's data is captured at 1/60 Hz (once a minute) from the internal temperature and RH sensors and passed through a simple Kalman filter to remove signal noise. To train the model, we have captured 24 hours of data from the room where the thermostat will be located. The following figure shows the proportions used to train, test and validation:

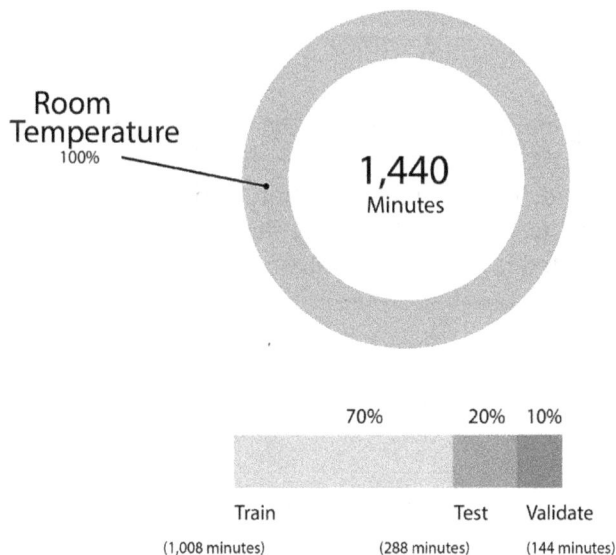

Figure 7.12: *Training dataset (Temperature prediction)*

Processing

The acquired data is split into chunks of 8 seconds and is labeled with the space temperature that the room will have 20 minutes later. Each different label will define a new class (just like in traditional classification). The temperature range of the room determines the number of classes. If we wanted to predict the temperature of a narrower range, we would need a temperature sensor that guarantees that the decimals are accurate enough. The cluster diagram shown in *Figure 7.13* illustrates that similar inputs produce similar outputs. The pattern formed by the samples represents the multidimensional relationships that the regression model needs to learn and capture.

Figure 7.13: Cluster diagram (Temperature prediction)

Model

We use a deep-learning model with an input layer of 8 nodes. Each one of the nodes will receive a reading from the sample. Remember that the sample is 8 seconds long, with one reading every second. The input layer is fully connected to a 20-neuron dense layer, subsequently connected to another 10-neuron dense layer (*Figure 7.14*). The output is a single node fully connected layer that will return the regression value.

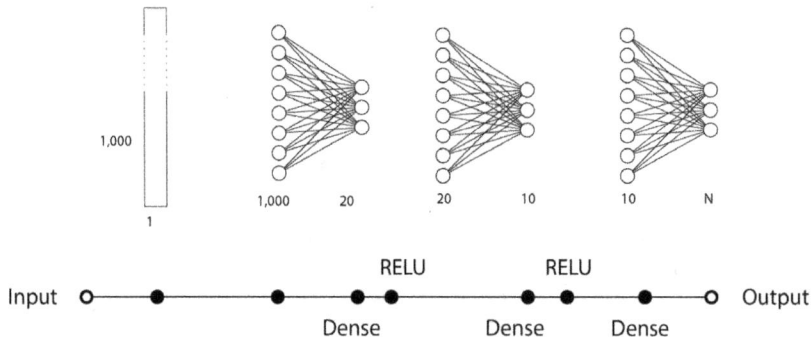

Figure 7.14: Regression model (Temperature prediction)

We are going to parallelize the input by providing a sequence of readings over time as the input. In other words, we will send the entire sample at once instead of only its most recent reading. This approach is equivalent to instructing the model to learn from the shape of the curve, enabling it to infer the future state.

An essential aspect of the **Dense Layered Neural Networks** is that they always return numbers, which is what we need for regressions. Since the last layer has only one node, calculating the error in every iteration is as easy as comparing the label with the output of that last layer. During training, the weights of each dense layer are adjusted automatically to reduce that error using a process called **backpropagation**. With enough data and iterations, the model learns to recognize patterns and infer future temperatures from data previously unseen. It is important to emphasize that because we trained the model with temperature data from a specific room, it only knows how to predict temperature from that room.

The results of training, validation and testing in *Figure 7.15* show that the validation stage achieves a loss of 0.03, indicating that the model has a low error on the validation dataset. In the testing stage, the model demonstrates 100% accuracy, suggesting it is perfectly predicting outputs on the test dataset. However, this unusually high accuracy for a regression problem raises potential concerns about overfitting, as the model may have learned patterns specific to the test data rather than generalizing to unseen data.

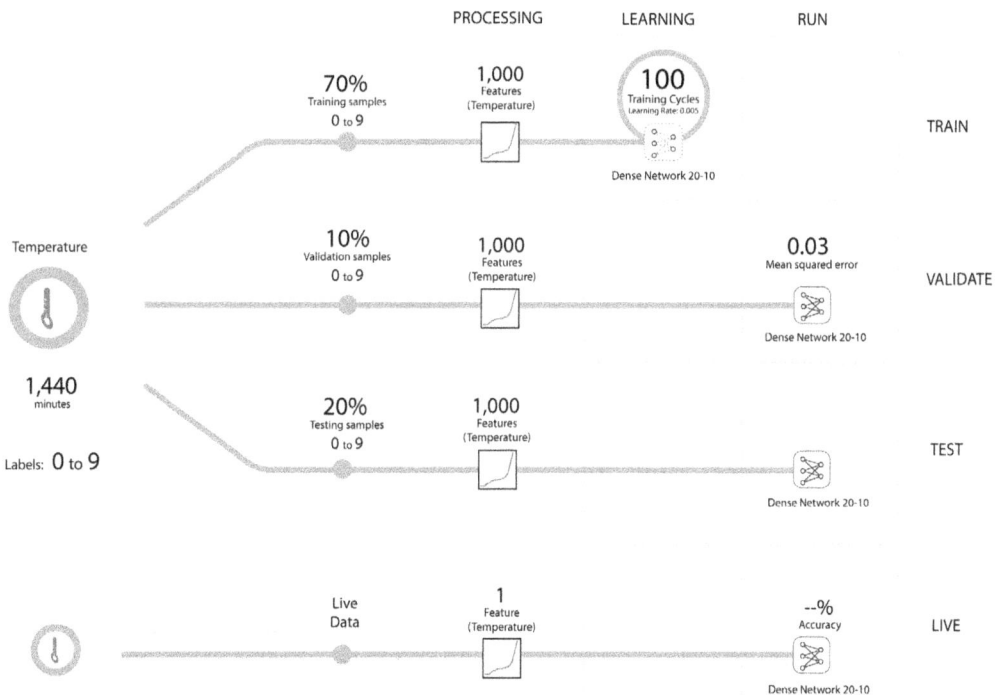

Figure 7.15: Training, validation and testing metrics (Temperature prediction)

System implementation

This solution has two different Blocks. Block 1 is the acquisition and regression device, and Block 2 is the **user interface (UI)**. The following figure shows the various components of each Block, along with their connections and power sources:

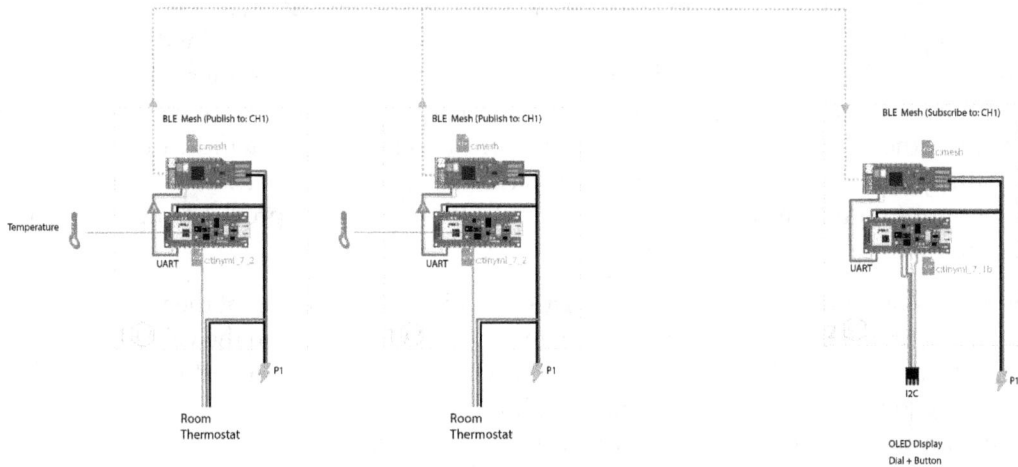

Figure 7.16: Connection diagram (Temperature prediction)

The application's requirements specify that it needs to have a way for users to establish setpoints per room and to provide visibility on the current and predicted state of the room temperatures. For that reason, the implementation of this solution assumes that every smart thermostat captures data and performs regression in the same device but, at the same time, sends out its status to a central display for the user to read the information and set room temperatures.

Block 1 uses an Arduino Nano 33 BLE Sense to capture the room temperature and run the regression model. A secondary microcontroller (NRF52840) sends messages to the Block 2 via a BLE Mesh Network. No additional sensors or peripherals are needed, as the Arduino board has an integrated temperature sensor.

Block 2 subscribes to all the Block 1 devices around the location and shows their status using an I2C OLED display. The user navigates across the OLED interface using a Dial/Button peripheral connected via I2C. One of the screens in the interface allows the user to enter the desired temperature per room. The Block 2 sends a command to the Block 1 (via the Mesh Network) to adjust the setpoint.

Block 1 features a PID control function that controls the heating/cooling unit (via its thermostat pins) proactively using the predicted temperature and the setpoint temperature established by the user.

Source code

The process goes as follows: The temperature is captured, the temperature is predicted and actions are recommended to reach the setpoint. In parallel, the current readings and the forecast are sent to a component that shows the metrics to the user via a display. If the user decides to change the setpoint, the user enters the new setpoint and its value is sent back to all the thermostats. The thermostats now plan their strategy around the new setpoint.

Table 7.9 illustrates the logic to capture data, perform inference and issue a control command. There are four main components in the logic of Block 1. The first is the Kalman filter, which removes noise from the readings. The second involves feature extraction, followed by running the data through the regression model, and finally, adjusting the output using a PID control function.

c:tinyml_7_2a	Code location: Arduino Nano 33 BLE @ Block 1
	Capturing the temperature, performing regression, communicating readings and results to the central UI. Pseudocode 1. Temperature sensor captures reading. 2. Value is passed through a simple Kalman filter to remove noise and outliers. 3. Convert readings to features and feed them to the regression model. 4. Pass regression result to PID control to determine actions needed to get to setpoint. 5. Send out readings and predictions to Block 2.

Table 7.9: Pseudocode for Block 1 to control temperature (Temperature prediction)

Table 7.10 illustrates the logic that helps display the metrics to the user. There are two main components in the logic of Block 2: the data buffer, which maintains a short memory of the temperatures reported to the thermostat, and the display driver, which serves as the main UI. It is important to note that this Block is purely for informational purposes and does not generate control commands.

c:tinyml_7_2b	Code location: Arduino Nano 33 BLE @ Block 2
	Receiving readings from all thermostats, displaying results to user. Pseudocode 1. Receive readings and predictions from all the thermostats that the device is subscribed to. 2. Translate data to a display buffer. 3. Refresh buffer to show new data in OLED display.

Table 7.10: Pseudocode for Block 2 to display setpoint (Temperature prediction)

The following table shows the logic that allows the user to enter a new setpoint and send it to the thermostats:

c:tinyml_7_2c	Code location: Arduino Nano 33 BLE @ Block 2
	User sets a new setpoint. Sending new value to the thermostat. Pseudocode 1. User modifies the setpoint of a thermostat using a Dial/Button interface. 2. The peripheral driver converts user input to a command. 3. Block 2 publishes a command to the channel the target Block 1 is subscribed to.

Table 7.11: Pseudocode for Block 2 to acquire setpoint (Temperature prediction)

The following table shows the logic to acquire and store the setpoint for further actions:

c:tinyml_7_2d	Code location: Arduino Nano 33 BLE @ Block 1
	Receiving new setpoint Pseudocode 1. Setpoint set command is received from Block 2. 2. Setpoint is loaded to volatile memory for PID function to use it to calculate control commands. 3. Additionally, setpoint is saved to permanent memory (SD Card) for backup in case of a power loss.

Table 7.12: Pseudocode for Block 1 to acquire setpoint (Temperature prediction)

Network

Assuming 3 rooms with a standalone smart thermostat. It is safe to assume that it would be impractical to lay cable between all the components. For that reason a wireless network is the best option. Multiple components communicating between each other also make the case for an asynchronous communication network. We use a wireless mesh network where the thermostats publish their state in their own channel. The UI device that serves the purpose of showing the metrics and acquiring setpoint changes from the user subscribes to each thermostat channel. Additionally, all thermostats are subscribed to the channel where the setpoint is published by the UI device. Refer to the following table:

Block(s)	Action	Channel
1a,1b,1c	Publish to	CH1,CH2,CH3
2	Subscribes to	CH1,CH2,CH3
2	Publishes to	CH4
1a,1b,1c	Subscribe to	CH4

Table 7.13: Network configuration (Temperature prediction)

Power analysis

The power for Blocks 1a, 1b, and 1c would come from the electrical register box where the thermostat is installed. This differs from traditional thermostats, which are typically battery-operated, due to the higher energy demands required for running regression models and wirelessly communicating with the UI device. Refer to the following table:

Power source	Device	Latent consumption	Active consumption	Notes
P1	Arduino Nano 33 BLE Sense	0.032A @5V	< 1A @5V	Arduino will be polling temperature, running regression and controlling heating and cooling units.
P1	NRF52 Dongle	0.04mA @5v	3mA @5v	Dongle is in charge of publishing and receiving messages from the network.

Table 7.14: Power analysis, Block 1 (Temperature prediction)

Similar to Block 1, the UI device (Block 2) needs to be installed in an electrical register box. While it could be powered by a battery, relying on batteries for a thermostat controller would be impractical due to the need for frequent recharging.

Power source	Device	Latent consumption	Active consumption	Notes
P2	Arduino Nano 33 BLE Sense	0.032A @5V	< 1A @5V	Receives readings from all thermostats, generates UI for user to read state and write setpoints
P2	NRF52 Dongle	0.04mA @5v	3mA @5v	Dongle is in charge of publishing and receiving messages from the network

Table 7.15: Power analysis, Block 2 (Temperature prediction)

Bill of materials

The bill of materials considers 3 rooms with thermostats and one display unit:

Description	QTY	Unit cost	Total
Arduino Nano 33 BLE	4	$30	$120
NRF52840 Dongle	4	$12	$48
OLED Display	1	$10	$10
Dial/Button	40	$40	$40
Power Sources	4	10	$40

Table 7.16: Bill of materials (Temperature prediction)

Approximate cost of materials is $258.

Use case: Estimating

Regression has been traditionally constrained to numeric inputs. Deep learning and convolutional networks open the possibility to multi-modal regressions. It is now possible to infer a number from an image, from a sound or even from an oral description. The following use case explores the concept of multi factor verification which illustrates a way to verify a measurement in multiple ways.

Weight estimation from images

Problem definition: A grain market is looking to automate its checkout process without increasing the risk of financial loss. It has been determined that the system should be able to verify the weight of the grains by using an alternative method in addition to the measurement returned by the weight balance. The solution should also be able to classify and infer the product's weight in almost real time to avoid delays in the checkout process. The following figure shows a conceptual diagram of the solution:

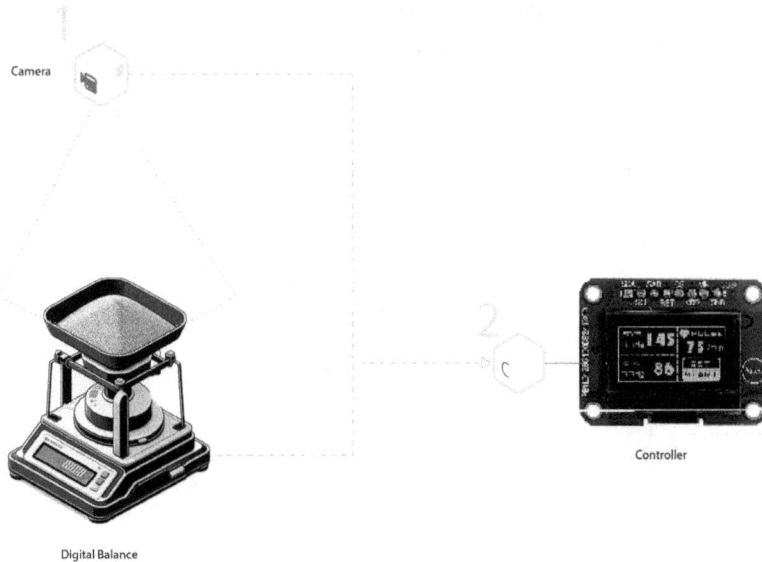

Figure 7.17: Concept diagram (Weight estimation)

Solution: The market is planning to introduce a dual-function verification system.

The primary function of this system is to classify the type of grain being weighed accurately. This classification process is crucial to ensure that each grain variety is correctly identified and associated with the appropriate product code, thereby preventing the recurrence of past errors. The system's second function involves estimating the grain pile's weight using an image-based regression model. This estimation will be based on images captured at the register. By analyzing these images, the system can independently assess the grain's weight, offering a reliable cross-check against the readings from the balances.

If a discrepancy in weight is detected, the system will activate a **Service** light that will notify a human assistant for further assistance. Additionally, a secondary light will indicate to the user to wait while the inference takes place, continue with the next item, or wait for a service assistant to help with the transaction.

Data acquisition

The data required to run the regression, and the classification models are images from a digital camera at the top of the self-check-out register. Images are captured at a ratio of 10Hz. The microcontroller does not store the history of images in memory. The model should be able to perform the inference and regression at a speed sufficient to avoid backlog. If a backlog takes place, newer images will overwrite old ones. Either way, once the classification results are back and approved, the user can move to the next item.

For the pilot of this use case, only one type of grain is used. As shown in *Figure 7.18*, the training set consists of 50 images per weight and class. The weight starts at 0g and gets incremented every 50g in every class up to 1000g. The data set contains 1000 images. Since this is a controlled environment, the supermarket requires the user to weigh the grains using a standard tray. Using the same tray makes the image-based regression much more accurate.

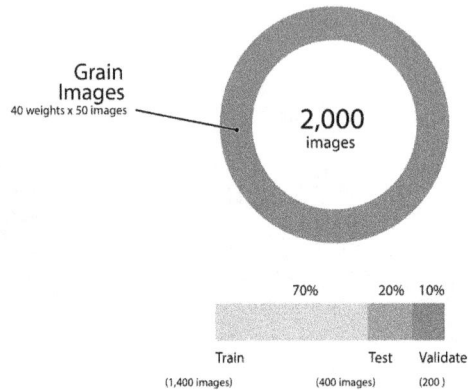

Figure 7.18: Training dataset (Weight estimation)

Processing

As with the *Image Classification* problem in *Chapter 3, Movement Classification,* we need to prepare the image before sending it to the model. First, we make it square, then scale it to 160x160. This use case is inspired by *Aditya Mangalampalli's* blog post, which describes how reducing images to 96x96 makes them too blurry for the model to be effective.

If light conditions are right, they will enhance the grain's color and details. All three-color channels are necessary, as color plays a significant role in grain classification.

The total number of features sent to the classification and regression models is 76,800. Every pixel is a feature (160x160x3 = 76,800). The following figure shows groupings of similar outputs which means that similar inputs return similar outputs which is what we are looking for:

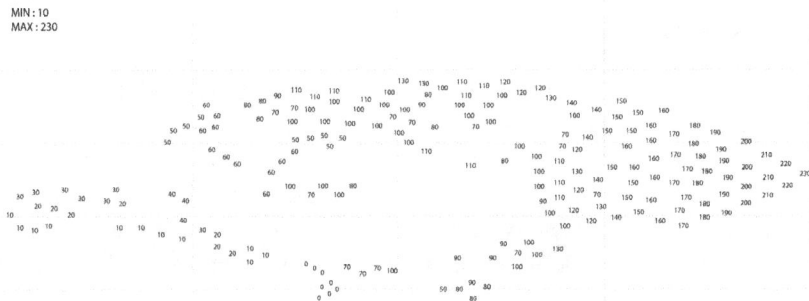

Figure 7.19: Cluster diagram (Weight estimation)

Model

Since we are using an image, it makes sense to use a **Convolutional Neural Network** to exploit the picture's spatial relationships.

The Neural Network consists of an input layer with 76,800 features fully connected to a 2-dimensional convolutional layer with 32 neurons. The kernel size of that layer is 3x3. We used padding to keep the same size after every convolution. Outputs are normalized and run through a ReLu activation function to introduce non-linearity. The following figure shows the diagram of the network:

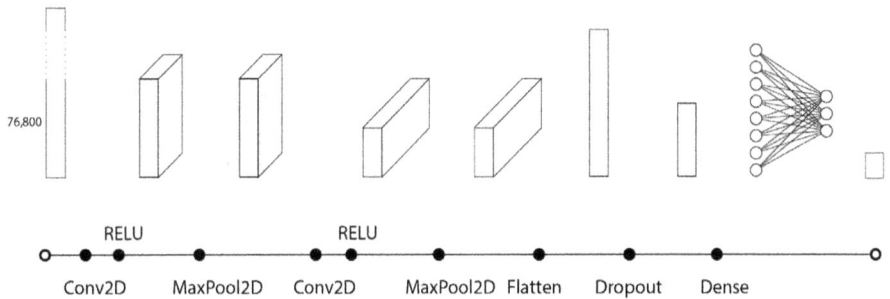

Figure 7.20: Image regression Neural Network (Weight estimation)

Immediately after the first convolutional layer, we have a **MaxPooling** layer that reduces the size of the parameters, by two, by keeping the value with the maximum value from every other pixel.

The second 2-dimensional convolutional layer has 16 neurons and a kernel of 3x3. It has the same parameters as the first convolutional layer: the same padding, normalization, and ReLu activation.

A MaxPool layer reduces the parameters' size in half. Then, the whole matrix is flattened, meaning all the parameters are made of a very long one-dimensional array. After that, we drop one of every four readings (we turn them to zero) to reduce overfitting. Notice that the dropping function will only be applied during training.

The last layer (the output layer) has a single node. This layer returns the inference result. The value is compared against the label using a *root mean square* function. During training, this error is communicated to the hidden layers to adjust their weights and improve in the following training iteration.

Something important to notice is that while all the labels could be integers, the output of the inference might have decimal points. Remember that every neuron represents a linear equation at the end of the day. Linear equations are multiplied by their slope and added to the offset. Returning decimals in the results is entirely normal. This is a characteristic of the regression function, which returns values between known points.

Figure 7.21 shows the results of training, validation and testing. It is shown that the model struggles to generalize effectively, as indicated by a high validation loss (135.12) and extremely low testing accuracy (1.22%). This suggests potential overfitting or insufficient learning due to the high feature-to-data ratio, with 76,800 features extracted from only 2,000 images. The CNN architecture, with just two convolutional layers, may be too simple for the task, and the dataset might lack sufficient diversity or size to capture variations in grain pile appearances. Improving the model architecture, increasing or augmenting the dataset, and optimizing feature representation could help address these issues and enhance performance.

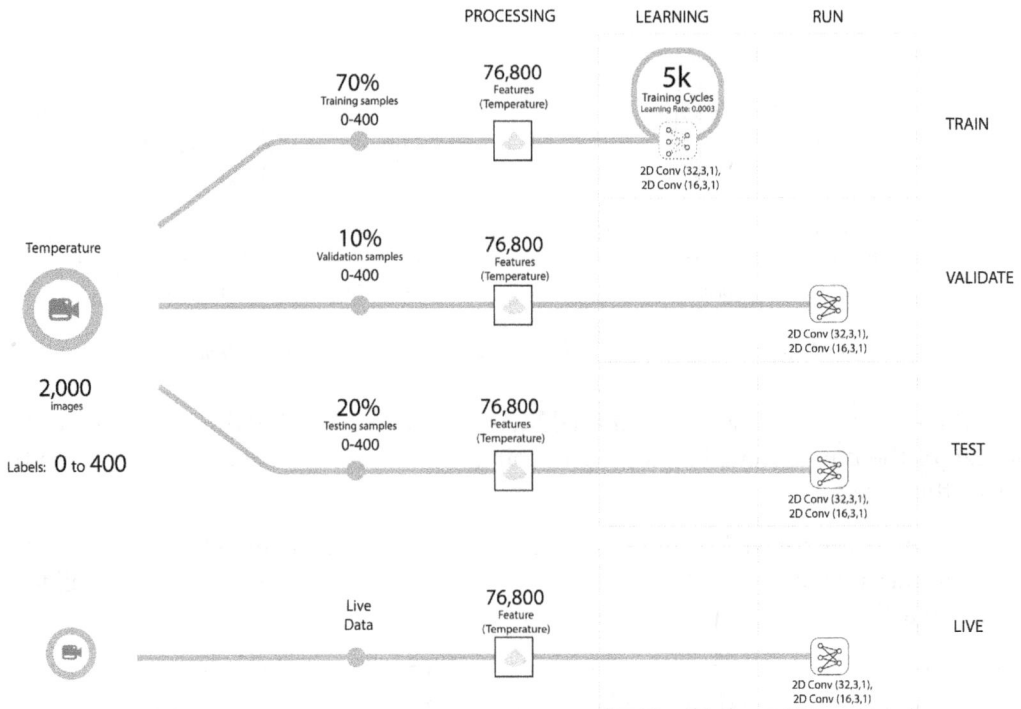

Figure 7.21: *Training, validation and testing metrics (Weight estimation)*

System implementation

The implementation as shown in *Figure 7.22*, consists of two Blocks. Block 1 captures data and processes the image-based regression. Results of the regression are sent out to a device (Block 2) connected to the balance weighing the grains. Block 2 compares both readings and determines whether there is a tolerable weight discrepancy or not. If the difference is significant, Block 2 sends an I2C command to an external light in charge of notifying a human service specialist in the store to handle the conflict.

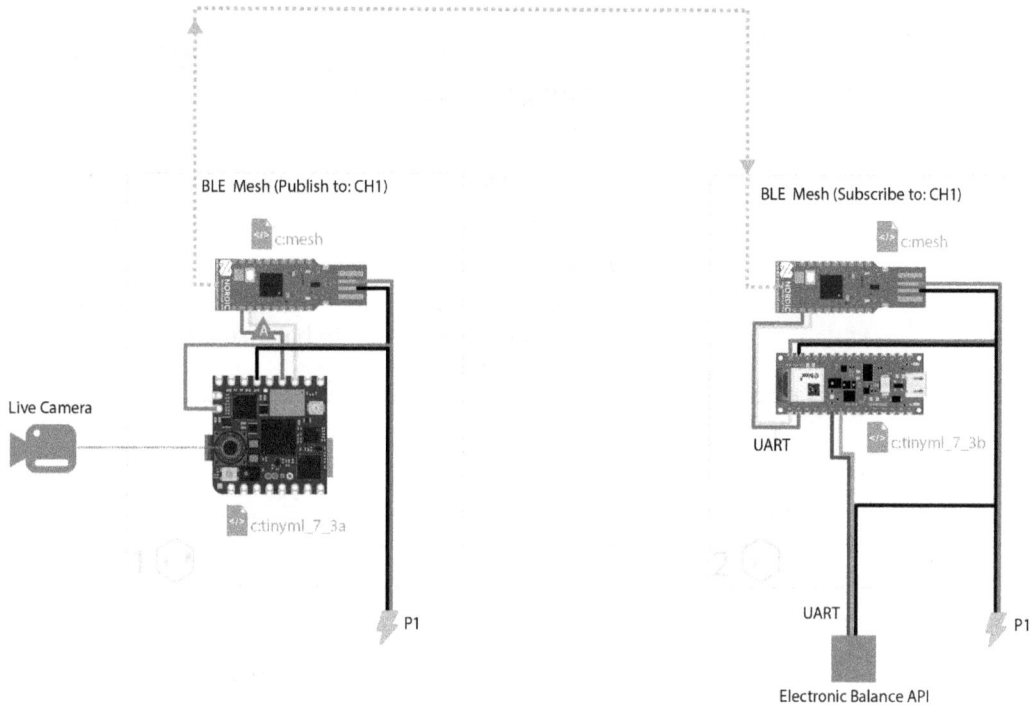

Figure 7.22: Connection diagram (Weight estimation)

Block 1 is implemented with a Nicla Vision running the regression model and notifying a secondary microcontroller (52840Dongle) in charge of publishing the conflict status to the network.

Block 2 is implemented using a combination of a 52840 Dongle and an Arduino Nano BLE 33. The former receives messages from Block 1 instances and sends its payload to the latter. The Arduino in Block 2 also keeps the state of all the events by storing them on an SD Card. The SD logger is an external component that receives commands and data via an I2C bus.

Source code

The logic in this use case consists of acquiring the weight of a product in two different ways, comparing them and alerting somebody if there is a significant difference.

The pseudocode for Block 1 shows a preprocessing component that extracts features from the data captured by the camera connected to the device. These features are then sent to the regression model, and the resulting inference is passed to a post-processing stage, which waits for a series of similar readings before outputting the final result. Refer to the following tables:

c:tinyml_7_3a	Code location: **Arduino Nano 33 BLE @ Block 1**
	Capturing image. Performing image-based regression Pseudocode 1. A camera captures an image of the checkout tray. 2. Image is processed, features are generated. 3. Image is run through regression model. 4. Result of regression is validated and sent out to device connected to balance for weight comparison.

Table 7.17: Pseudocode for Block 1 (Weight estimation)

The pseudocode for Block 2 illustrates the process of acquiring the value from the inference, obtaining the reading from the weighing balance, performing a comparison, and triggering an alert if a conflict is detected.

c:tinyml_7_3b	Code location: **Arduino Nano 33 BLE @ Block 2**
	Capturing balance from weight measuring device. Receiving result of inference. Performing comparison, notifying conflict Pseudocode 1. Reading from the inference is received via the Mesh network. 2. Reading from the electronic balance is acquired. 3. The algorithm normalizes both measurements and sends both readings to the Comparison function. 4. The algorithm compares measurements and determines whether there is a significant weight difference (conflict). 5. If there is a conflict, alert lights are activated.

Table 7.18: Pseudocode for Block 2 (Weight estimation)

Network

A wireless mesh network enables the communication between both Blocks. The Block one in charge of capturing the image and inferring the weight of the product, publishes a message to a channel that the comparison Block is subscribed to.

Block(s)	Action	Channel
1	Publishes to	CH1
2	Subscribes to	CH1

Table 7.19: Network configuration (Weight estimation)

Power analysis

Any device performing computer vision continuously like in this use case consumes a considerable amount of energy. It is recommended to connect it directly to the electric grid. The commercial setting where this balance will be installed is likely to provide an easy connection without big installation costs.

Power source	Device	Latent consumption	Active consumption	Notes
P1	Arduino Nicla Vision	0.032A @5V	< 1A @5V	
P1	NRF52 Dongle	0.04mA @5v	3mA @5v	Active when publishing messages as a **client**.

Table 7.20: Power requirements Block 1 (Weight estimation)

Same as with Block 1, the Block 2 should be powered directly but the electric grid. This device will be placed in close proximity to the balance.

Power source	Device	Latent consumption	Active consumption	Notes
P2	NRF52 Dongle	0.04mA @5v	0.3mA @5v	Receives regression results from Block 1.
P2	Arduino Nano 33 BLE	0.034mA @5V	< 1A @5V	Receives readings from balance and regression. Compares results. Notifies about conflict.

Table 7.21: Power requirements Block 2 (Weight estimation)

Bill of materials

This bill of materials considers a simple setup of one camera-based inference Block and one validation Block with a visual alert peripheral.

Description	QTY	Unit cost	Total
Arduino Nicla Vision	1	$85	$85
Arduino Nano 33 BLE	2	$30	$60
NRF52840 Dongle	2	$12	$24
Alert Light	1	$20	$20
Power Source 1A @5v	2	$10	$20

Table 7.22: Bill of materials (Weight estimation)

Approximate cost of materials is $209.

Conclusion

This chapter introduces an alternative approach to traditional regression and demonstrates three distinct applications of deep learning regression. The first involves replacing traditional control systems, the second focuses on transforming reactive devices into proactive ones through forecasting and prediction, and the third explores how regression can be applied to non-numeric inputs.

In the next chapter, you will learn what is anomaly detection and its many applications.

References

- *Paradiso, R., Proietti, S. Light-Quality Manipulation to Control Plant Growth and Photomorphogenesis in Greenhouse Horticulture: The State of the Art and the Opportunities of Modern LED Systems. J Plant Growth Regul* **41**, *742–780 (2022).* **https://doi.org/10.1007/s00344-021-10337-y**

- *Li, Y.; Li, T.; Lv, W.; Liang, Z.; Wang, J. Prediction of Daily Temperature Based on the Robust Machine Learning Algorithms. Sustainability 2023, 15, 9289. https://doi.org/10.3390/su15129289* **https://www.mdpi.com/2071-1050/15/12/9289**

- *141 - Regression using Neural Networks and comparison to other models* **https://www.youtube.com/watch?v=2yhLEx2FKoY**

- *Estimate Weight From a Photo Using Visual Regression in Edge Impulse, Aditya Mangalampalli.* **https://edgeimpulse.com/blog/estimate-weight-from-a-photo-using-visual-regression-in-edge-impulse/**

- Regression use case 1: **https://studio.edgeimpulse.com/public/368122/live**

- Regression use case 2: **https://studio.edgeimpulse.com/public/368150/live**

- Regression use case 3: **https://studio.edgeimpulse.com/public/368559/live**

CHAPTER 8
Anomaly Detection

Introduction

Anomaly detection is a technique used in data analysis to identify patterns that differ significantly from expected behavior. In TinyML systems, these unusual patterns, referred to as anomalies, outliers, or exceptions, may arise due to various reasons such as hardware failure, system disturbance, or novel occurrences due to new or unknown environmental conditions. Anomaly detection is particularly useful in edge devices, where early detection and immediate resolution are critical in real-time applications. To detect anomalies, statistical, machine learning, or deep learning methods are used to build models that understand the normal behavior of a system and can then identify deviations. *Figure 8.1* illustrates a common method for anomaly detection based on distance. In a multidimensional space where multiple parameters define behavior, similar data points tend to form a cluster representing typical behavior. An anomaly is identified as a point that deviates significantly from this cluster, with a large enough distance to be considered separate from the normal pattern. The distance is also known as the **anomaly score**.

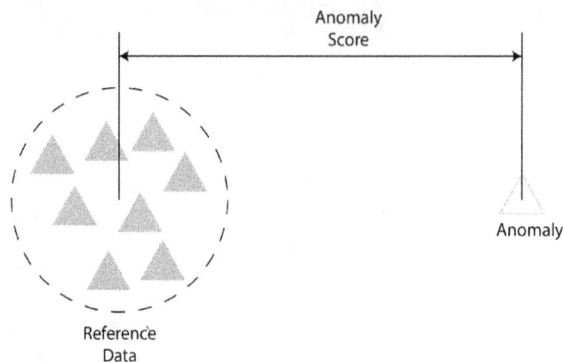

Figure 8.1: *Anomaly score*

Structure

The covers the following topics:

- Types of anomalies
- Precision versus recall
- Distance calculation
- Feature importance
- K-means clustering and anomaly detection
- Use case: Movement
- Use case: Sound
- Use case: Time

Objectives

The objective of this chapter is to introduce you to the concept of anomalies, what they are and how are they detected. By the end of this chapter, you will learn the types of anomalies, the theory behind them and the implementation details to design a system that can flag them in a real time scenario. You will also understand the difference between precision and recall, what are the different ways to calculate distance and how do you determine what features to pay attention to find an anomaly.

Types of anomalies

Anomalies can be categorized into two types: **Univariate** and **multivariate**. Univariate anomalies are detectable from a single variable. On the other hand, multivariate anomalies require the simultaneous analysis of multiple correlated variables. For example, a household's power consumption may seem normal at first, but it may be atypical when additional factors such as seasonality indicate excessive energy usage on days that do not require heating or cooling.

Figure 8.2 portraits anomalies in different dimensions. Each dimension represents a variable that contributes to determining whether an anomaly is present.

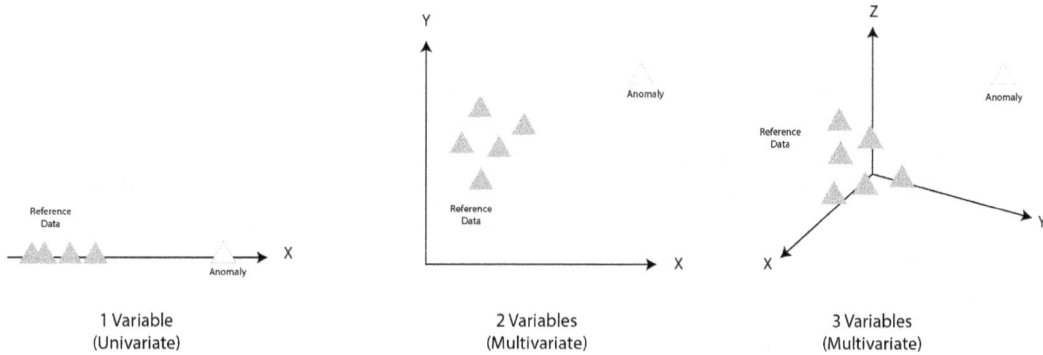

Figure 8.2: *Univariate and multivariate anomalies*

Anomalies can be detected through two main methods: distance and statistical approach. The distance approach involves measuring the separation between regular readings and the point in question, with greater separation indicating a higher probability of anomaly. On the other hand, the statistical approach calculates probability distributions from the data and identifies points with low probability as anomalies. The following figure is an abstraction of both types of anomalies.

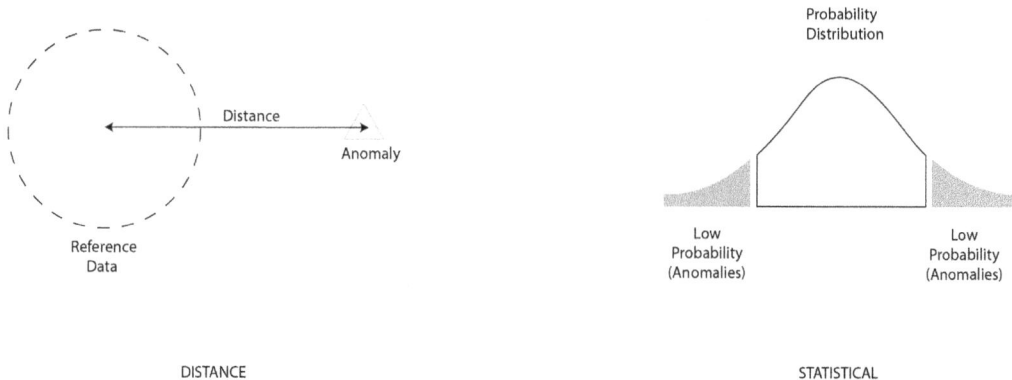

Figure 8.3: *Distance and statistical based anomaly detection*

Beyond univariate and multivariate anomalies, there is a third category known as **collective** anomalies. These anomalies are characterized not by singular data points but by a collection of points over a period of time. For instance, consider an event typically occurring once daily that suddenly begins to occur multiple times. While no individual occurrence is anomalous in isolation, the frequency and pattern indicate an anomaly. This collective nature highlights a different aspect of anomalous behavior, focusing on the unusual aggregation of events rather than isolated incidents.

Precision versus recall

Balancing recall and precision are crucial in the realm of anomaly detection. Overemphasizing one can negatively impact the other. For example, if you use a TinyML application for defect detection using an embedded camera, a system with high recall will detect all real anomalies but may also misidentify non-defective items as anomalous. This approach is useful when avoiding defective outputs is critical, even if it means discarding some good items. On the other hand, a system with high precision ensures that flagged items are truly defective but may miss some defects. This approach is preferable when cost optimization is crucial, and replacing defective items is easy. *Figure 8.4* shows both cases. In the high recall low precision diagram, all the positive samples (blue triangles) are inside the anomaly threshold at the expense of also including anomalies (white triangles). In the low recall high precision diagram, the anomaly threshold only includes positive samples and no anomalies at the expense of leaving some positive samples out.

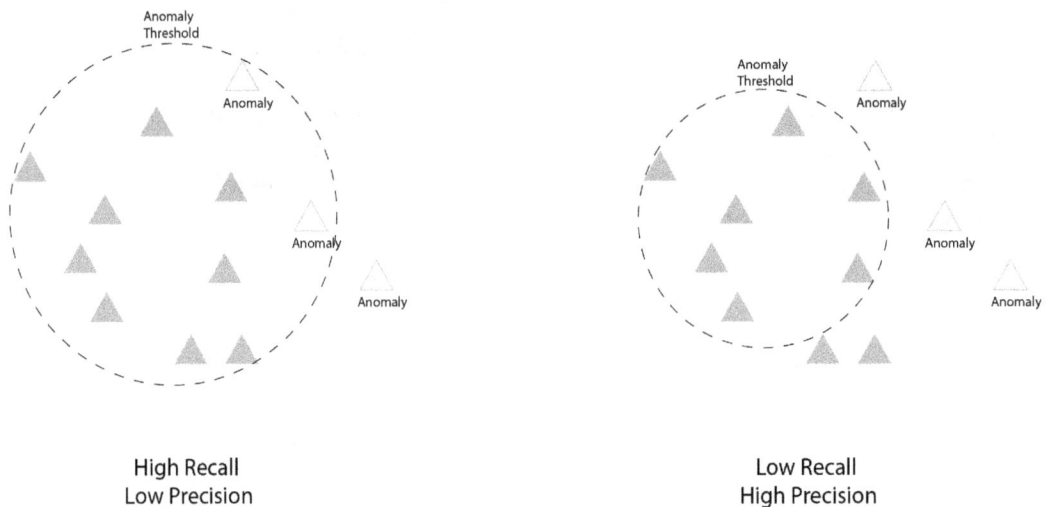

Figure 8.4: High recall, low precision versus low recall, high precision

In practical applications within TinyML, anomaly detection is often employed alongside a classifier model. Initially, the classifier attempts to categorize the data into known patterns. However, due to the inherent design of classifiers, they will assign even unfamiliar patterns to a class. This is where anomaly detection plays a crucial role. It evaluates the data and assigns an anomaly score, indicating the degree of deviation from established classes. Should this score surpass a certain threshold, the system overrides the initial classification and relabels the data as an **anomaly**. This tandem approach ensures that the system identifies known patterns and is adept at flagging new, potentially significant deviations.

Distance calculation

Calculating distance is a crucial tool for measuring the deviation of data points from normal patterns or expected behavior. By determining the distance between a particular data point and the rest of the dataset, we can identify anomalies as those that significantly diverge from most of the data. This quantification helps anomaly detection algorithms systematically evaluate the uniqueness or unusual nature of individual data points, enabling the identification of potential anomalies. Additionally, distance metrics provide a means to reduce the dimensionality of high-dimensional data, thus making it easier to visualize and understand complex datasets.

When calculating distance, it is necessary to measure the deviation or dissimilarity of a data point from the expected behavior or reference distribution. The techniques used to calculate distance depend on the type of data and the anomaly detection algorithm being used. The following are some common approaches to calculating distance:

- **Euclidean distance**: This is a simple metric that calculates the straight-line distance between two points in an n-dimensional space. It is particularly useful for numerical data. In a two-dimensional space *Figure 8.5*, the **Euclidean** distance between points (x1, y1) and *(x2, y2)* is calculated as $\sqrt{((x2 - x1)^2 + (y2 - y1)^2)}$. This metric assumes that the features are independent and equally weighted. Refer to the following figure:

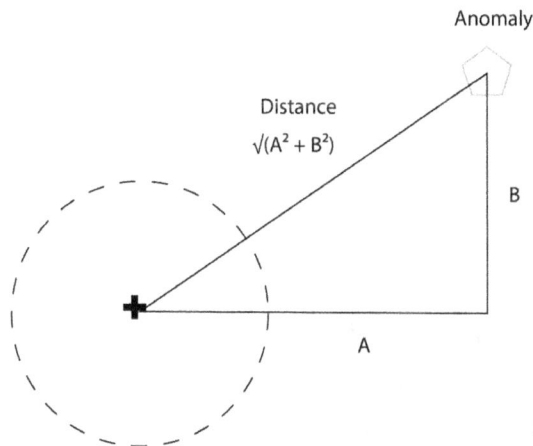

Figure 8.5: Euclidian distance

- **Mahalanobis distance**: This is a generalized form of **Euclidean** distance that accounts for correlations between features and different scales. It is especially useful when the data is not spherical or when features are correlated. The **Mahalanobis** distance (*Figure 8.6*) is calculated as the distance of a point from the center of a distribution divided by the spread of the distribution along each dimension.

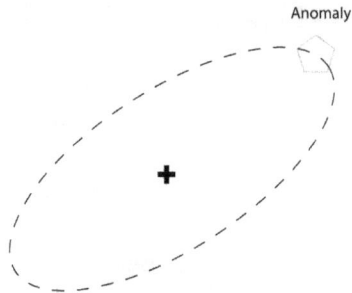

Figure 8.6: Mahalanobis distance

- **Manhattan distance (city Block distance)**: This metric calculates the distance between two points by summing the absolute differences between their coordinates (as shown in *Figure 8.7*). It is useful when dealing with non-continuous data or when there are grid-like structures, such as images or text data.

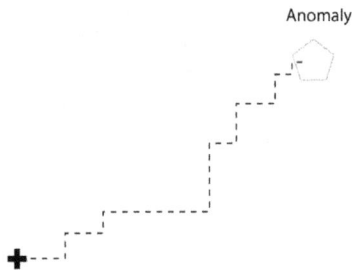

Figure 8.7: Manhattan distance

The choice of distance metric depends on the nature of the data, the underlying distribution, and the specific requirements of the anomaly detection task. Different algorithms and methods may utilize different distance metrics to detect anomalies effectively.

Feature importance

Determining the importance of features is crucial in detecting anomalies as it helps to identify the most influential attributes in distinguishing between normal and anomalous behavior within a dataset. By knowing which features contribute the most to the detection of anomalies, it becomes easier to select the most relevant attributes, thereby reducing computational complexity and enhancing detection accuracy. Additionally, understanding feature importance aids in interpreting and explaining the detected anomalies, providing insights into the underlying factors driving anomalous behavior. This process optimizes anomaly detection models by focusing on key features and enhances their robustness by excluding irrelevant attributes, ultimately leading to more effective and efficient anomaly detection systems. *Figure 8.8* is an example screenshot from Edge Impulse showing of a list of features ordered by feature importance:

Feature importance ⑦   All data ⌄

accX RMS

accX Peak 1 Height

accZ Spectral Power 2.0 - 5.0

accY Spectral Power 2.0 - 5.0

accX Peak 1 Freq

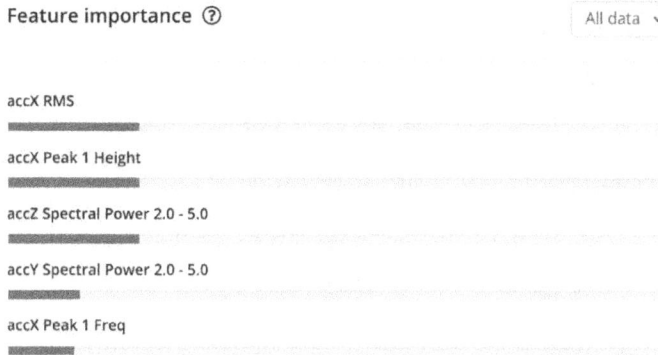

Figure 8.8: Feature importance example (source: Edge Impulse)

K-means clustering and anomaly detection

K-means clustering is a technique used for unsupervised clustering, where it groups similar data points into pre-defined clusters. Although it is not specifically designed for detecting anomalies, K-means clustering can be adapted for this purpose by calculating the distance from centroids. After clustering data into clusters using K-means, anomalies can be identified as data points that are far from the centroids of all clusters. If a data point is distant from any cluster centroid, it may be considered an anomaly. The sensitivity of anomaly detection is influenced by the distance metric used, such as Euclidean distance. *Figure 8.9* is an example of the output of K-mean clustering. Each round area is a cluster. The samples that are not inside a cluster are considered anomalies.

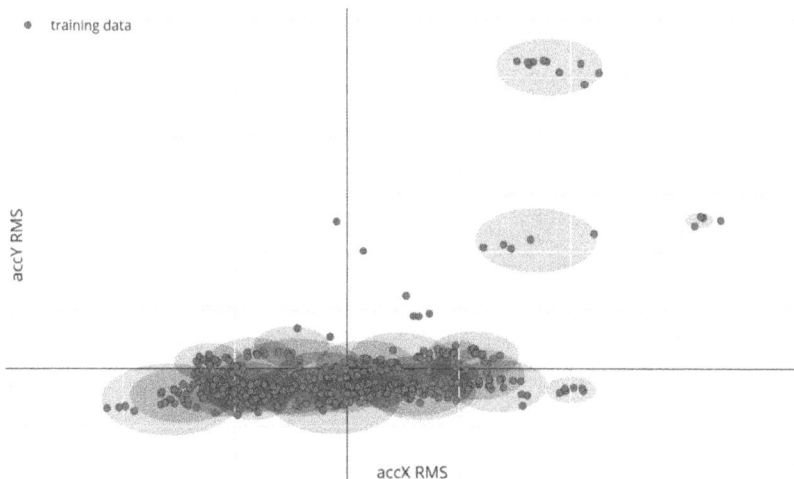

Figure 8.9: K-mean clustering (source: Edge Impulse)

Steps to detect an anomaly

To systematically detect an anomaly, we assess how far a given piece of information deviates from what is considered normal. This involves plotting the data in a multidimensional space and measuring its distance to the nearest cluster. Let us look at the key steps in this anomaly detection process:

1. From the reference data that shows nominal behavior, create the clusters that define its space using k-means. Calculate the centroids of each cluster (*Figure 8.10*).

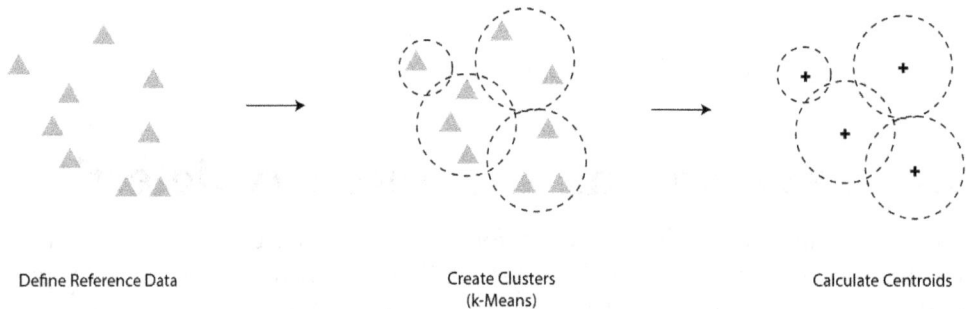

Define Reference Data   Create Clusters   Calculate Centroids
                               (k-Means)

Figure 8.10: Process to calculate centroids

2. Every new data point is evaluated. Calculate its distance to each one of the cluster centroids (*Figure 8.11*).

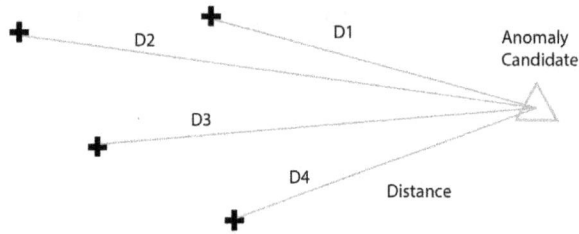

Figure 8.11: Distance calculation

3. Determine whether the data point is an anomaly by selecting the shortest distance and comparing it against the anomaly threshold. If the distance is greater than the threshold, you have found an anomaly.

Use case: Movement anomalies

A popular use case for anomaly detection is to provide instantaneous feedback to a system or user to indicate that something is not okay. This can be extended to navigation systems, control systems, manufacturing, ergonomics or any process that can benefit from real time correction.

Rowing machine anomaly

Problem definition: A gym wants to monitor the performance of its athletes by tracking quantitative metrics generated during their workout. The rowing machine is one of the most used machines at the gym, but it is also frequently misused, which can result in reduced exercise benefits and injuries. The gym owner desires to provide instant feedback to the user without the need for a trainer.

Solution: To address this issue, a small accelerometer gyroscope will be installed in the handle of the rowing machine. This device will detect if the athlete is using the machine incorrectly and send a wireless message to a status light in front of the user. If the machine is being used correctly, there will be no indication. However, if a stroke is ineffective, a *red* light indicator will light up, prompting the athlete to correct their posture. The following figure depicts a conceptual diagram showing the components of this solution:

Figure 8.12: Concept diagram (Movement anomalies)

Data acquisition

We installed an **Inertial Measurement Unit** inside the tubular handle of a rowing machine to collect the data. The device has a Logger that captures the time series from six different readings: The X, Y, and Z axis from the accelerometers and gyroscopes. We worked with five athletes and collected 40 minutes of data, with each athlete performing the same sequence, starting at 50% and increasing by 10% every minute. A video of each athlete was filmed to cross-reference each stroke with its label (regular versus defective). The data is split into three subsets: 70% is the training set, 20% is the testing set, and 10% is the validation set shown in the following figure:

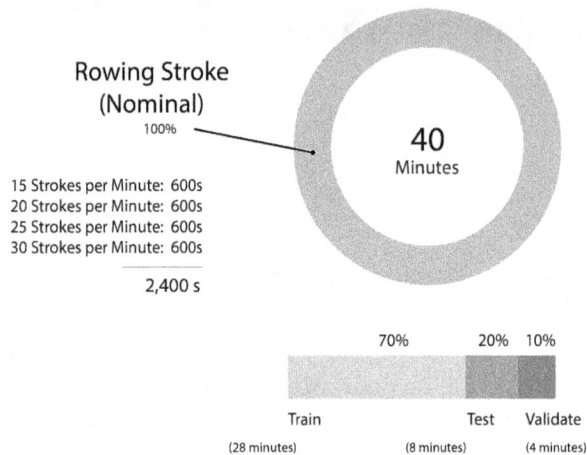

Figure 8.13: Training dataset (Movement anomalies)

Processing

The dataset is split into samples of 1000ms, with each sample containing six time series, each with 13 features. This adds up to 78 features per sample. Of the 13 features, eight describe spectral power, and the other five are RMS, kurtosis, spectral kurtosis, skewness, and spectral skewness. The anomaly detection model works in tandem with a classification model. The cluster diagram in *Figure 8.14*, shows the cluster with samples that demonstrate the correct use of the rowing machine. Notice how we do not have samples of incorrect use of the machine. That is going to be detected by the anomaly detection model.

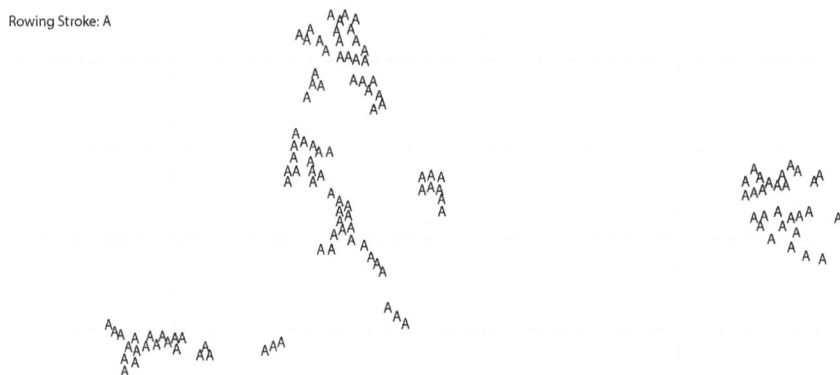

Figure 8.14: Cluster diagram (Movement anomalies)

Model

A classification model is used to identify between two classes, correct and incorrect. It involves two dense layers, the first with 20 parameters and the second with ten parameters.

Each layer has a ReLU function at the output. At the output of the second layer, we have a SoftMax activation layer that converts the output values into a probability distribution that shows what class is more probable. We declare the class with higher probability as the inference.

If we leave it as is, this would be a supervised version of anomaly detection. However, we would not be able to detect incorrect movement that has never been seen before. For this reason, a second stage uses a modified version of **K-means clustering** to determine a score for each point based on the distance between the reading and the centroid of the rest of the samples.

According to the model scorecard shown in *Figure 8.15*, the model demonstrates strong generalization, with high testing accuracy (94.86%) and low validation loss (0.27), indicating its effectiveness in distinguishing between normal and anomalous rowing machine usage without overfitting. The use of K-means clustering with 32 clusters and a threshold of 0.3 adds robustness by capturing deviations not perfectly aligned with the model's predictions. However, this approach assumes well-defined clusters, which could lead to missed anomalies near the threshold or false positives if the training data does not fully represent normal usage scenarios. To optimize performance, it is important to fine-tune the threshold based on live data feedback and ensure the training dataset covers a wide range of normal behaviors to enhance generalization further.

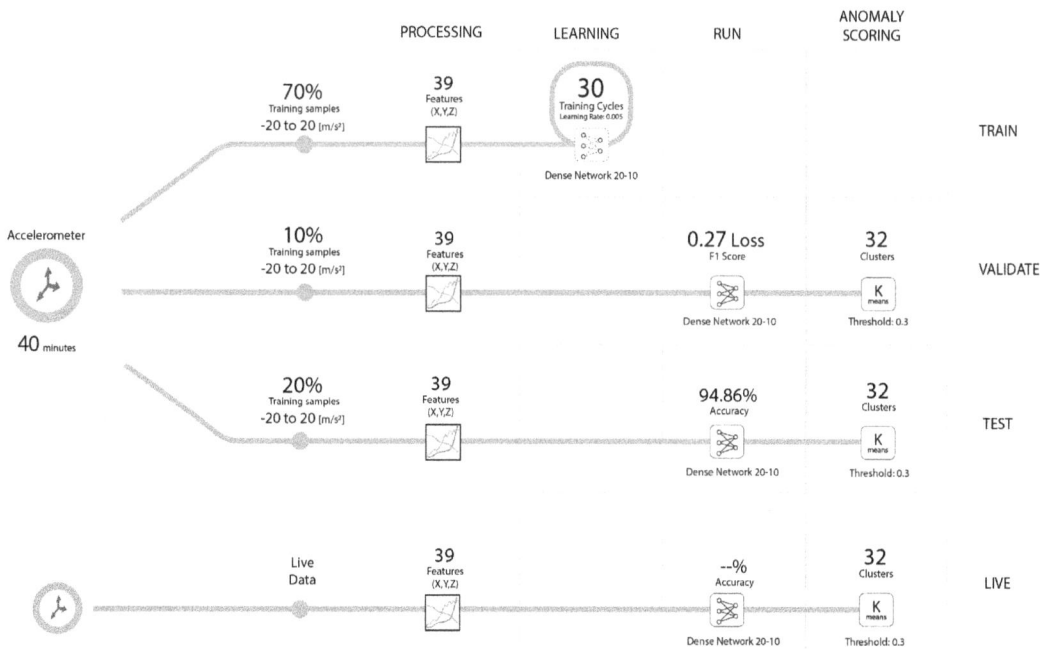

Figure 8.15: Training, validation and testing metrics (Movement anomalies)

System implementation

The implementation consists of two Blocks: the movement tracker and the status notifier as shown in *Figure 8.16*. The first Block is located inside the rowing machine's tubular handle, while the latter is attached to the screen that shows the machine metrics to the user.

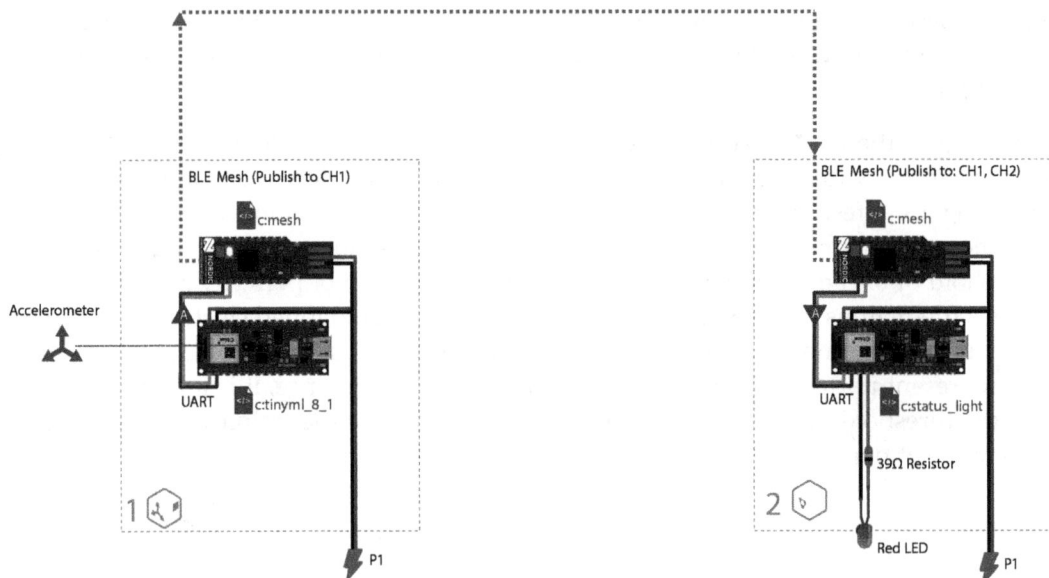

Figure 8.16: *Connection diagram (Movement anomalies)*

The first Block has been implemented using an Arduino Nano 33 BLE powered by a small 600MHa battery. The Arduino captures the accelerometer and gyroscope readings and sends them to the microcontroller. The microcontroller contains, among other things, the model trained to recognize the two movement classes (Correct and incorrect). A function reads the model output and calculates the anomaly score using the k-means function. If the anomaly score exceeds a predetermined threshold, the MCU issues an event to a secondary microcontroller attached to the Arduino. The secondary MCU is an NRF52840 dongle that sends status messages to the mesh network. An external antenna is implemented in the microcontroller to allow the signal to escape the metal cage formed by the rowing machine handle.

The second Block receives the message containing the machine's status and activates a pin connected to a red **light-emitting diode (LED)**. The red LED communicates to the user that the model in the first Block detected an anomaly in the movement.

Source code

The process that needs to be programmed into the Block 1 is an infinite loop that is continuously capturing accelerometer readings, classifying them and then calculating their anomaly score. If the score is high enough, the Block 1 will publish an alert message. Refer to the following table:

c:tinyml_8_1	Code location: Arduino Nano 33 BLE @ Block 1
	Capturing data, processing it, classifying movement, generating anomaly score. Pseudocode 1. Device captures accelerometer readings. 2. The readings are converted into 39 features. 3. The model classifies the features. 4. The **anomaly score** is calculated. If there is an anomaly, a message is sent out to the Mesh Network.

Table 8.1: Pseudocode for Block 1 (Movement anomalies)

Network

Since the anomaly detector will be inside of the handle, the only feasible solution is to get its messages wirelessly. The components use a wireless mesh network where the data producer (the anomaly detection) publishes messages to a channel that the data consumer (the alerting component) is subscribed to. Using a mesh network seems to be an overkill however it allows for upgrades to the system. An upgrade example is to create a central node that would detect anomalies from all rowing machines that are being used at the same time during a class.

Block(s)	Action	Channel
1	Publishes to	CH1
2	Subscribes to	CH1

Table 8.2: Network configuration (Movement anomalies)

Power analysis

The nature of the use case requires the anomaly detection component (Block 1) to be battery operated since it will be housed inside of the rower handle.

Power source	Device	Latent consumption	Active consumption	Notes
P1	Arduino Nano 33 BLE Sense	0.032A @5V	< 1A @5V	
P1	NRF52 Dongle	0.04mA @5v	3mA @5v	Active when publishing messages as a *client*.

Table 8.3: Power profile of Block 1 (Movement anomalies)

For Block 2 batteries would also be useful to keep the anomaly detection components integrated to the rowing machine. To optimize the battery, a movement sensor can be used to wake up the component during use and letting it sleep when idle.

Power source	Device	Latent consumption	Active consumption	Notes
P2	NRF52 Dongle	0.04mA @5v	0.3mA @5v	Active when receiving messages as a *Server*.
P2	Arduino Nano 33 BLE	0.034mA @5V	< 1A @5V	Drives Status LED

Table 8.4: Power profile of Block 2 (Movement anomalies)

Bill of materials

The bill of materials considers one sensor and one alerting component.

Description	QTY	Unit cost	Total
Arduino Nano 33 BLE Sense	1	$45	$45
Arduino Nano 33 BLE	1	$30	$30
NRF52840 Dongle	2	$12	$24
LiPo Batteries	2	$30	$60

Table 8.5: Bill of materials (Movement anomalies)

Approximate cost of materials is $159.

Use case: Sound anomalies

Detecting anomalies does not need to be a binary event, instead, you can classify the event first, and then use a specialized classification model to determine whether that event is an anomaly of not. The following use case shows the implementation of a system that classifies an event first and then performs a targeted anomaly detection.

Machine sound anomaly

Problem definition: A small workshop specializes in making car replacement parts and owns a CNC router that cuts aluminum pieces. The owner of the workshop has noticed that the experienced operators can identify when something is not right with the machine by the sound it produces while cutting materials. However, since the workshop is operational 24*7, it is impossible to have an operator by the machine all the time. To prevent material loss, the workshop wants to find a way to automatically shut down the machine when it does not sound right so that an operator can inspect it.

Solution: A microphone will be placed near the machine to capture real-time sounds. The sounds will be sent to a sound classification model on the device to classify them. The sound sample will also be analyzed by an anomaly scoring function to determine if it deviates from the typical operating sound. If the score goes beyond a set limit, the MCU will send a message to a switch to turn off the machine and alert the operator. The following figure shows a concept diagram that illustrates the closed loop between the microphone and the machine emergency switch:

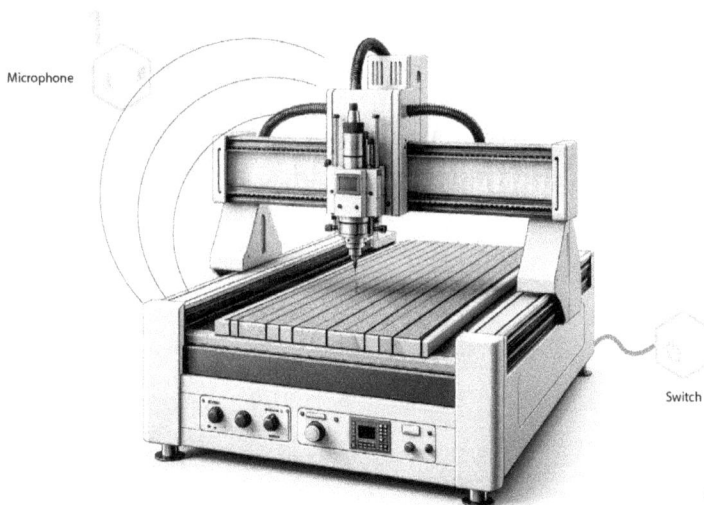

Figure 8.17: Concept diagram (Sound anomalies)

Data acquisition

To train the model, we generated a dataset by recording the machine under normal conditions. The recorded sounds encompass all known states that are considered normal. The following nominal states were considered: machine cutting **Material A**, machine cutting **Material B**, machine running **empty**. *Figure 8.18* shows that the training set includes ten minutes of each state. As we are not training the classification model to recognize anomalies, no anomalous sounds are required.

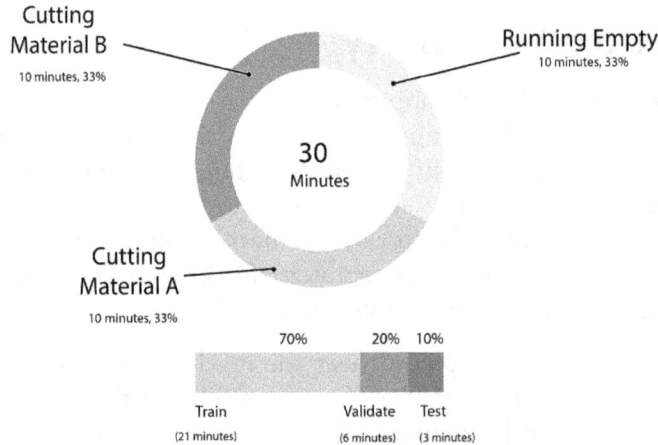

Figure 8.18: Training set (Sound anomalies)

Processing

The audio signal is divided into one-second segments, with each segment consisting of 50 frames. Each frame represents a duration of 0.02 seconds and has a stride of 0.01 seconds. The frames are then transformed into frequencies using a **Fourier Transform (FT)**, which results in 128 frequencies per frame. Therefore, each sample has a total of 6,400 features (50 x 128). The cluster diagram (as shown in *Figure 8.19*) shows clearly defined groups of samples:

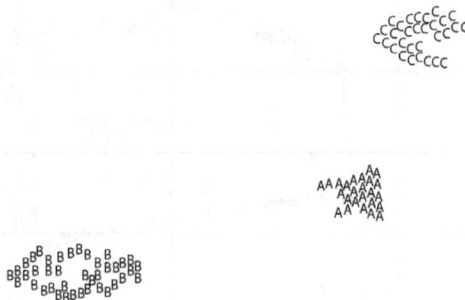

Figure 8.19: Cluster diagram (Sound anomalies)

Model

We utilize a **Convolutional Neural Network** comprising of eight layers. The first layer reshapes the spectrogram to fit the convolutional layers. The first convolutional layers use a kernel of 3x3 with eight filters activated by a ReLU function. MaxPool layers are utilized to decrease the size of the array by selecting its most representative values. Dropout layers minimize overfitting (for detailed information on how this model operates, refer to *Chapter 2, Sound Classification*). At the end, a Softmax function converts the network output into a probability distribution that displays the likelihood that the sample is typical.

However, the problem with classification models is that they must assign a probability to every sample, even if it needs to be corrected. For that reason, we have the second stage, a modified K-means algorithm. A fundamental feature of K-means is determining distances to respect a centroid. The modified K-means algorithm determines how far each sample is from the regular class. The result is a score. The higher the score, the farther the sample is, and the higher the probability that an anomaly has been detected.

The scorecard in *Figure 8.20* shows that the model achieves perfect validation loss (0.0) and testing accuracy (100%), which suggests it has learned the dataset extremely well but raises concerns about potential overfitting, especially if the data lacks diversity or if the training and testing sets are too similar. The use of Mel filter banks for feature extraction is robust and appropriate for audio data, while the inclusion of K-means clustering with a threshold of 0.3 adds an additional layer of refinement for anomaly detection. However, the model's perfect performance is unusual for real-world scenarios, particularly in anomaly detection, which often involves noisy or edge-case data. This indicates the need for further validation with diverse live data to ensure generalization and effectiveness in capturing subtle anomalies.

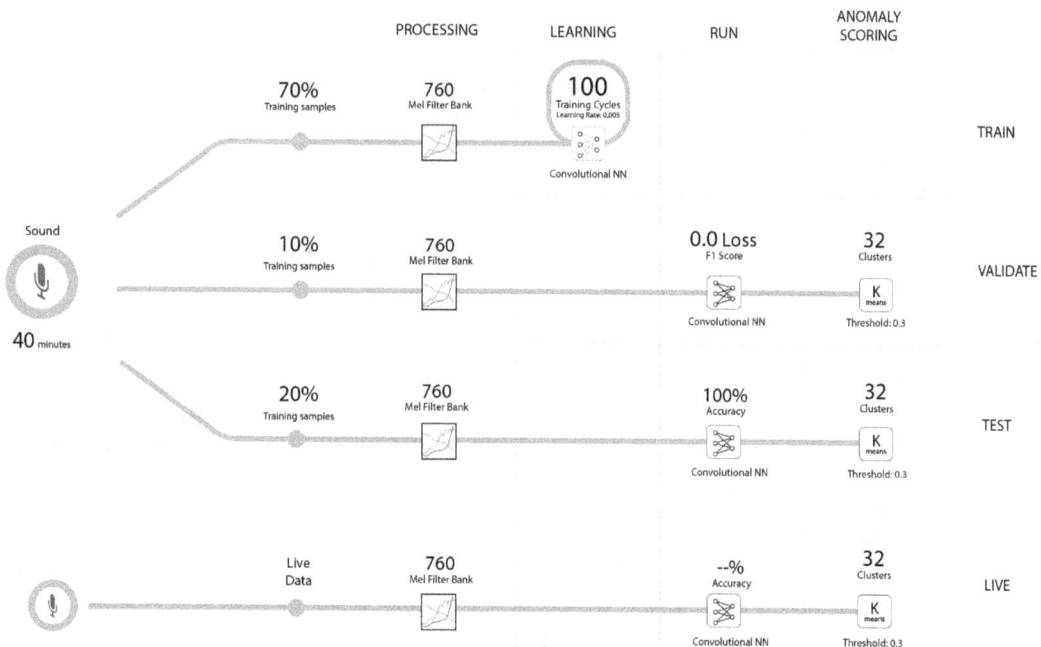

Figure 8.20: Training, validation and testing metrics (Sound anomalies)

System implementation

The implementation consists of three Blocks. The first Block is responsible for listening to and processing the machine's sounds to determine if there is an anomaly, while the second Block is responsible for turning the machine off if an anomalous situation is detected. The third Block generates visual and auditive alerts for the operator in the event of an anomaly. The following figure shows the connections between the Blocks:

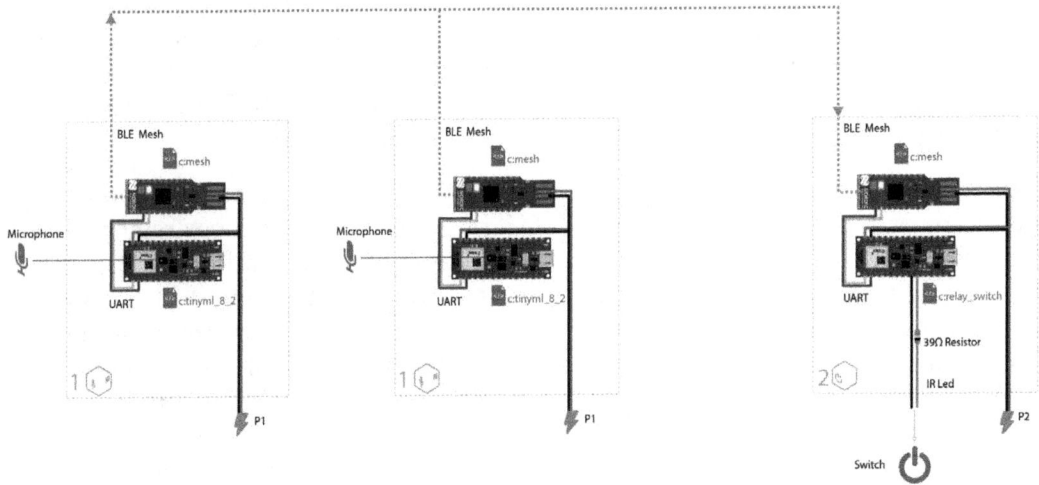

Figure 8.21: Connection diagram (Sound anomalies)

Block 1 is implemented with an Arduino Nano 33 BLE Sense with an integrated microphone. Sounds are captured and then sent to the microcontroller, which runs a TinyML classification model to determine the class the sound sample belongs to. Immediately after that, a K-means function assigns an **anomaly score** to the sample. If the anomaly score exceeds a predetermined threshold, the device sends a message announcing the anomaly. The network communication is implemented via a NRF52840 Dongle that communicates with the primary microcontroller via UART. Block 1 acts as a BLE Mesh Server, publishing to a channel dedicated to anomaly detection messages.

Block 2 of the machine monitors for anomaly messages and shuts down the machine using a relay switch to avoid locking it. It also has an on/off switch that allows the operator to enable or disable anomaly detection shutdown manually. This Block is implemented using an Arduino Nano 33 board in conjunction with a NRF52840 Dongle to receive network messages.

Block 3 (optional, not shown in the diagram) is responsible for notifying the operator of an anomaly event. It listens to the anomaly messages sent by Block 1 and activates a light and sound alert when an anomaly is detected. The Block uses an Arduino Nano 33 board to communicate with the light alert through the I2C protocol. It generates sound via its I2S output, which is amplified directly from a secondary power source. Block 3 also employs a NRF52840 Dongle to subscribe to the anomaly notification channel in the Mesh Network.

Source code

The logic implemented in Block one consists of capturing the sound, extracting its features and then classifying the sound. Based on the class, the sample is sent to the specialized anomaly detection model. Refer to the following table:

c:tinyml_8_2	Code location: Arduino Nano 33 BLE @ Block 1
	Capturing sound sample, processing sample, classifying sample, scoring for anomaly, sending anomaly notification. Pseudocode 1. The sound is captured by the microphone. 2. The sound is processed and converted to features. 3. The model output is sent to the anomaly detection function. 4. The K-means function determines the **anomaly score** of the sample for a specific class. If an anomaly is taking place, a message is sent out to the network with an alert.

Table 8.6: Pseudocode for Block 1 (Sound anomalies)

Network

In order to avoid extra cables in a high-risk environment, a wireless network is a viable option. In this use case, a wireless mesh network is used. Only if the Block 1 detects the anomaly a message is published to a channel that the Block 2 is subscribed to. Once the message has been validated by the Block 2, the emergency switch is activated. Refer to the following table:

Block(s)	Action	Channel
1	Publishes to	CH1
2	Subscribes to	CH1

Table 8.7: Mesh network configuration (Sound anomalies)

Power analysis

Block 1 is powered from the electric grid to avoid interruptions given the criticality of the mission:

Power source	Device	Latent consumption	Active consumption	Notes
P1	Arduino Nano 33 BLE Sense	0.032A @5V	< 1A @5V	
P1	NRF52 Dongle	0.04mA @5v	3mA @5v	Active when publishing messages as a *client*.

Table 8.8: Power profile, Block 1 (Sound anomalies)

Block 2 is also powered by the electric grid to ensure that all messages are received, especially in the event that the machine needs to be shut down.

Power source	Device	Latent consumption	Active consumption	Notes
P2	NRF52 Dongle	0.04mA @5v	0.3mA @5v	Active when receiving messages as a *server*.
P2	Arduino Nano 33 BLE	0.034mA @5V	< 1A @5V	Drives shut-down switch

Table 8.9: Power profile, Block 2 (Sound anomalies)

Bill of materials

This bill of materials considers one sound anomaly detection Block and one emergency switch.

Description	QTY	Unit cost	Total
Arduino Nano 33 BLE Sense	1	$45	$45
Arduino Nano 33 BLE	1	$30	$30
NRF52840 Dongle	2	$12	$24
Power Source 1A @5v	2	$30	$60

Table 8.10: Bill of materials (Sound anomalies)

Approximate cost of materials is $159.

Use case: Anomalies across a period of Time

Some events are not anomalies if they happen instantaneously, however they will become an anomaly if the event stays in a state for a certain period of time. In order to detect this type of anomaly, you need to input a time series to the anomaly detection model instead of a single point in time. The following use case illustrates a situation where an anomaly across time is detected with the help of sensors and short-term memory.

Room temperature anomaly

Problem definition: A commercial real estate company is facing complaints from tenants about rooms being too hot or too cold. Typically, by the time a complaint is received, the tenant is already upset, and it takes longer to solve the problem as the room has been outside the comfort threshold for a while. The building operator wants to detect temperature anomalies in real-time, so they can provide a quick response and solution before the tenant is even aware of the issue. However, the current system only has a few temperature sensors per floor, making it difficult to identify anomalies in specific areas or rooms. Therefore, the company needs a solution that can detect temperature anomalies in every room in real-time.

Solution: The proposed solution comprises of sensors that can capture the temperature in their surroundings and detect any unusual activity or anomaly using a combination of a classifier model and an anomaly scoring system. Each room on the floor will be able to communicate with a central device placed in the middle of the floor that can send a signal over the internet to the cloud, which in turn will alert the building's operators in case of any irregularities detected by the sensors. The concept diagram (as shown in *Figure 8.22*) shows the general idea of the solution with sensors connected together via a network in which one of the nodes has the ability to send the data out to the cloud.

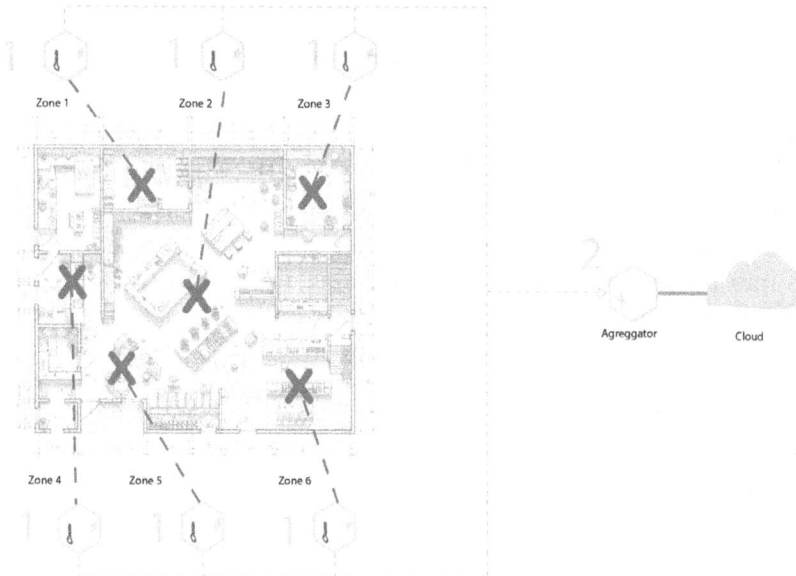

Figure 8.22: Concept diagram (Room temperature anomalies)

Data acquisition

To ensure accurate monitoring of commercial spaces, it is recommended to capture space temperatures in every area that will be monitored for anomalies. This allows for the creation of explicit models for each space, rather than relying on a generic anomaly detection model that processes data in the cloud. By running TinyML models on the edge, anomalies can be detected locally. Room temperature does not change instantly, for that reason, capturing temperature data every minute is sufficient. The initial model is trained with 24 hours of data, but future versions could be trained with data from multiple days under varying weather conditions. The data partition is shown in the following figure:

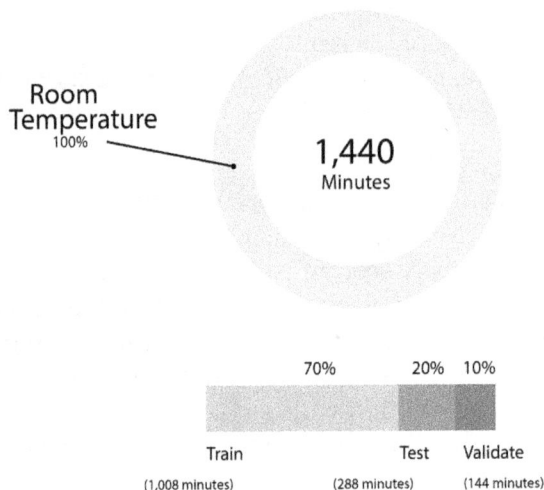

Room
Temperature
100%

1,440
Minutes

70%   20%   10%

Train   Test   Validate
(1,008 minutes)   (288 minutes)   (144 minutes)

Figure 8.23: Test dataset (Room temperature anomalies)

Processing

The temperature signal is a series of measurements taken at $1/60$Hz frequency. To measure the rate of change of temperature over time, we buffer the last ten readings. Before we feed the readings into the TinyML model, we need to check for gaps, changes in frequency (such as receiving three readings instead of one), and outlier values that may be caused by a faulty sensor rather than an actual temperature anomaly. To do this, we use a **Kalman filter** that follows simple physics rules to determine the accuracy of the reading. If the sensor does not provide the data in Celsius degrees, we convert the raw byte data to Celsius. The ten most recent readings are resampled at a frequency of 1Hz (one data point per second) and sent to the TinyML model, resulting in 600 features.

Model

We use a tandem configuration of a classification model and k-means function to identify anomalies in room temperature. The classification model takes in the 600 features that represent the last 10 minutes of room temperature and feeds them into a fully connected dense layer. The next layer is a dense layer with 20 parameters, which is activated with a ReLU function. The third layer is another dense layer with 10 parameters, also activated with a ReLU function. Finally, the output is passed through a SoftMax function, which transforms the output of the dense network into a probability distribution. This distribution shows the likelihood that the sample represents normal behavior.

After this initial classification, we then run the sample through the K-means function to determine its anomaly score. This score is determined by calculating the distance between the cluster centroid representing normal operations and the sample based on its most essential features. This process allows us to identify any anomalies in the room temperature readings.

As shown in *Figure 8.24*, the model demonstrates strong performance in identifying temperature anomalies, with a low validation loss of 0.27 and a high testing accuracy of 94.86%, indicating it is well-trained and capable of generalizing to unseen data. The use of K-means clustering with 32 clusters and a threshold of 0.3 enhances the model's ability to refine anomaly detection by classifying points based on their proximity to cluster centers. The compact representation of the time series into 7 meaningful features suggests effective feature engineering, reducing dimensionality while preserving critical information. However, while the metrics are promising, the model's ability to detect subtle or edge-case anomalies should be validated further during live deployment to ensure robustness in diverse, real-world scenarios.

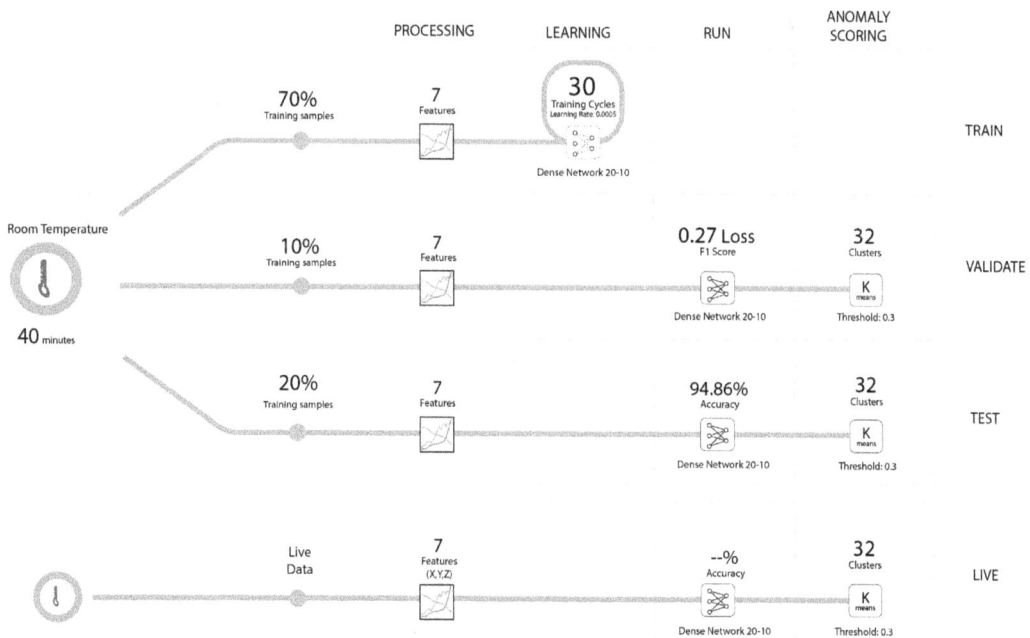

Figure 8.24: *Training, validation and testing metrics (Room temperature anomalies)*

System implementation

The system comprises of two different types of Blocks. Block 1 is responsible for capturing temperature readings and determining their anomaly score. You can replicate Block 1 as many times as there are rooms in the space that you want to cover using this solution. On the other hand, you only need one Block 2, which receives the status (not the readings) of all the Block 1 devices. It then sends this information to an alert system using an internet connection. The flow of information via the wireless network is shown in the figure implementation figure:

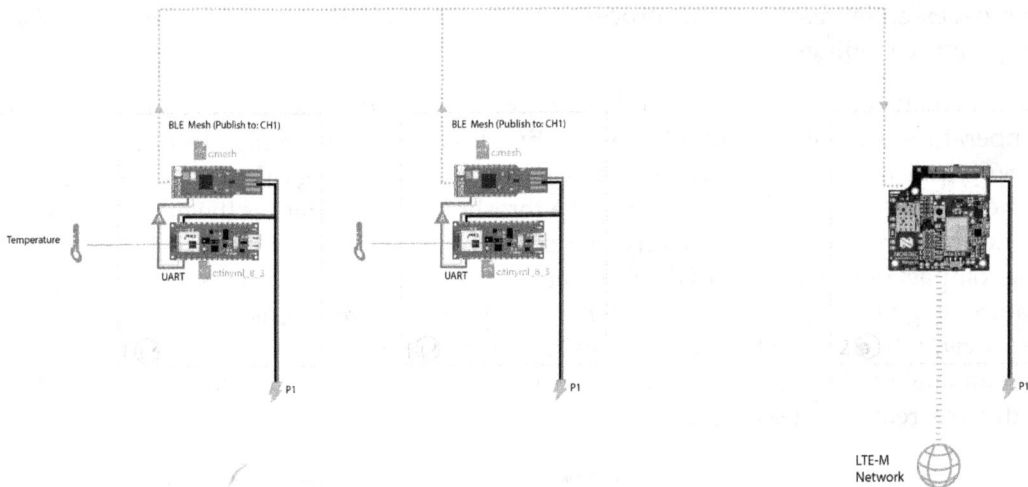

Figure 8.25: Connection diagram (Room temperature anomalies)

Block 1 is built with an Arduino Nano 33 BLE Sense, which has an integrated temperature sensor and an ARM-M microcontroller capable of running both the TinyML classification model and the K-means function. Block 1 uses a secondary microcontroller (NRF52840 Dongle) to transmit messages to a Bluetooth Mesh Network.

Block 2 is built with a Thingy9160 that features dual processors. The first one (an NRF52840) receives status messages from the BLE Mesh Network, and the second one (NRF9160) connects to the NRFCloud using an LTE-M connection.

Source code

The logic implemented in Block one consists of capturing the temperature at regular intervals, storing it in a buffer and then sending a series of readings to the classification and anomaly detection models at once. Refer to the following table:

c:tinyml_8_3	Code location: Arduino Nano 33 BLE @ Block 1
	Capture temperature, process readings, classify sample, determine anomaly score. Pseudocode 1. Temperature is captured by sensors and then saved to volatile memory. 2. Temperature history is converted to features. 3. The classification model classifies the sample. 4. The **anomaly score** is determined. Status message is sent out to network.

Table 8.11: Pseudocode for Block 1 (Room temperature anomalies)

Network

The distributed nature of this solution requires the use of a wireless network. Since the anomaly detection process takes place in the device, there is no need to send out every temperature reading. The only messages that go out are flags that indicate that an anomaly is present. The low bandwidth nature of this solution is a good match for a low energy mesh network. All messages are published to the same channel. The aggregator node can identify the message sender by an id in the metadata.

Block(s)	Action	Channel
1	Publishes to	CH1
2	Subscribes to	CH1

Table 8.12: Mesh network configuration (Room temperature anomalies)

Power analysis

This solution offers the optionality to power sensors (Block 1) directly from the electric grid of using a battery.

Power source	Device	Latent consumption	Active consumption	Notes
P1	Arduino Nano 33 BLE Sense	0.032A @5V	< 1A @5V	
P1	NRF52 Dongle	0.04mA @5v	3mA @5v	Active when publishing messages as a *client*.

Table 8.13: Power profile Block 1 (Room temperature anomalies)

The aggregation Block (Block 2) will require a power source connected to the electric grid as it will perform long range communication with the cloud.

Power source	Device	Latent consumption	Active consumption	Notes
P2	NRF9150 Thingy	0.04mA @5v	0.3mA @5v	Active when receiving messages as a *server*.

Table 8.14: Power profile Block 2 (Room temperature anomalies)

Bill of materials

This bill of materials considers two anomaly detectors (covering two rooms) and one aggregator Block.

Description	QTY	Unit cost	Total
Arduino Nano 33 BLE Sense	2	$45	$90
NRF9160 Thingy	1	$150	$150
Power Source 1A @5v	2	$30	$60

Table 8.15: Bill of materials (Room temperature anomalies)

Approximate cost of materials is $300.

Conclusion

The ability to detect abnormal events or readings has countless applications. In this chapter, we introduced the concept of distance calculation as a method to determine how close something is to being normal. However, this is just one approach to anomaly detection. Another powerful method is statistics-based anomaly detection, which offers a rich framework for identifying unusual events. Additionally, convolutional networks can be used to analyze the shape of a curve or figure to determine if something is amiss. This chapter only scratches the surface of this vast topic, and we encourage readers to explore it further.

References

- Anomaly detection use case 1: **https://studio.edgeimpulse.com/public/378012/live**
- Anomaly detection use case 2: **https://studio.edgeimpulse.com/public/378013/live**
- Anomaly detection use case 3: **https://studio.edgeimpulse.com/public/378014/live**

Index

www.ingramcontent.com/pod-product-compliance
Lightning Source LLC
Chambersburg PA
CBHW061807210326
41599CB00034B/6914